To: Courtney,
May the Lord richly bless you indeed
and enlarge the place of your tent.

Paul 03/10/2016

# THE AGE OF
# THE PROPHET
# BRANHAM

GW00504080

**"What is the Age of the prophet Branham?"**

Whether you are the Bride of Christ, Message believer, born again Christian, church member or someone in pursuit of man's search for meaning, you certainly can gain an understanding of the extent to which historical events are made clear by prophecy with the help of this book on the history of Christianity past, present and future. This book seeks to answer the following questions:

What is the origin, meaning and development of Christianity, civilisation, culture and religion?

What did the prophet have to say about the birthplace of Adam and Eve, and where Eden is geographically situated on the map of the world?

What was prophesied about the Middle East, Israel, the Palestinian situation, and the rise of India, Iran and China?

What part did the Babylonian and Egyptian Mystery Systems play in the origin and growth of modern Christianity?

What is the connection between the first Jesuit pope elected by Roman Catholicism in the twenty first century and his fellow Jesuits in the past?

What has the changing face of Roman Catholicism and the one world system of government to do with the closing of our age and the end of the world?

Why did Enoch build the Great Pyramid and what is its link to the Eternal City in the New Jerusalem in the Book of Revelation?

**Paul C Boyd** is a historian and like other Christian believers past and present holds the view that the Bible is the inspired Word of God; and that God first reveals His Word to His servants the prophets.

# THE AGE OF
# THE PROPHET
# BRANHAM

Paul C Boyd

QEC
PUBLICATIONS

First Published in Great Britain 2014 by
QEC Publications, PO Box 3368, London N20 0UQ

© Paul C Boyd, 2014
First Edition

ISBN 978-0-9534273-1-4 [print]
ISBN 978-0-9534273-2-1 [Kindle]

Jacket illustration: The montage covers images of Life in Ancient times in Egypt, Greece, and Rome are by courtesy of Common Ground. And photographs of modern day living, buildings, currencies, CNT Tower, White House, gold bars, US dollar, the sphinx and the pyramids of Giza, in the major cities of the world are reproduced by permission of Mensa, Chandler and Boyd. We are also grateful to visual artist David Christie for copyright permission to reproduce the photograph of Big Ben. The tanks, scales, man on the moon, aeroplanes, and jet planes are accredited and sourced from www.public-domain-image.com. Quotes from Reverend Branham in this book were printed with the permission of Voice of God Recordings, Jeffersonville, Indiana, USA. Through Heaven's Eyes, from THE PRINCE OF EGYPT, Words and Music by Stephen Schwartz, Copyright © 1998 DWA SONGS, All Rights Administered by ALMO MUSIC CORP. All Rights Reserved. Used by Permission. Reprinted by permission of Hal Leonard Corporation. The author and publisher would like to thank ©The British Library Board for permission to reproduce the following sources: YC.1990.b.3038, 3624.c.5, m01/32770, vol 1, m01/32769, vol 2, m01/32768, vol 3, m01/32767, vol 4, YC.2005.b.156, 3125.df.15, 3052.dd.19, 3939.bb.41, 4808.h.10, 4857.ff.10, 04034.ee.34, 85/09243, X13/0416, 0900.316000, vol 6, 85/07682, 3940.i.18, 4907.aa.42, 4324.cc.25, P.P.790.ga, MRF/3008,1,reel 55.5, RB.23.b.2992, 1126.k.18, 4650.a.12, RB.23.a.6678, Wq6/0371. 4415.cc.18, 4414.d.2. Special thanks are due to the writer J. Paul LaFontaine, and The LaFontaine Family for permission to quote and reproduce the song "I Feel the Pull", published by J. Paul LaFontaine © 1990 Out of the Fountain Music BMI. Every effort has been made to contact copyright holders, and the publisher apologise for any omissions which they will be pleased to rectify at the earliest opportunity.

Cover Design Cherene Lawmann

Printed in the UK by Russell Press Ltd, Nottingham

Dedicated to the Bride of Christ
of all nations and people and tongues

# CONTENTS

Preface and Acknowledgements      ix

## Chapter One  Introduction:
### A Modern Prophet for A Modern Age      1
What is the meaning of the word prophet?
Why did God send a prophet to this age?
"This is the sum"

## Chapter Two  A New Age      7
The age and its meaning
History in the making
Relevance of authentic history in our age
The correct way to view history
Typology
Determinism or predestination

## Chapter Three  Organised Religion      19
Origin of religion
Babylon past and present
Break up of Roman Catholic Church
Road to pentecostalism

## Chapter Four  The Pentecostal Movement      31
Organised religion revisited
Origin of the holiness movement
How did pentecostalism begin?
What exactly is pentecostalism?
Baptism of the Holy Spirit with sensation
Speaking in tongues
The 1906 Azusa Street Outpouring
The warning

## Chapter Five  Civilisation                                45
Civilisation past present and future
Meaning of civilisation
Where did civilisation first begin?
Nimrod's civilisation
The Pyramids of Giza
Greek civilisation
The Renaissance
The meaning of culture
The Age of Enlightenment
Science
Darwin's death bed confession

## Chapter Six  Meaning and Origin of Rights        61
What do we mean by rights?
Where did rights first come from?
British claims to origins of rights
Elective love

## Chapter Seven  Protecting Human Rights          73
The rights and wrongs of rights
Nelson Mandela
Politics
Viktor Frankl
Psychology
Universal rights
The Laodicean Age

## Chapter Eight  A New Dawn                         89
The Dark Ages and our age
The first Jesuit pope: "A Man of Peace"
A modern approach for a modern age
Roman Catholicism's continuing rise to power

Chapter Nine  The Changing Face of
    Roman Catholicism                       101
The Jesuit way
The pope can do no wrong
Mysticism

Chapter Ten  The Countdown                  111
The Seals
The antichrist
What the four horse riders represent

Chapter Eleven  Signs of The Times          119
The fullness of time
The world economy
Palestine (Israel) God's timepiece
Signs in the sky

Chapter Twelve  Closing of the Age          131
The tribulation
The great millennial reign
The great white throne judgment
The eternal city: a new heaven and a new earth

Summary and Conclusion                      139

Appendices                                  152
Notes                                       184
Bibliography                                217
Recommended reading and websites            233
Glossary                                    235
Index                                       284

# THROUGH THE EYES OF THE PROPHET

Owen Jorgensen, the author of an extensive biography on Branham, summed him up in one word, "supernatural" in his book titled, *Supernatural: The Life of William Branham (1909-1965)*. He described Branham as coming from a poor Kentucky home. Jorgensen says that Branham traces his father's ancestral lineage to Ireland and his mother's to the native Indians in America. He informs us that Branham, whose life was "plagued by poverty and rejection", was a "nervous child". Branham himself confessed that he only received a seventh grade education. According to Jorgensen his research on Branham "drew most of the information from the personal testimony of William Branham himself". He concluded that William Branham was

> ... one of the most influential Christian leaders of the twentieth century – and one of the most controversial. His ministry saw more miracles than any other in recorded history. That much can be verified.[1]

It is not surprising that with such a groundswell of support[2], and "upwards of 2 million people worldwide" believing his message,[3] that Branham is considered to be a prophet and his teachings and messages are deemed to be the vindicated Word of God.[4] Even his most virulent critics noted that the manifestations of the supernatural were "unparallel"[5] in modern times and that divine healings displayed in his ministry "are still held in awe"[6] by Christians today. The printing of some 160 million of Branham's books interpreted into 70 languages and distributed to about 175 different countries since 1984 is no doubt another reason for the assertion that Branham was a prophet.[7]

What I am attempting in this book to show is that the prophet William Marrion Branham, the seventh angel and end-time prophet messenger came to tell us and show us the mysteries that are in the Bible. There is nothing William Branham said about the Lord that is not in the Bible. He came to tell us our position in relation to God, to the Lord Jesus Christ His Son and what will happen until the establishment of His Kingdom on the face of this earth. This was described to Daniel in Chapters 9, 10, 11, and 12 and other places in the Bible. In these chapters of Daniel we see the type of kingdoms and power that will be upon the face of the earth; the movement of civilisation from the east to the west; how the end will come. And finally we witness in Daniel 12 his description of the interplay of politics, religion and civilisation.

The prophet said that in his "third vision" The King of the North referred to in Daniel 12 came within "the realm of world politics". Politics we know is inextricably bound with government, money and the economy. All this was described in symbolic form in the Book of Daniel. Daniel was told to seal up all these things so that the meaning will be made known at the end time. This was undoubtedly the prophecy of the coming of the seventh angel in Revelation 10:7 which clearly states that: "in the days of the voice of the seventh angel when he shall begin to sound the mystery of God should be finished". This is what we are trying to convey to you in *The Age of the Prophet Branham*: that William Marrion Branham was fulfilling Revelation 10:7 thus making the Scriptures plain and known to us.

The *Age of the Prophet Branham* makes use of the prophet's

books, tapes and messages to examine some key events of the past and present which he prophesied would take place. The book therefore begins the process of pointing the reader to the primary and original sources in the Bible and the prophet's message. This is to enable you to examine for yourself what he said would take place. You are given the opportunity in *The Age Of The Prophet Branham* to compare the events I have mentioned in this book with those that have already happened and those Branham prophesied will come to pass.

I also hope that this book will help us to probe further into our divine heritage. Since the prophet's message is based on inspiration and revelation and the King James Version of the Bible, I shall regard such sources as authentic and relevant for this book. I am fully persuaded that the prophet's work is authentic, and that the Bible is an accurate and reliable historical record of God's Word. In fact, the Bible declares that, "All scripture is given by inspiration of God, and is profitable for doctrine, for reproof, for correction, for instruction in righteousness."[8]

I once read that when we say that the Word of God was given by inspiration and revelation it meant that "God simply dictated the whole Bible, so that human contribution was that of the secretary or the tape recorder and transcriber."[9] This view of Biblical history tells us that God's prophet is His mouthpiece and acknowledges that God reveals His secrets to His prophets.[10] That is why we are able to gain insight, make connections and recognise similarities between a range of Branham's prophecies and key past and present historical events.

*The Age of the Prophet Branham*, therefore, is much more than what we ordinarily understand by historical facts as described by the Dickensian character Gradgrind in *Hard Times*: "What I want", declared Mr Gradgrind "is Facts ... facts alone are wanted in life." The meaning of history adopted throughout this book has the same meaning as revelation the prophet attributed to the Greek word "apocalypse", which he says is, "the unveiling". "This unveiling", he continues, "is perfectly described in the example of a sculptor unveiling his work of statuary, exposing it to the onlooker. It is an uncovering, revealing what was previously hidden. Now the uncovering is not only the revelation of the Person of Jesus Christ but it is the revelation of His future works."[11]

In fact, I would suggest that The *Age of the Prophet Branham* views history from what historians call a teleological perspective. The idea of teleology comes from the Greek word "telos" meaning "end" or "purpose" in that God begins with the end in mind and continues until He achieves His purpose. There have been dissenting opinions on the idea of teleology, namely, that world history is heading towards a final end. But in my view such an approach of looking at biblical history from the perspective of inspiration and revelation is relevant. For it takes the personal experience into account. It will therefore help individuals to critically "test the spirits whether they are of God".[12] Such spirits will include "atheists" and "chronologists", and proponents of "natural genesis" or "evolution".[13] These dissenting voices use their own intellect or "carnal conception"[14] to interpret what the prophet is saying to the age.

As a former history teacher, head of a history department in a comprehensive school in the United Kingdom, and historian, I would suggest that the meaning of history as "uncovering" or "unveiling" not only of everything that has happened, but the actual record of ourselves and our heritage, helps us identify with the prophet's assertion that we come from eternity and are going back to eternity. According to the prophet, we are "attributes" of God, because we were in His thinking, and we will never be part of Him, that is the Word, unless we were in Him at the beginning. Branham uses the Greek expression *en morphe*, meaning to change masks like an actor that plays many parts, to demonstrate the different roles God has played in the lives of His children throughout the ages. At one point he uses Shakespeare to draw comparisons from the play *As You Like It*. In that play the character Jacques declared: "all the world is a stage and all the men and women merely players. They have their exits and their entrances; and one man in his time plays many parts. His acts being seven stages". In *Who Is This Melchisedec?* Branham developed his theme by saying that God was *en morphe* in the Pillar of Fire, in a Man called Jesus, and in you, His Bride. When Melchisedec (God) appeared to Abraham, the prophet declared, He was showing or revealing to Abraham all of His attributes His sons and daughters would be manifesting in the last days. They would be like Him and do exactly as He did, Branham said. This means, he continued, that the sons and daughters of God will be changed from mortality to immortality and will one day be raptured like Christ and have glorified bodies like His.

According to the prophet, it is only through man that history is made. One of the aims of this book is to show how the prophet revealed that God was using man to shape and mould biblical history. Viktor Frankl in *Man's Search for Meaning* (1946) writing after the II World War demonstrates that natural man has throughout history been in search for the purpose for which he came to this earth. I discuss his work later in this book. It is therefore important, I think, that we first find out who we are, where we come from, where we are going and the purpose of us being on this earth. At one level this is what the prophet's message is about.

Readers would benefit from consulting the extensive references which appear in the notes for each chapter at the back of the book. Many of these references are taken from The Table, Version 2005, Voice of God Recordings, and contain some 1200 of the prophet's message. You can look up what has been said from this source or in the Bible, the prophet's printed and published Message or the secondary sources using the reference in the notes at the back of the book. You may wish to check the accuracy of a quote or fact or you may wish to do some more reading or research on the subject. There is also a bibliography which you might find helpful. I have also used secondary sources to look at some key historical events made clear by the prophecy of William Branham. I have pointed out in one secondary source that economic historians such as Martin Jacques suggests that by 2050 the developing world, particularly in eastern Asian countries like China, would be the largest economic power in the world outstripping the United States.[15] Moreover, I have suggested that Jacques' observation in his book *When China Rules the World* (2012) appears to be a confirmation of Branham's 1956 prophecy that China, one of the world's oldest civilisations[16] will be on the rise again.[17] Eastern nations, proclaimed the prophet, will, according to the Bible, once again "blossom like a rose and would bring forth her abundance".[18]

I have painstakingly checked the British Library for the original references and rare books the prophet consulted which are reproduced in Voice of God Recordings Books InfoBase in *The Table*, Version 2005. Many of these references appear in the notes for each chapter at the back of the book. You are at liberty to follow up these references and the website links in the notes at the back of the book for further research and more detailed investigation. The © British Library Board have given permission to reproduce the original source/ reference of these books. They can be found in the British Library which I have included under Appendix A titled "Branham's Original Sources".

Many of these ancient books date back from the fifteenth century to the beginning of the twentieth century, and are listed in the British Library. They were written by believers, historians and other writers of high academic qualifications and impeccable reputation. A number of these books have more than one edition and I have endeavoured to select the oldest editions for reference which are listed in the back of this book under the heading "Branham's Original Sources." It has not been possible to ascertain which of the many editions the prophet used. Nevertheless I have used these books to support my belief that what the prophet has to say is both authentic and relevant and should be explored further by the reader if you so wish. You will also see that I have created a Glossary of biblical and other names and terms. Many of these were selected from the original sources he used including his 1200 messages recorded in *The Table* (2005) to reflect the most up to the minute meanings and usages of words and expressions the prophet spoke by inspiration and revelation. In addition, the recommended reading and website is compulsory reading and viewing for readers who wish to gain a deeper understanding of what the prophet has to say.

I have drawn up a template which is inserted in the back of the book showing 40 countries in the four continents of Africa, Asia, America and Europe which are contacts and hosts of the prophet's messages including books, tapes and other products. The contacts email addresses and telephone numbers are also included if you would like to know where to get in touch in the area where you live.

I am eternally grateful and indebted to Victor Lawmann and the brethren of Shalom Bible Study Fellowship for their tireless encouragement, unstinting support, and practical and helpful comments. Needless to say without the contribution of any one of them I would never have completed the work. I would like to extend a special thank you to Cherene Lawmann for the cover design. The montage is a masterpiece and reflects her expertise, dedication and commitment to the work.

I am deeply indebted to Olayinka Ibidunni for his IC

commentaries and recordings on the closing of the age. I am also grateful to my own sister Rose Boyd for her inspirational thoughts and the books and other resources on the Welsh Revival she contributed. I owe a deep debt to Peter Chandler of the Local Christian Assembly who was unwavering in his support. I am more moved than I can say at the great amount of time he spent on my work, amounting to many hours on the telephone at times. I am most grateful to Mary Lawmann for her close scrutiny of the work in terms of spelling, punctuation and grammar; and her helpful reminders that the text must be written to captivate the minds of the ordinary person in the common language of our global citizens. My gratitude also extends to Albert Djanmah whose contribution has added greatly to the simple causal connections based strictly on the Word of God; and his passion that the work should be a legacy in leadership for the youth in our present and future generations.

Last but not least, I owe an incalculable debt to my wife Sila and daughters Rebekah and Hannah for their patience and emotional support and for devoting a considerable amount of time reading and commenting on the manuscript despite their other commitments.

Chapter One

# INTRODUCTION: A MODERN PROPHET FOR A MODERN AGE

*The great man of the age is the one who can put into words the will of his age, tell his age what its will is, and accomplish it. What he does is the heart and essence of his age; he actualizes his age.*
– Georg Wilhelm Friedrich Hegel, *Philosophy of Right*, 1942[1]

Once I gave the above quote to a message believer to read and asked her to explain what it was about. She read it and said that she had no idea what it meant. The quote was taken from the well known philosopher and historian Hegel. The point of the quote was to explain why great men are great. Hegel's view is that the great man is one who sees the world in a mess; and in chaos. He first tells the world what mess they are in, why they are in that mess, and what they can do to get themselves out of that mess. In fact the great man defines the age. He gives the age a remedy for its sickness, and diseases.

We are talking here about a great man in the natural realm. He gives natural solutions to natural problems. However this definition of the man we call great in this world is a type of the characteristics we can use to identify a great man of God to whom the Word of God comes to give us spiritual solutions to our problems. The prophet of our age is this great man of God.

## WHAT IS THE MEANING OF THE WORD PROPHET?
The prophet said that "a prophet is a man who's born and

predestinated and foreordained for that generation".[2] "At the end of this age", the prophet insists, "a prophet will come",[3] but the people will miss his coming because of their wretchedness and blindness. In fact so often when we are reading or listening to the prophet's message we notice that William Branham did not want to say outright that he was a prophet, but sometimes he did say under inspiration: "Do you believe I'm His prophet ...?"[4] In *The Anointed Ones At The End Time* he made it clear that, "The Holy Spirit is the prophet of this hour; He [is] a vindicating His Word, proving It. The Holy Spirit [was the] prophet of Moses' hour. The Holy Spirit was the prophet of Micaiah's hour. The Holy Spirit, which wrote the Word, comes and confirms the Word."[5] He pleaded in the following words for the people to accept that he was merely a vessel used by God to do His will. "Always remember this", declared the prophet. "God takes His man off the earth, but never takes His Spirit. His Spirit comes right back down this a way. It come upon Elijah, went off of Elijah onto to Elisha, off of Elisha It come on John the Baptist, off of John the Baptist, and is predicted to come again in the last days, the same Spirit. See? It's God's Spirit. The Holy Spirit was upon the Church at Pentecost, come right down through the age and right on down through the age to the Lutheran, Baptist, Methodist, and on down through, on into this age here. It's still the same Holy Spirit."[6]

Now, how does the great natural man find out the cause or causes of the problems facing our generation? He always looks into the past to find out how he can help solve the problems we are facing at present. That is how Hegel was able to know what great men do by studying what great men did in each age of history. The prophet, a man of God, did the same thing when he wanted to find out what was wrong with those sick people who came before him. He looked into their history, their past. He saw (through the eye of the prophet), what the problem was, where it came from, when it first begun, how it started, and why the "patient" was in that sick condition. He was able to probe into the darkest areas of a person's life. Once he knew the cause(s) of the problem he was able to tell the person what they could do about it. He used the same approach to investigate and comment on church history, world history, and current affairs. In other words he was commenting on what was happening at that particular moment in time in the areas of religion, politics, and the moral and social state of the people and society. Many of us ought to follow the example of the prophet by studying about the past and knowing our day and its message. He was well read; He had historians as his friend. Thus good background knowledge of the age of the prophet, could help us understand the time in which we are living.

The purpose of this book is to enable us to gain a much more in-depth insight into the age in which the prophet came and lived. It will attempt to answer questions such as: What problems and events were taking place when the prophet came on the scene? How and where did all this trouble start in the first place? What was the prophet saying about our modern world and what problems were we likely to face in the future? In answering these questions this book aims to examine the extent to which the prophet's message would be able to demonstrate to his and future generations those modern events which he said would come to pass. We shall be identifying at the end of this introduction and throughout this book a few of those key events. These include events relating to: religion, science and civilisation.

## WHY DID GOD SEND A PROPHET TO THIS AGE?

Many children and young people often asked us at Sunday school, why did God send a prophet to our generation? We would tell them that before the prophet came on the scene in the first half of the twentieth century the whole world was in a mess. We explained that at the time, a large number of people held false beliefs just as they do today. We said that at the beginning of the twentieth century there were wars, diseases, disasters and other terrible events taking place in our world. They listened. They questioned. They wanted answers. Sometimes we thought they asked too many hard questions; questions which made us read the message more and seek the face of the Lord for help.

We told them that these events were a clear sign that we were drawing to the close of the age; and that the reason God sent the prophet was to answer the very questions they were asking – questions about the wars, earthquakes, poverty, filth and "moral decay" which we still see in the world today. Questions about other religions and the many beliefs held by the different Christian churches were fired at us. We understood why they asked these questions because they had friends at schools and in the community that held different Christian and other religious beliefs who were asking them such questions. I remember one little girl of five years of age asking, "What if the things we are told about the prophet are not true?" and "What if the prophet is not telling us the truth?" Whilst her peers were surprised at the questions she posed, these were very profound questions which challenged her Sunday school teachers. For by the time her peers reached their teens they were not satisfied to be told that the reason God sent a prophet to this age was "to introduce the Messiah and to tie up the loose ends."

They saw the contradictions and confusion in the Christian world with their friends attending different denominations and multi-faith organisations. Our young people wanted clear answers to the very real problems that they were facing in society and to be told that God sent a prophet to explain the Bible from Genesis to Revelation and to deliver a modern message for a modern age clearly did not cut ice with them when they had to face the big, bad, wide world. This little girl is now in her twenties. She was prudent enough to search the scriptures and studied the prophet's message to be fully persuaded in her mind that what was presented to her is the truth. She did not take it on the say so of her Sunday school teachers or parents that God sent a prophet. She needed to have an individual experience with God. And today she is a very devout Christian and understands the contradictions and confusion in what many in the denominations pay lip service to as Christianity.

Thus we would suggest that the reason God sent us the end time prophet messenger was to "call out a Bride", to answer many questions left unanswered in Christendom, and to make clear teachings on the Godhead, Water Baptism, Original Sin, Predestination, the Seven Seals, The New Birth, and so on. These truths were restored in our age. The aim of the prophet's message was to prepare the Bride of Jesus Christ in every nation to recognise that God has come in the flesh to put us back in the position we would have been in had the fall not taken place. And to get us ready for the rapture which is the second coming of the Lord. What we really must have in mind when thinking about the background history of the age, is that the prophet was sent to shed light on the chaos in which he found the world and to restore the Word – the Truth, to the children of God.

**"THIS IS THE SUM"**
The following biblical expression is the opening statement that explains the purpose of this sub-section of the book. "Now of the things which we have spoken this is the sum."[7] I am merely using this scripture to suggest that what I am about to say is a summary of this chapter. For its purpose is to demonstrate that the aim of the book is to enable us to see how this single thread, namely, the summary, fits into the grand story or tapestry from which *The Age of the Prophet Branham* is woven or written. The central theme running through this grand story or single thread is Christ. The thread

is a type of the age, and the age here means the beginning of time to the end of time. The prophet talks about events throughout the ages from the beginning to the end of time when the age melts into the Great Age which is eternity. Thus though we focus on the twentieth century because the prophet came in that age, we will, like the prophet, consider "the age" to embrace other ages throughout the annals of history including that Grand Age, he refers to as "eternity". I hope that the excerpt from the Lyrics quoted below, "Through Heaven's Eyes", sung by Brian Stokes Mitchell who acted as Jethro, high priest of Midian, in *Prince of Egypt*, supports the point I am making that this single thread represents the age in the broadest sense of the word, that is, the beginning of time until the closing of the age when there will be "time no longer", and the ushering of the age into that Grand Age called eternity. The Lyrics are sung by Jethro at a time when we see Moses questioning whether he is of any worth at all after fighting off the "attackers" or "bully boys" who were threatening the high priest's daughters.

A single thread in a tapestry
Though its colour brightly shine
Can never see its purpose
In the pattern of the grand design

And the stone that sits on the very top
Of the mountain's mighty face
Does it think it's more important
Than the stone that forms the base?

So how can you see what your life is worth
Or where your value lies?
You can never see through the eyes of man
You must look at your life
Look at your life
Through heaven's eyes.

Chapter Two

# A NEW AGE

*It was the best of times, it was the worst of times, it was the age of wisdom, it was the age of foolishness, it was the epoch of belief, it was the epoch of incredulity, it was the season of Light, it was the season of Darkness, it was the spring of hope, it was the winter of despair, we had everything before us, we had nothing before us, we were all going direct to Heaven, we were all going direct the other way – in short, the period was so far like the present period, that some of its noisiest authorities insisted on its being received, for good or for evil....*
– Charles Dickens, A Tale of Two Cities, 1859

## THE AGE AND ITS MEANING

At the end of the Introduction we saw that the age could have many meanings. The birth of the twentieth century prophet William Marrion Branham on Tuesday 6 April 1909 signalled the continuation of a new age which arrived in 1906. What exactly does this mean? Of course we have a story to tell. We called it the grand story in Chapter One. However, the story we have to tell about the age would not make sense unless we told it in the right order. Thus one of the first things historians do is to tell us about what took place in the order it happened. Historians are not the only ones who are interested in what happened or what is going to happen. We too need to be certain in our everyday lives about what is likely to happen. This is why our ancestors thought of calendars to help us work out the time something is likely to happen. In the United Kingdom the calendar divides time up into days, weeks, and months. When we come to use the calendar we see that they have made it easier for us to use it by dividing it up again. The days are given names and numbers, the months are given names, and the years numbers. For example, we say that the prophet William Marrion Branham was born on Tuesday 6 April 1909.

We know that the study of time and dates is called chronology, that is, to organise events so that first things come first, and last things come last. Chronology is just a first step in saying what happened in the past and why. We know that in biblical history time begun when God first spoke the Word "Let there be."[1] I was once asked to think very carefully about my claim that time started when God first spoke the Word. Like a good researcher I combed through the prophet's entire message to find out what he had to say about the beginning of time. He made it clear that where the Bible says "in the beginning, that's when time started, when Eternity broke down into time..."[2] Historians need to find some way of dividing up the time so that we know what "bit" of time they are talking about. Suppose, for example, someone were to ask you where you live, it is unlikely that you would say "the universe" then walk away. You would probably tell them the continent, in which you live, and the country, county, city, town, village, or street and indeed house number. A list of events in date order by itself would not help us to understand the full story. Now we know that there are different ways to divide up time. The prophet has divided up time in the same way that historians have divided up time. Historians talk about periods or ages in history. For example, the prophet talks about the Ephesian Church Age (53-170) and the Philadelphian Church Age (1750-1906). The prophet in his book *An Exposition of the Seven Church Ages* insists that in fact there are seven church ages.

We can see from reading the prophet's message that "the age" has at least three meanings. The first meaning of the age is where it refers to a certain or fixed period of time like in the church ages where each age is divided into "bits". The second meaning of the age is when we say that it is the period from the beginning of time to the end of time. Thus, the use of the term "the age" might be more than the years covering the birth and death of the prophet. It could refer to the entire period of existence of planet earth from its beginning to the end of the world as we know it.

The prophet also talks about the age as meaning that great age when we will be in eternity with our Lord. He had no doubt that there would be "the second coming of our Lord to receive us into His glorious Kingdom where there'll be no end to that great age."[3] For the purpose of this book the age of the prophet covers the past, present and future. We will focus on the age in which the prophet lived, namely the twentieth century, bearing in mind that the age embraces the history of earlier centuries, the twenty first century and beyond into eternity. We will therefore extend its meaning to cover that "Great Age" which melts into eternity.

## HISTORY IN THE MAKING

I once read a saying by a great man who said that: "a people without the knowledge of their past history, origin, and culture is like a tree without roots". Natural man has from the beginning of time wanted to find out where he comes from and where he is going. Even before history was written men studied the things that survived which our ancestors used as tools such as stone, bronze or iron to find out about our origin. We also notice that there are other records used by historians to find out about where we come from. These records include scrolls, temples, the pyramids, and oral records, for example, they would ask the oldest living person on earth to tell them what their parents and grandparents told them about what happened in the past. There is always a hunger, a thirst for us to find out about our family tree. Once when I was teaching history in a state school in the United

Kingdom the pupils asked me where I came from. I told them that I was born in an island called Dominica in the Caribbean.

My father was a native of the Caribbean. When Africans were brought to the Caribbean during the time of slavery Africans and Caribbeans married each other. My culture and history is therefore African Caribbean. I also told my pupils that my grandmother was French from the French colony of Martinique in the Caribbean. This was due to the French taking Africans to the Caribbean as slaves. So where did the name Boyd come from? My pupils were very keen to know. Ah! It came from Scotland, I told them. Like young adults who love history they listened in awe and excitement. We had real fun studying a unit of British history which gave us the opportunity to find out where we came from.

Just as natural man is always striving to find out where he comes from, spiritual man, the man of God, the Christian strives day and night to find out his spiritual origin. We have already seen how the prophet looked into a person's past to find out why they were sick. Similarly history testifies that "as a prophet, as a seer that sees things before it comes to pass and what's going to be afterwards",[4] he could confidently say by his use of the scriptures that you were in Christ before the foundation of the world. So you can confidently say, "I come from God, and I go to God" – that's where you first came from, that's your origin.

I remember once after reading *Christ Is The Mystery of God Revealed* by the prophet, I said to one of the brethren in conversation that Christ was the history. The point the prophet was making is that Christ is the creator of everything. And He is history for according to the Bible; He is the same, yesterday, today and forever. He is the Maker of meaning. Indeed He is History in the making. He is the "Author". He is the "Alpha". He is the "Finisher". He is the "Omega". "History is life itself",[5] and life is the very essence of Christ. "History", declared one writer whilst still a US ambassador, "is the torch that is meant to illuminate the past". In biblical history, that "torch", that "light" is Christ. And so the prophet continuing his theme on history concludes: "He [Christ] was the history, see, and He is the Prophet. He is the Psalms. He is everything. And if you can't make Him everything, and the same, where, what's your picture look like? Do you see it?"[6] But The Prophet was careful to warn that in the physical realm, "history only tells us what we have read, of what has been. And what's in the future lays in the hand of God".[7]

## RELEVANCE OF AUTHENTIC HISTORY IN OUR AGE

The prophet uses the expression "authentic history"[8] to signal that an historical event was "real", "genuine", and "infallible" like the Word of God, that is, "having the origin supported by unquestionable evidence". Authentic history is infallible. In the previous section we noted that the prophet declared: "[Christ] was the history." Now if Christ is the history, and Christ is "the same yesterday", then it is an absolute fact that if we look at history through the eyes of the prophet, the eyes of the eagle, as it were, then what he says as the mouthpiece of God is history in the making, and therefore infallible. For the Word of God is the absolute. We could imagine the children whom I taught in England bringing their authentic or real photographs of themselves to show the class what they looked like when they were first born; or asking their ninety year old granny to explain to the class what it was like during the First and Second World Wars. Although you might question whether we can rely on granny's memory being authentic, it would be more difficult to dispute the fact that the photographs presented to the class by pupils of themselves when they were born were authentic. You could possibly think of lots and lots of examples to explain the meaning of the word authentic history such as old tools, stones, weapons and written records that were there at that particular moment in time the historian was writing about. The prophet

makes use of "biblical" and "profane" history[9] to help us
develop a knowledge of chronological events and prophecies
in the Bible which have taken place from the beginning of
time and will take place in our world and the world to come.
"Profane history" are records of events not recorded in the
Bible, but help us develop an understanding and awareness of
biblical and other historical events.

In *Modern Events Are Made Clear By Prophecy* the prophet
demonstrates how Jesus when he met the two disciples on
their way to the village of Emmaus uses biblical history to tell
them about Himself. "Beginning at Moses and all the
prophets" the Bible states, "He [Christ] expounded unto them
in all the scriptures the things concerning Himself."[10] Luke
did not mention any specific scriptures or historical events
relating to Christ when he used the word "expounded".

Nevertheless, the Bible recorded that He expounded "all
the scriptures", from Moses up until the present time. The
prophet sought to identify and list twenty such scriptures
Jesus was referring to as having taken place "beginning at
Moses"[11] that is, from the time man was first created. He listed
prophecies and historical events from the Psalms, Isaiah,
Zechariah and Malachi. This was in an attempt to help us
fully appreciate what Jesus was saying about Himself
concerning His birth, death, burial and resurrection.
Evidence that such events took place no doubt demonstrates
the true meaning of authentic history. For history, according
to one notable source is: "everything that has happened", and
"our actual record of what has happened".[12] Christ was
therefore telling the two disciples everything concerning
Himself. In fact He was telling them the history of his past. In
Christendom, our only authentic or true history is found in
the Bible. Profane history can only be the truth if it is
supported by evidence of the scriptures. So, how then do we
know what is true and what is false. We would have to rely
on the Holy Spirit to lead us into all truth. And this would be

evident in the life of the believer, in the words of the prophet, "after being baptized with the Holy Ghost ... would have the Teacher come and teach all truth. But that Teacher was an INSIDE teacher, not an outside teacher. If the Spirit wasn't inside, you wouldn't hear the truth and receive it by revelation if you heard it every moment of the day".[13]

The prophet frequently read and quoted historians who told the truth about biblical and profane history to support prophecies which came to pass or historical events he was preaching or writing about. Such historians included James Ussher (1581-1656) and Alexander Hislop (1807-1865). Where history supports what the Bible is saying it is a testimony; for a testimony is the evidence we get from a witness who makes a statement to say that something is true. We know that the Gospels were written by men of renown who knew full well how to present testimonies of people, events, time and places of the historical period in which they lived. For example, we have eye-witness testimonies of the historical event of the risen Christ, we trust them, and cling to the story of the risen Christ including the testimonies of those who followed in His footsteps.[14] In fact where the history in this book agrees with what the prophet says it is a testimony.

THE CORRECT WAY TO VIEW HISTORY
How then do we view some of these major events which relate to the age of the prophet? The correct way to view history would be through the mind of Christ or Holy Spirit, namely the eagle "that looks far off and sees the great time coming".[15] In the following quote the prophet has no doubt that we should change our seeing, and look at the world, through the Eagle's Eye, namely, the Holy Spirit, which is Christ in us, the hope of glory:

... now it's in the eye time, the seeing. See? Now, there isn't one moving faculty beyond the eye. Is that right? The next is the intelligence, which is Christ Itself, Who controls the whole Body. No moving, motion beyond that. See? Everything else has moved. See? Move your feet, move your muscles in your legs, move everything. ... Your ears can move, your nose, your lips, and so forth. But after your eyes, there is nothing moves.[16]

Once the prophet knew and understood that the correct way to view History is through the eye of the Holy Spirit, the eye of Christ, he explained in the following extract the way in which he approached the study of the history of the seven Church ages in order to find out what happened throughout those ages.

Since this study was to be the most serious one I had ever undertaken up to this time, I sought God for many days for the Inspiration of the Holy Spirit. Then only did I read the Scriptures on the Church Ages and delve into the many church histories written by the most unbiased historians that I could find. God did not fail to answer my prayer, for while I read the Word and the histories, I was enabled by the Holy Spirit to see unfolded a pattern that runs through the centuries and right into this present, last day. The key given me of the Lord whereby I was able to determine the messenger for each age is a most Scriptural one. In fact it might be called the Keystone of the Bible. It is the revelation that God never changes, and that His ways are as unchangeable as He is.[17]

Many people[18] including historians[19] and Christians alike have been trying to find out about the truth of historical events throughout the ages. "What is truth ask some historians?" Jesus clearly had the final Word on the matter when He declared, "I am the way The Truth and The Life."[20] Bible commentators, Bible believers, and Bible historians, tend to view biblical history and indeed the history of the world from a biblical stand point, that is, that God knows the end from the beginning, and therefore He begins with the end in mind. Theologians have also invented a word from Greek to refer to Biblical History to explain the scripture which declares that "to everything there is a season, and a time to every purpose under the heaven".[21] The word they use to explain this is called teleology. They say that "telos" in Greek means "purpose" or "end". So God has a purpose for his creation of the world and the human race. No wonder the age appears to be continuous from the beginning of time to end of time where there is "time no longer" and in the end time melts into eternity.

## TYPOLOGY

The prophet, historians and Bible commentators of our age are agreed that one way to test whether our world view is correct is to use types. "Everything that God has, everything in the natural types the spiritual",[22] declares the prophet. And we know that type means a figure or symbol of a place, person, event or thing in the Old Testament which is a shadow of things to come in the New Testament. The shadow of a person is a symbol that there is an actual person in existence. That there is a natural world means that there is a spiritual world also. The prophet said that he is a "typologist" because he believed that was the correct way to view the world and get at the truth with the help of the Holy Spirit.

Communism is one of those major events in world history in modern times in our natural world which mimics or copies Christianity in the spiritual world. In fact the prophet commented that "this is the age of the communist where all men are supposedly equal".[23] Communism is merely a higher form of socialism and in the words of the prophet, "according to our liberal theologians Jesus was a socialist and the early church under the guidance of the Spirit practised socialism and thus we ought to do so today".[24] It is not surprising therefore that many communists suggest that the way in which they view the world is correct and that others should use this as a symbol or model through which they should view or see the world. No wonder the prophet in his condemnation and rejection of communism remarked in a federal court that, "If communism had Christianity in it, I'd be a communist. But I can't be, because it denies Christianity."[25] Moreover, he concluded, "there's nothing written in the Scripture about communism ruling the world".[26] "Romanism" he insists, "is going to conquer the world".[27]

## DETERMINISM OR PREDESTINATION

The word "antitype" is used many times in the prophet's Message. I rather suspect that some of us are familiar with the word and others are not. I asked a "Message believer" the other day whether they knew what the word antitype meant and they did not know what I was talking about! Antitype means the original, for example, the original pound note or dollar bill. The "type" is a copy of the original. In the Bible the type was "a shadow" of what was going to take place in the New Testament. For example, the killing of the lamb as a sacrifice in the Old Testament was a symbol of Christ who was going to come to the earth to be sacrificed as we have read in the New Testament. The "type" is merely a carbon copy, "a shadow", symbol or representation of the original or prototype. Thus whilst predestination is a genuine spiritual representation of an event or person which is "foreordained"; determinism is the natural representation of a person or event which will come to pass. Predestination is the antitype or real thing and determinism is the type or copy. The trees we see on earth are a type or shadow or copy of the antitype or real tree which exists in the spiritual realm. The natural tree will be done away with. The spiritual tree will remain throughout eternity.

The prophet said that God Being God knows the end from

the beginning. "Predestination looks to destiny".[28] Determinism on the other hand has a meaning similar to predestination. Determinism in our natural world means that whatever is there in the universe to happen will take place. To put it bluntly, determinism is used by communists and Marxists in the age of the prophet to suggest that everything is due to natural causes or laws. For example, the Greeks at one time thought that laws made by man are given to him by nature. They therefore believed that the laws we make must be based on nature alone. The idea of determinism gives the communists the excuse to deny that God exists. They say that what happens in the world or universe is due to nature or natural events or causes as they are there to happen anyway. In 1967 a communist writer and historian who believed in determinism exclaimed it thus: "I am wholly what I am. I do not have to look for the universal."[29] "And so it is not I who make a meaning for myself but it is the meaning that was already there, pre-existing, waiting for me."[30] The writer in question, an atheist, was drawing his inspiration from the following words of his icon Karl Marx whom he worshipped:

> Men make their own history, but they do not make it just as they please; they do not make it under circumstances chosen by themselves, but under circumstances directly encountered, given and transmitted from the past.[31]

"Each generation" declares this disciple of Marx and communism, "must, out of relative obscurity, discover its mission, fulfil it, or betray it".[32] Here, this servant of communism and determinism is suggesting that each individual is born to fulfil a certain mission in life, which he must first discover and then carry out. The ideas of this god of communism, Karl Marx, stepped out of the nineteenth century into the age of the prophet. He no longer believed that we are free moral agents. He believed everything that happens to us is there to happen.

There is nothing we can do about it, it is our fate, our destiny, he said.

Marx warned, that: "history does nothing, it possesses no immense wealth, fights no battles. It is rather man, real living man who does everything, who possesses and fights".[33] He finally gave up the ghost declaring that "human beings enter into definite and necessary relations which are independent of their will".[34] He was making the point again that everything man does is due to natural laws or the result of natural causes, and that he has no say in the matter. These ancient and nineteenth century man made ideas in the form of communism spilt over into the age of the prophet. They are still having an impact on our present generation. Here the prophet reminds us of the Bible prophecy that in our "day ... knowledge shall increase ... the wise shall know their God, in that day, and shall do great exploits in that day. But the wicked will not know the God of Heaven".[35] The rise of communism, one of the world's most revered ideologies is, amongst other things, the fulfilment of this prophecy. Moreover, the ideology of Karl Marx appears to have lost much of its popular appeal as the alternative to man's search for meaning in this world and the one to come.

## Chapter Three

# ORGANISED RELIGION

*Now, the book of Genesis is the beginning. The very word "Genesis" means "beginning". Now, everything begin [s] in Genesis. Evil begin in Genesis; good begin in Genesis. Life begin [s] in Genesis. Death begin [s]in Genesis. The creation begin [s] in Genesis. Every religion begin [s] in Genesis. Every spirit started in Genesis.*
– William Branham, *God Keeps His Word*, 1957[1]

You may well ask, what on earth has the above quote got to do with religion in the age of the prophet? Of course it would take a seer to respond in the words quoted above that "everything's got a religion";[2] for this is what the prophet had to say about religion in our age. Religion is a belief in something or the worship of something or the obedience to some natural or supernatural power,[3] good or evil, that has control over our lives. For the German theologian Rudolf Otto, "all religion" is "wholly emotional" and accepted by its disciples "as a blind and overpowering force, or spirit".[4] It is generally formal and something we do over and over again in honour of an object of worship. It usually involves rituals or ceremonies which are more often than not formal and practised in an organisation or institution such as a football stadium, or other gathering such as churches, lodges or the sun worship temple Stonehenge in Britain.

In many people's mind religion has something to do with a belief system, in God, that is holy, sacred, spiritual or divine which has become their traditional way of life. In the prophet's view, "Religion means a covering." Thus a person may have a Baptist, Presbyterian, Methodist or Pentecostal covering[5], and what is more their covering could be Socialist, Fascist, Nazi, Atheist or Communist to fit the wider meaning of the prophet's definition of the word religion by his expression that, "everything's got a religion"?

## ORIGIN OF RELIGION

The prophet tells us that the idea of religion started in heaven by Satan who got a group of angels to worship him. He and his fallen angels were thrown out of heaven by God, and landed on earth at "the world's headquarters in the garden of Eden, in Egypt",[6] to use the words of the prophet. There were two trees in the middle of the Garden of Eden, declared the prophet. One of these represented the Tree of Life which was Christ and the other the Tree of Knowledge of good and evil, which was Satan. Satan's aim, he said, was to use scientific Knowledge, intellectual knowledge, theological knowledge "to build a greater Christian civilisation."[7] This was the "knowledge of good and evil" which first originated in the Garden of Eden through organised religion, he said. So, how was Satan going to achieve this? Witness the scene in Genesis 3 in the Garden of Eden:

> Now the serpent was more subtil than any beast of the field which the LORD God had made. And he said unto the woman, Yea, hath God said, Ye shall not eat of every tree of the garden? [2] And the woman said unto the serpent, We may eat of the fruit of the trees of the garden: [3] But of the fruit of the tree which is in the midst of the garden, God hath said, Ye shall not eat of it, neither shall ye touch it, lest ye die. [4] And the serpent said unto the woman, Ye shall not surely die: [5] For God doth know that in the day ye eat thereof, then your eyes shall be opened, and ye shall be as gods, knowing good and evil. [6] And when the woman saw that the tree was good for food, and that it was pleasant to the eyes, and a tree to be desired to make one wise, she took of the fruit thereof, and did eat, and gave also unto her husband with her; and he did eat.[8]

However, as "he has no creative powers", declares the prophet, "the only way for Satan to accomplish what he wanted to do was to enter the serpent in Eden even as he entered by evil spirits into the swine at Gadara".[9] It was in this way that he entered the human race by speaking to Eve through the serpent and caused man to disobey the Word of God. Moreover, declared the prophet, Satan sought to achieve his aim through the seed of the serpent, namely Cain. Thus Cain brought fruits before the Lord as an offering of sacrifice.[10] The Lord turned down his man-made ideas, his man-made religion. But this did not discourage Satan. In Genesis 6 he went ahead with his scheme to "pervert"[11] God's plan of creation. He therefore set up his own kingdom on earth. He wanted people to worship him. This was for him to gain total control over the whole of God's creation on earth. In the process of time, the Bible proclaims, "when men began to multiply on the face of the earth, and daughters were born unto them,[2] That the sons of God saw the daughters of men that they were fair; and they took them wives of all which they chose".[12] "We find out", says the prophet, "that they become great scientists, great workers of wood: great, smart, educated people. And they had a great economy, and they lived in such a scientific age until they built pyramids that we couldn't build today."[13]

**BABYLON PAST AND PRESENT**
Thus we can track "the trail of the serpent"[14] from Egypt[15] to Babylon. In Babylon Satan continued his scheme through Nimrod who led God's children astray. Nimrod's father was Cush. He was the son of Ham, one of the three sons' of Noah.[16] Nimrod's great grand uncle was Shem. Ham and Shem were the sons of Noah. The Bible says that Nimrod "was a mighty hunter before the Lord ... and the beginning of his kingdom was Babel".[17] He assembled the people together to build the Tower of Babel. The aim was so that its "top may

reach unto heaven".[18] He would therefore be able to " ... get out of the way of all the floods and destructions, and find his way back on this tower, in Babel, back to God".[19] According to historian Diop, the Tower of Babel was like the "step pyramids in Saqqara, Egypt".[20] In fact Alexander Hislop in *The Two Babylons*, a book the prophet frequently referred to, suggests that it was Cush who "built or founded Babylon", but it was his son Nimrod, who erected The Tower of Babel.[21] Hislop concluded that Nimrod or Ninus (the son) and his wife Semiramis in Babylon were also known as Osiris and Isis in Egypt. They were, he said, the same Mother or Madonna and Child worshipped in our day under the name of Jesus and Mary by the followers of Roman Catholicism.

Nimrod's great nephew, Abraham, a gentile,[22] was an idol worshipper in the city of Ur, in Babylon. It was the Babylonian system that was practised in Egypt, Greece and Rome which was borrowed by the Roman Catholic Church. The three leading Church Fathers Tertullian (155-222) and Cyprian (249-258) both from Carthage, and Augustine (354-430) from Numidia in North Africa practised idol and Babylonian forms of worship.[23] These three members of the North African Church are said to be the pioneers in establishing organised Christianity as the official religion of the Roman Empire. When Constantine "the great" (306-337) became Emperor of the Roman Empire, Christianity was already well established by the "Church Fathers". Therefore, on his conversion to Christianity he decreed that Christianity should be the official religion under a united East and West Roman Empire. In 325 he called the First Council of Nicaea, now present day Iznik in Turkey. This is where the bishops met who set up "the organisation of the great universal Christian church, that is, the Roman Catholic Church".[24]

It was here at the Nicene Council that the idea of the trinity was first introduced – the doctrine of the three persons in one God: God the Father, God the Son and God the Holy

Ghost including the worship of the Mother and Child. The endorsement of this doctrine by the Nicene Council prompted the prophet to comment that it was at this time "pagan Rome became papal Rome",[25] in that Constantine united "the church and state together'.[26] In the prophet's view Constantine gave control of the state to the Roman Catholic Church.[27] It in turn wielded a great deal of power over many nations all over the world. Children in British schools learn about the grip the Roman Catholic Church had in England and Europe.

By 1066 when William the Conqueror landed in Britain the whole of the country was already divided into parishes. Each parish had its own church and its own priest. The Church was the largest gathering, the largest organisation within the community outside the family, not only in Britain, but Europe as a whole. It was responsible to a much larger organisation in Rome. Around 1500, for example, the Roman Catholic Church exerted a powerful influence on village life in Britain. The Church was the largest building in the villages apart from the manor and formed the centre of people's social life in the villages. It was the largest organisation in Europe before the Industrial Revolution.

According to one historian: "sitting in the 10,000 parish churches of England at every service, Sundays and Saint days, holy days, that is, or holidays as we now call them",[28] everyone went to church. In the hierarchy of the Roman Catholic Church during this time every official was ranked according to their status in the Church. For example: "Over a group of priests was a bishop. Over a group of bishops was an archbishop. Over all the archbishops was the pope in Rome, because the Church stretched across Europe."[29] In our ancient and far distant past there was one united Church of Europe, that is, the Roman Catholic Church with the pope at the top. All the kings, princes and emperors of Europe were ruled by Rome.

## BREAKUP OF ROMAN CATHOLIC CHURCH

Martin Luther (1483 – 1546), a German priest, has been credited with starting the Protestant Reformation by bringing to an end Rome's stranglehold over the kingdoms of the world. He strongly disagreed with many of the doctrines of the Roman Catholic Church such as its teachings that the communion was the "literal body of God";[30] their belief that the Church has the power to forgive sins, and that people would not be punished for their sins if they paid money to the Church for them.

Other men of God in Europe like Huldrych Zwingli (1484 – 1531), a pastor in Switzerland, followed Luther's example. Zwingli challenged certain practices within the Roman Catholic Church. He protested against the practices of fasting during Lent and the display of images in places of worship. The French theologian and pastor John Calvin or *Jean Cauvin* (1509 – 1564), with his beliefs in predestination and grace inspired by the actions of Luther and Zwingli broke away from the Roman Catholic Church. However, the Dutch Reformation influenced by Jacob Arminius (1560 –1609), the Dutch theologian, joined the Protestant Reformation. He focussed on preaching a doctrine on law. This was in sharp contrast to Calvin's doctrine on grace. England too joined the Protestant Reformation in 1530 by cutting links with Rome. But, this protest against the Roman Catholic Church was for no other reason than the fact that the pope refused to grant King Henry VIII a divorce. In 1534 he got Parliament to make him Supreme Head of the Church in England and Wales (Anglican Church). He was well aware that once the Church was no longer ruled by the pope in Rome he would be fully in charge of the affairs in England. All disputes in law and the making of rules and doctrine for the Church of England were now handled by Henry VIII.

The Roman Catholic Church no longer received money from England which now had the last word on how bishops were appointed. However, the Church of England became the church for only the rich and powerful. The Baptist church founded 1609 in Amsterdam by the Englishman John Smyth, its pastor, extended its influence in England as a protestant church during the reformation also became a church for the well to do. Smyth's church rejected the Roman Catholic doctrine of the baptism of infants or "sprinkling". The prophet declared that "sprinkling" is against the Word of God. It is not in the scriptures, he said.[31] Ireland on the other hand was a strictly Roman Catholic country and did not break away from the Roman Catholic Church during the Reformation. Over in Scotland, however, John Knox (1510 – 1572), a Scottish clergyman and founder of the Presbyterian Church saw his opportunity to protest against the practices of the Catholic Church and finally left it.

The spread of the Protestant Reformation meant that the Roman Catholic Church was no longer one big unit, which had absolute power over whole nations and states. The impact of the Reformation resulted in it being split into a number of smaller units with each unit having its own name and Head of Unit. Each unit was a denomination like a £1.00 divided into a hundred other units. Each of these organisations, for example, Lutherans, Calvinists, Anglicans, Presbyterians, Baptists and so on is known as a denomination. The prophet said that these men of God were "reformers". The reason for this, he said, is because of the change or reform they brought about. Such a change altered religion and religious practices in the world for generations to come. Because the followers of these denominations protested against the Roman Catholic Church they were called Protestants. Though for the first time for generations the United Church of Europe, namely, the Roman Catholic Church was split into many pieces Satan still remained firmly in control of these sister churches since his intervention in the Garden of Eden when he reigned in the "children of disobedience".

## ROAD TO PENTECOSTALISM

The historian Peter Laslett in his book *The World We Have Lost* (1965) states that up to the seventeenth century "all our ancestors ... were Christian believers"[32] because they all went to church. By the time people started to move away from their cottage industries into the cities to work in factories at the beginning of the Industrial Revolution in 1750 the village church no longer had control over the people as it did in the past. John Wesley (1703-1791), a Church of England priest supported by his brother Charles became a powerful force in the Protestant Reformation. By the middle of the eighteenth century it was clear that the Church of England attracted only those higher up in society.

Wesley and his fellow Anglican students of the Church of England got together on the Oxford University Campus and began to study the Bible by using a certain religious method. The group included John Wesley, Charles Wesley, and George Whitfield. Their fellow students mocked them calling them names such as "the Methodists" because of the strict rules or methods they followed to study the Bible in detail, worship, and to live their lives. He founded the Methodist Church. Whilst his teachings were based on the Armenian doctrine of law, those of George Whitfield were based on Calvinism, the doctrine of grace. Wesley in turn was influenced by the Moravians who believed in the Christian having an experience or personal relationship with God through their senses. He taught that Christians should receive a "second blessing" after they were converted which he called sanctification or "perfect love".

He and his followers believed that the Church of England had lost touch with the common people. They took the message of Christianity to the cities, and to miners and factory workers. The Methodist Church appealed to the "better type" of the working class. These working men stuck to a strict religious way of life. They did not smoke, drink or gamble or use bad language. Those who followed these strict moral codes of conduct saw themselves as better off than many of their neighbours. They lived their dreams and became very successful through their own efforts. These self-made men began to look down on those who were worse off than them, that is to say, those who gambled, drank and did not practice religion as a way of life.

Wesley himself was not in favour of organisation.[33] When he died his followers organised the Methodist Church.[34] But as we have already seen organised religion began in the Garden of Eden when Cain tried to approach God with his own man-made ideas. Organised religion from the time of Cain in the Garden of Eden through to the building of the Tower of Babel and the establishment of the Roman Catholic Church was evident in the prophet's research of church history. It still dominates our religious way of life in the twenty first century. From Paul, Ephesus (53-170), to Irenaeus, Smyrna (170-312), to Martin, Pergamos (312-606), to Columba, Thyatira (606-1520), to Luther, Sardis (1520-1750), to Wesley Philadelphia (1750-1906) and right down the road to modern day Pentecostalism we find that people and groups organised their lives and places of worship in a big way.

Believers over time were therefore always making up what they thought the Bible said by injecting their own man-made ideas into Christianity; thus creating more confusion. "In the Dark Ages", declares the prophet, "the Word was almost entirely lost to the people. But God sent Luther with the WORD. The Lutherans spoke for God at that time. But they organized, and again the pure Word was lost for organization tends toward dogma and creeds, and not the simple Word. They could no longer speak for God. Then God sent Wesley, and he was the voice with the Word in his day. The people who took his revelation from God became the living epistles read and known of all men for their generation. When the Methodists failed, God raised up others and so it has gone on through the years until in this last day there is again another people in the land, who under their messenger will be the final voice to the final age."[35]

God therefore kept his promise he made in Malachi 4 to send a prophet in our age to make everything plain in order to clear up the confusion caused by Satan because everyone had their own interpretation of what was written in the Bible. Thus whilst our ancestors called these many denominations churches, the prophet made it clear that we should not call these organisations churches. We should instead call them "lodges", he said; because they were man-made organisations with man's own ideas and interpretations of the Word of God. God sends His prophet as his mouthpiece at the end of the age to tie up the loose ends and make the Word of God plain. He challenges the reader to examine carefully the ministry of the prophet when he comes on the scene by using the following guide or criteria:

"... Find out how He will manifest Himself at the end time. It's written. See, He never does anything unless He reveals it first. He said so in the Scripture, 'He does nothing, except He reveals to His servants the prophets.' And He has revealed It. And this is His prophet. This is a Book of prophecy. It's the complete revelation of Jesus Christ, all the way through. Nothing to be added to, or taken from It. And we ought to search It and see what day we're living in, 'cause we might be caught in the same trap."[36] In the Bible when the message of a prophet goes forth it militates against the spirit of the age. Its only appeal is to "one in a million"[37] in a world where "the Children of disobedience"[38] resist the Word of God; for they are "ever learning, and never able to come to the knowledge of the truth".[39] Thus the idea of creation as a fact[40] which was spelt out at the beginning of this chapter has been resisted in the twenty-first century by the education authorities in England.

They have given into the forces of resistance that the

teaching of creation as a fact cannot in our modern society be accepted in our schools as a scientific fact. This has been endorsed in a country where in the past, as we have already seen, everyone was a Christian and where everyone went to church every Sunday – a country which you may recall was the satellite for spreading the Christian gospel to the world. The prophet on the other hand, has always rejected Darwin's idea of evolution by declaring that: "man evolutes [evolves] from himself". We do not all come from "one cell", he insists, that is, "every seed" and "living creature" "bring [s] forth after its kind", for example, "a bird has been a bird ever since God made him a bird, and a monkey's been a monkey; a man's been a man".[41]

Historically religion, as we have already seen, was conceived in heaven by the archangel Lucifer, "God's right hand man".[42] The manifestation of his religion was evident in his son Cain, "born of that wicked one",[43] which he used as a vessel to offer the "fruit of the ground" to the Lord. He continued his scheme to form a religious denomination when Jesus came to the earth over two thousand years ago. For example, on Mount Transfiguration when Peter said unto Jesus, "Master, it is good for us to be here: and let us make three tabernacles; one for thee, and one for Moses, and one for Elias: not knowing what he said."[44] We know that Jesus ignored Peter. Again, after Paul preached the full gospel or the "whole counsel of God",[45] Satan led "the children of disobedience" to form a large religious organisation at Nicaea, namely, the Roman Catholic Church. Then came reformers such as Luther to get the Children of God back to the Word but Satan continued with his plan to control the human race by forming religious organisations, religious denominations.

We have already seen that following the Protestant Reformation the Roman Catholic Church was fractured and split up into little pieces such as the Lutherans and Anglicans. The churches which "split" or "denominated" were autonomous. They in turn split and denominated. This splintering of church after church kept happening time and again throughout the centuries. The continuity of this splintering is evident throughout the twentieth century until our present time in the twenty-first century. In light of this fracturing within Christianity which continues unabated in Chapter Four, the next chapter on the Pentecostal Movement, it is not difficult to understand why the prophet sought to explain *Why I'm Against Organized Religion*[46] in a message he delivered in 1962.

Chapter Four

# THE PENTECOSTAL MOVEMENT

*The movement[Pentecostal], they say, is characterised by its unique teaching that "speaking in tongues is the initial, physical evidence of Baptism in the Holy Spirit"[1]... this doctrine was not developed in that form until a dozen years after the 1906 Los Angeles revival that marked the rise of the movement to national and international significance. And, at that time, this doctrine was the occasion for a division in the movement because not all Pentecostals accepted it, nor do all accept it today.*
– Robert Mapes Anderson, *Vision of the Disinherited*[2]

### ORGANISED RELIGION REVISITED

I have already indicated in the previous chapter on Organised Religion that working men and women and middle class men and women who attended churches throughout the ages were unhappy with the cold and formal worship within their place of worship. The prophet made this observation of our modern day form of worship when he "indicted this generation for the second crucifixion of Jesus Christ",[3] and for "having a form of godliness but denying the power thereof".[4] He said that this "organisation of Christianity" was in essence the very definition of religion because it is, "unscriptural" and "unorthodox".[5]

He is emphatic that religion started in Eden with Adam who used it as a covering; and, "certainly made it himself out of fig leaves, and it didn't work".[6] It is the Spirit active in the individual living the Life of Christ through that individual demonstrating the worship of God in Spirit and in Truth that is the mark of a true Christian, insists the prophet. "The Spirit is not active in any denomination. It's not interested in making organisation, because the Spirit Itself is contrary to the organisation. The organisation is looking for worldly things, the mind of the world, and they make big temples...",[7] declares the prophet. Men such as William Booth, a Methodist, were very much aware that churches were failing to reach the down and out, lower working class who were at the bottom of society. They did not feel welcome in a church building or chapel. Booth found a way to get to the hard to reach down town members of society. They lived in the slums of the towns and cities of Victorian England in the nineteenth century. He took the gospel directly to them in the streets of Britain. He held open-air meetings. Hecklers, rabble rousers and protestors started to make lots of noise whilst those poor folks were singing hymns. Booth therefore introduced bands to lead the singing to drown out the noise of the mob. If tho old hymns were thought too boring he wrote new hymns. "Why should the devil have all the best tunes?" he boldly asked.

William Booth condemned sin and unbelief. He waged war against that "sinful and adulterous generation" by forming the Salvation Army. Many of us in the United Kingdom today still see the bright uniform and the noisy bands of the Salvation Army marching through our streets. Booth's Salvation Army was only one of the many movements which tried to take the gospel to the poor. They lived in the worst conditions in the slums of towns and cities in nineteenth century Britain. But the Salvation Army was not the only group that was unhappy with the way in which the gospel was preached. The prophet had already observed that throughout history when a church became cold and formal in a particular age the Lord raised up a messenger at the end of that age. That messenger was filled with the Holy Spirit. His ministry was to bring the people back to the Word of God. For example, "when the Methodists failed, God raised up others and so it has gone on through the years".[8]

## ORIGIN OF HOLINESS MOVEMENT

There is no doubt John Wesley's idea of taking the Word of God to the masses was failing to reach the poor and oppressed. Other groups of people within the Methodist Church were becoming deeply concerned that the gospel was not reaching the common people. The Holiness Movement grew out of the Methodist Church to address this concern. The Pentecostal Movement in turn first grew out of this nineteenth century Holiness Movement because a number of people were unhappy with the Holiness Movement. Its members, they said, were becoming like people in the world, that is, "worldly". The Holiness Movement was concerned that the masses were not living a life of "holiness".[9] Their aim was to take the gospel to the ordinary people. This would enable them to live a holy life: to get back to the pure Word of God, back to innocence, back to a literal interpretation of the Bible, back to experiencing the move of the Holy Spirit. Above all they wanted to make sure that believers experience a "second blessing" in their Christian life. We will recall that Wesley preached a message of sanctification. According to the prophet the word "sanctify" and "clean" has the same meaning as the word "holy".

The word "sanctify" means "clean and set aside for service",[10] he says. He concludes that, "you could be clean, and pure, and sanctified without having the Holy Ghost."[11] The prophet commented on what has come to be called the "three works of grace". He said that Wesley preached on the second work of grace which his followers called "the second blessing". that is, sanctification. Moreover, says the prophet, Wesley taught against "speaking in tongues and gifts of the Spirit".[12] The prophet therefore sought to explain why he thought that Wesley's message lost its popular appeal to the masses. They organised, he said, and the Holy Spirit moved on. As for "the three works of grace" he reminds us that: "there was justification, sanctification, the baptism of the

Holy Ghost, not three different dispensations, not three works of grace, but one work in three different manifestations. Same Holy Spirit was with Luther, under justification was under Wesley with sanctification; in the Church now, in the baptism of the Holy Ghost: the same Holy Spirit, not two Holy Spirits, the same Holy Spirit".[13]

## HOW DID PENTECOSTALISM BEGIN?

It is difficult to see how the American people would have had the freedom of religious movement and expression had there not been an American Civil War (1861-1865) to end slavery once and for all. For once slavery was abolished the Holiness Movement grew out of Methodism. And this Movement in turn then gave birth to the Pentecostal Movement. It opened up the way in the long term for inter-racial religious worship in the United States.

The American Civil War was a war to free the slaves in America once and for all. It was a war of emancipation, a war between the states in the north that believed slaves should have their freedom, and those states in the south which did not believe that slaves should be free. In short, it was a war which signalled, I think, that slaves should not only be physically freed from the plantation but that they should be freed from religious organisation. This is because before the American Civil War slaves felt bound by the system of religious organisation which was created by their masters. They were cautious about the way they worshipped in public. But once they knew that they had the freedom of religious expression they did so openly and freely. They worshipped without fear of being bound by any religious organisation or creed. However, both the plantation slave and the slave to organised religion had a choice to be free or remain a slave.

An example of the choice a slave could make as a free moral agent is recorded in the Bible where they were advised that "... if the servant shall plainly say, I love my master, my wife, and my children; I will not go out free: Then his master shall bring him unto the judges; he shall also bring him to the door, or unto the door post; and his master shall bore his ear through with an awl; and he shall serve him forever".[14] Thus as the prophet declared, not even a "pardon" from Abraham Lincoln, the very President who issued the emancipation proclamation to free all slaves could save a man from execution who had refused to accept his freedom which President Abraham Lincoln personally signed at the time. Thus after the American civil war members of the Holiness Movement formed the National Holiness Association in 1867, New Jersey. This Association included Methodists, Baptists and Presbyterians. It was a Methodist Holiness minister namely, Abner Blackmon Crumpler, whose church, the North Carolina Holiness Association formed in 1897, that first used the word Pentecost as part of its name. Thus his Holiness Association became known as the Pentecostal Holiness Church when the first congregation met in North Carolina, 1898. For Pentecostals, the term Pentecostalism means receiving the "baptism of the Holy Spirit" with sensation followed by the "gifts of the Holy Spirit", especially speaking in tongues, as the initial evidence of the Holy Spirit. According to Pentecostals, speaking in tongues means "the power to speak supernaturally by the Holy Spirit, in a language not known to the one possessing the gift".[15]

The expression "Pentecostal" comes from the experience of the apostles and others on the Day of Pentecost in the Book of Acts when believers in Jerusalem were "all filled with the Holy Ghost, and began to speak with other tongues, as the Spirit gave them utterance".[16] This doctrine or belief that the initial evidence of the Holy Spirit is speaking in tongues and the belief in what the Methodist Church called the "second blessing" created a split in the Holiness Movement. Those who believed in the "second blessing" remained in the Wesleysan Methodist Church. Those who believed that the initial evidence of the Holy Spirit is speaking in tongues became "Pentecostals".[17] The Baptists also played a part in the birth of Pentecostalism, through Benjamin Irwin, once a Baptist preacher who helped to organise the International Pentecostal Holiness Church which grew out of the Fire Baptised Holiness Association in Iowa, 1898.

## WHAT EXACTLY IS PENTECOSTALISM?

By now you might be able to guess that the way to identify Pentecostals or Pentecostalism is what they believe about the "Baptism in the Holy Spirit". Pentecostals believe that you must prove that you have two qualities. First, that you have received the baptism of the Holy Spirit with sensation. Second that you spoke in tongues which demonstrate that speaking in tongues is the initial evidence of the Holy Spirit. However, not everyone agrees with them. This is because many preachers say that the way the Pentecostals believe you should receive the Holy Spirit is not in the Bible. So what are these two qualities Pentecostals believe you should show to prove that you have received the Holy Spirit?

## BAPTISM OF THE HOLY SPIRIT WITH SENSATION

Many Pentecostals often feel that the best way to explain the first quality is through the example set by the evangelist and Presbyterian Charles Finney's (1792-1875) testimony of his emotional and "mighty baptism of the Holy Spirit". This, they say means that they too should be overcome by their emotions when they receive the Holy Spirit. The Memoirs of Mrs. Mary B. Woodworth-Etter gives scores of examples of people in the 1880s and 1890s coming to "the altar screaming for mercy and multitudes falling to the ground as dead, shouting, talking, and weeping". "Sinners were converted"[18] she said. According to the prophet there were people in the Bible who received the baptism of the Holy Ghost without sensation.[19] For example, in Acts 8 the Samaritans,[20] John the

Baptist and Elisabeth the mother of John received the Holy Ghost without speaking in tongues.[21] Moreover, some Pentecostals believed that Matthew 28:19 should be literally interpreted and that baptism with water should be "in the name of the Father, and of the Son, and of the Holy Ghost". The prophet has called this form of baptism "extreme trinitarianism", namely, "water baptism" in which converts are baptised into the "titles of Father, Son, Holy Ghost". They, he insists, should be baptised into the name of the Lord Jesus Christ "for the remission of sins" according to Acts 2:38, and they "shall receive the gift of the Holy Ghost".[22]

## SPEAKING IN TONGUES

Pentecostals believe that the second quality you should possess to show that you have received the baptism of the Holy Spirit is that you first spoke in tongues when you received the Holy Spirit. "It is not ye that speak", cried the early Pentecostals, "but the Holy Ghost, and he will speak when he chooses".[23] In *Debate On Tongues* the prophet made it quite clear that speaking in tongues is not necessarily evidence of the Holy Spirit as he had seen witches speak in tongues. "Now, tongues", he thundered, "is a gift of the Holy Ghost. There's no Scripture in the Bible that says it is the Holy Ghost. It's a gift of the Holy Ghost".[24] "We don't believe [in the Pentecostal doctrine] that the speaking with tongues makes you filled with the Holy Ghost", he continued, " ... We believe that you receive the Holy Ghost by an experience, not by mythical intellectual conception of the Scriptures, but by an experience that you alone know. Now, if you want to know whether it was the Holy Ghost, watch how your life patterns after that; it'll tell what kind of a spirit come into you".[25]

Thus whilst the believers of Pentecostalism were talking about natural sensations as evidence of receiving the Holy Spirit, the prophet was warning believers of the dangers of relying on the senses or emotions as the only proof of

receiving the Holy Spirit. He was reminding us yet again that
the believer must have a real spiritual experience like the one
witnessed by believers on the Day of Pentecost when they
received the "baptism of the Holy Ghost without sensation".
He therefore exhorts us not only that this is the kind of
experience we should have, "but the Person of Christ per-
forming in" us "the same works that He did".[26]

## THE 1906 AZUSA STREET OUTPOURING

In 1900 Charles Parham once a Methodist minister received
the Holy Spirit by the laying of hands and speaking in tongues
at a prayer meeting. He became convinced that the initial
evidence of receiving the Holy Spirit was by speaking in
tongues. Parham was the first minister to say that speaking in
tongues or "glossolalia" was the initial experience of
receiving the Holy Ghost. This doctrine of glossolalia, that is,
speaking in tongues, is what identifies Pentecostalism as
different from any other church organisation. In 1905
William Seymour, an African American minister, heard him
preaching and was fully persuaded that Parham's teachings
on glossolalia was correct.

Thus in that great move of the Holy Spirit in Los Angeles
at a house prayer meeting in Azusa Street[27] Seymour, a Black
man, and pastor and his mostly Black followers were "struck"
by the Holy Spirit. They broke out speaking in tongues amidst
rejoicings, continuous loud noises and prayers. This great
outpouring of the Holy Spirit attracted huge numbers of
people from all racial backgrounds at a time in America
where in many states there were segregation laws. Under
these laws Blacks and Whites were not allowed to mix. If they
did they would be punished for breaking the law. Huge
numbers of people from around the world came to Azusa
Street to be baptised with the Holy Spirit. Similarly in 1904
when the Welsh Revival[28] broke out thousands joined in the
event which was broadcast across the world. In fact Pastor

Joseph Smale, of the First Baptist Church in Los Angeles travelled to the event in Wales. He attempted to bring the revival to his congregation on his return to the United States. His efforts were in vain. A year later, 1905, mini revivals broke out in North Carolina accompanied with healings and speaking in tongues. However by this time Smale was so disappointed with the response he got from his brethren he left them at the First Baptist Church to found the First New Testament Church.

By 1906 the Azusa Street outpouring had touched thousands of souls across the world. Parham was credited for introducing people to the Holy Ghost experience of speaking in tongues. On the other hand Seymour, not Parham is said to be the true founder of this Pentecostal experience. It is said that once the outpouring of the Holy Spirit was on the way Parham tried to "control" the move of the Holy Spirit. It is claimed that he held deeply racist views of the Klu Klux Klan, whom he regarded as "those splendid men",[29] and was therefore rejected as leader by the people. "There was a beautiful outpouring of the Holy Spirit", he cried, commenting on the Azusa Street outpouring, "then they", referring to the worshippers, "pulled off all the stunts common in old camp meetings among coloured folks ... That is the way they worship God, but what makes my soul sick, and make[s] me sick at my stomach is to see white people imitating unintelligent, crude negroism of the southland, and laying it on the Holy Ghost".[30] He was therefore forced to remove himself from the scene and was never again seen in public.

However, the truth of the matter is that the move of the Holy Spirit had nothing at all to do with men. It was a move of God. Man attempted to interpret this move in the "conceit of his own imagination" and in his own way. The Holy Spirit moved on. The prophet therefore came to bring clarity to this dying world, a world, an age, where people were breaking out speaking in tongues from every corner of the earth. They were relying on this as the only evidence of receiving the Holy Spirit. It is not surprising; therefore, that Pentecostalism was increasingly called "the tongues movement".[31] It is a modern Babel like Nimrod's generation. In our generation people all over the world were breaking out in confusion speaking in tongues just as they did in Nimrod's day. Thus rejecting outright that the initial evidence of the Holy Ghost is speaking in tongues the prophet asserted that: "The Holy Ghost is the Word of God in you, that identifies Itself by accepting that Word. Outside of that, it can't be the Holy Ghost. If it says it's the Holy Spirit, and denies one Word of that Bible, it cannot be the Holy Spirit. That's the evidence whether you believe or not."[32] In plain English, the evidence of having the Holy Spirit is one's ability to receive the revealed Word for the age in which one lives, that is, to hear directly from God the message for their time and season.

During the Reformation a number of groups such as the Anabaptists, Shakers, Quakers and Mormons experienced the earlier manifestations of spiritual gifts and speaking in tongues well before the birth of pentecostalism. The age of the prophet, was again demonstrating that Satan was in its many "church" organisations. In those organisations he is seen "exalting" or making "himself above all that is called God". He has been sitting in "the temple of God"[33] such as the Assemblies of God and the Pilgrims Holiness and in well over its twenty six Pentecostal denominations which arose out of the Azusa Street outpouring or experience. But it is not only at Azusa Street that Satan was going about like a roaring lion trying to kill, steal and destroy, but across the world whenever there were signs that there was a big move of the Holy Spirit.

Take for example, places such as West Africa, Chile and India where there were great stirrings of the Holy Spirit in the souls of the people for the Word of God. There were revivals in these people's Native Lands in our generation. However, like Babel in ancient times, Satan entered into the movement and broke out in tongues in a big way amongst many of the people. This is not to say that there were not those who genuinely spoke in tongues. "I've seen devils speak with tongues", declared the prophet, "I've seen witch doctors speak in tongues. I've seen them drink blood out of a human skull and speak with tongues. I've seen pencils lay on the table, and write in an unknown tongues, and witches read it. That don't mean that they're a Christian", thundered the prophet.[34] The prophet was clear that speaking in tongues was not the evidence of receiving the Holy Spirit; neither did the individual receive the Holy Ghost when they receive the holy Eucharist or "wafer" which the Catholic Church serve as Holy Communion; nor is the Holy Ghost received when you shake hands or put your name on the book as the Protestant Church proclaims.[35] "Here's what Jesus said", declared the prophet, "'Except a man be borned of Spirit and of water he will in no wise enter the Kingdom.' Whether he's Catholic, Methodist, Baptist, or whatever, you'll have to be baptized in water for the remission of your sins and receive the baptism of the Holy Ghost, or you're lost. That's Jesus' own Word. So now, if you're Methodist and have received the baptism of the Holy Spirit and been baptized in water, Jesus said you'll enter heaven. If you're Catholic and have done the same thing, you'll enter heaven. But if you're just holding on to that creed of the Catholic Church, or the Methodist, or the Baptist church, you're still lost."[36]

Now, to make sure that the prophet left no doubt in the mind of the person who desires to be "baptized", he makes it clear that the way in which people are "baptized" "In the name of the Father, In the name of the Son, and In the name of the Holy Ghost" is wrong because "that's not even in the Scripture".[37] He says that the Scripture here in Matthew 28:19 is the only place in the Bible where these titles are mentioned. And in any event, declares the prophet, the name used here is "singular", and that name is Jesus Christ referred to in Acts 2:38 which calls on the sinner to: "Repent, every one of you, and be baptized in the Name of Jesus Christ for the remission of your sins, and you shall receive the gift of the Holy Ghost. For the promise is unto you, and to your children, and to them that's far off, and even as many as the Lord our God shall ever call."[38] He insists that from the Day of Pentecost and throughout the New Testament the disciples baptised people in the name of the Lord Jesus Christ. But that this practice was changed by the Roman Catholic Church when it began to baptise its converts in the titles of Father, Son, and Holy Ghost.

## THE WARNING

Clearly the warning of the prophet to the age is that history repeats itself; that as it was in the beginning so shall it be in the end. That Satan was kicked out of heaven because of his unbelief in God's Word and has entered the children of disobedience in every age up until now is evident from our brief study of the trail of the serpent. From the religion of Cain, to Babylon, to Rome, to the World Council of Churches, headed up by Rome, the second Babylon, that is, our modern man made religion from the old Babylonian Empire and Rome, is a sign of the time in our age. The Babylonian practice of the worship of the Mother and Child, in Egypt as Isis and Osiris, in India as Isi and Iswara, in Asia as Cybele and Deous, and in Rome, China, and Chile,[39] are religious rituals, customs and traditions which continue in one form or the other in the age of the prophet, that is, the age of the prophet's message.

The prophet came to the world to warn people against organised religion whether it is in the lives of individuals or institution of the "Church". Likewise he warned us that speaking in tongues is not necessarily evidence that we are filled with the Holy Spirit. He was sent to this age to the people of the four corners of the earth. He visited the continents and he met people from the United Sates and the Caribbean, Africa and Asia, Europe and Australia. These people from the four corners of the earth belonged to many different religions and denominations. In his own ministry he was no stranger to the many religions and worshippers of a variety of religions including the Seventh-day Adventist,[40] Mormons,[41] Amish,[42] Islam,[43] Mohammedanism,[44] Buddhism,[45] Hinduism,[46] Jains,[47] Jehovah Witness,[48] Sikh,[49] Judaism,[50] snake-worshippers,[51] cow-worshippers[52] and Sun worshippers.[53]

The prophet said that Pentecostals "organized" "and went right back into death again",[54] and "death", he insisted, "means separation, separation from God".[55] In his condemnation and rejection of organisation and organised religion he cried, "no wonder our Pentecostal system is done, and so is the Methodist's, Baptist's, World Council of Churches, and all! They're being swallowed up in the Council of Churches, making a mark or an image unto the beast, to give it its power".[56] So the prophet warns against a life of religion, a life of organisation, a life of tradition, a life of rituals. His Message is to the religious organisations as well as to each individual who claims to be a fellow citizen of the Kingdom of God. What kind of experience should the individual of this age have then? The prophet sets this out very clearly in the *Church Ages* which should leave the believer in no doubt:

> ... when a man experiences the depth of God in his life, it is an actual personal experience of the Spirit of God indwelling him, and his mind is illuminated by the wisdom and knowledge of God through the Word. But the depth of Satan will be in that he will attempt to destroy this. He will as always attempt to make a substitute for this reality of God. How will he do it? He will take away the knowledge of the truth of God – destroy the Word by putting forth his own, "Yea hath God said?" He will then substitute the personal Christ in our spirits. He will do it, as he caused Israel to do the same; by a human being reigning as king

instead of God. The born-again experience will be rejected in favor of church joining. The depths of Satan had been entered into in that age. And the fruit of that depth of Satan which are lies, murders and horrible crimes came forth from it.[57]

The final few words in the above quote from the prophet reminds me of a notable historian called Cheik Anta Diop who wrote a book titled *Civilization or Barbarism*,[58] which title appears to be expressing the sentiments of the prophet that "civilization" and murder and cheating, and lying, and filth and moral and spiritual decadence and blindness in our modern society are really one and the same thing. Mention in the book, *Civilization or Barbarism*, that "very crude people" with a "culture" who lived a "nomadic" life who had "literally erased" and "destroyed" "a civilization" is partly responsible for leading me to make the comparison between what the prophet said in the quote about "civilization", and the title of Diop's book.[59] But the very meaning of civilisation will become clearer in the next Chapter, Chapter Five when we examine fully its history and meaning, and the prophet's response to the modern events of our age.

Chapter Five

# CIVILISATION

*This is a great time. Everybody has got money. Everybody can do this, and everybody can do that, and money flowing every way, and big cars, and everything. There won't be one of them in that City. There won't be one car, one airplane. No. It'll be a altogether a different civilization. It'll be again a civilization not of knowledge, not of science, but of innocence, and faith in the living God.*
– William Marrion Branham, *Satan's Eden*, 1965[1]

### CIVILISATION PAST, PRESENT AND FUTURE

The prophet in the above quote is talking about two different meanings of the word civilisation. The first meaning is concerned with this world and the things of this world. The second meaning of the word civilisation is to do with our "future home",[2] that is, the "Holy City".[3] The last few words from the Lyrics "Through Heaven's Eyes", sung by Brian Stokes Mitchell who acted as Jethro, high priest of Midian, in *Prince of Egypt*, makes the point so clearly that we should always see the world through the Word of God. He first asks the question, "so how can you see what your life is worth or where your value lies?" Then he goes on to answer this question by insisting that "you can never see through the eyes of man; you must look at your life, look at your life through heaven's eyes". I personally like this quotation for though the film itself has not been authenticated by some notable historian I believe that these words hold a kernel of truth for us all.

In the first definition of civilisation the prophet hints at how natural man finds natural solutions to the problems he faces in this world. He does this through "knowledge" which is from "Satan's Eden" (the kosmos or our existing world view) then as it is now for it causes 'death'. In fact to drive home the point more forcefully he warns us that "knowledge and civilization, and true Christianity, have nothing in common".[4] And that these including "science" and "education" are "the greatest hindrances that God ever had". In rejecting this modern sin sick "civilization" the prophet gives his final verdict on natural "civilization" and the spiritual "civilization". "God will set up His own kind of civilization on earth, when He takes it over", the prophet continues. "This is Satan's world; he is god now of his worldly scientific knowledge. But God will set His Own kind of civilization up. It won't be a civilization like this. You just remember that. It won't be the kind of civilization we got today. No, no. It will be according to His Word and His purpose. For, the god of this present evil age will be destroyed, and his kingdom with him .... The god of this world has become knowledge, denomination, science, 'having a form of godliness, but denying the Power thereof.'"[5]

## MEANING OF CIVILISATION

If I were to ask you what you would expect to find in a country, nation or state that has an advanced civilisation, you would probably say that you would expect the people to believe in God; that they are refined, polished, well presented, like the arts, well cultured and so on. And you would probably say that the people in a civilisation that is not so advanced might behave like savages, are not cultured and behave like wild animals. According to Webster, civilisation refers to "a group of people in an advanced stage of development".[6] In the Oxford dictionary civilisation is "a developed or organised way of life".[7] I think you will agree with me that these definitions of civilisation are not what we always experience in our modern civilisation. The civilisation in our modern world is more like the one the prophet defines at the beginning of this chapter. In our modern civilisation many people are more "worldly", "lovers of pleasure more than lovers of God".[8] It was this "advanced state of human society" or civilisation after the American Civil War that caused many worshippers to leave denominational churches such as the Baptists and Methodists and set up Holiness and Pentecostal churches. Once the people were liberated from church organisation after the Civil War and they exercised the freedom of worship for some time, they again organised and began to treat the church as big business, investing in property and running it as a business enterprise. Thus the number of people attending church between 1870 to 1890 rose by some 130 percent and the value of church building rocketed by nearly 100 percent. For example, in the Methodist Church alone membership rose by 57 per cent during this period.

There were an additional 800,000 members in each decade from 1870 to 1910 that went to church. The Social Gospel and the Gospel of Wealth were received with a hunger and a passion by the members of these congregations for their new found religion. Some of their critics remarked that such members had a "friendship with the world" and "enmity with God".[9] Satan once again slipped in very subtly into these denominations. This resulted in many splits in church movements; for example, the formation of organised religion such as the Holiness and Pentecostal we have already cited in the previous chapter. Civilisation, that is, the things of the world had replaced the Holy Spirit in men's souls and the Word of God in our churches.

## WHERE DID CIVILISATION FIRST BEGIN?
The prophet appears to be in agreement with Scofield that "the first civilization", like religion started with Cain.

According to Scofield "every element of material civilization" such as "city and pastoral life, and the development of arts and manufacturers" is "Cainitic in origin".[10] After consulting Schofield the prophet sought to reinforce what Scofield had to say about the origin of civilisation. "Now to show where civilization come[s] from", declares the prophet, "let us read Genesis over here, in the 4th chapter of Genesis, and the 16th verse".

> And Cain went out from the presence of God, and dwelt in the land of Nod, on the east side of Eden. And Cain knew his wife; and she conceived, and bare Enoch: and he builded a city, and called the name of the city, after... his son, Enoch ... here in my Scofield Bible, it says, "The first civilization." Notice, then he begot sons, and they made organs and music. The next one begot sons, and he begin to do other things, wonders, build cities, and make instruments of brass, and all kinds of things. See, that's what he did, become the first civilization, which was Cainite. He's done the same thing down through the ages.[11]

It would seem therefore that the twins Cain and Abel were brought up in Egypt at the time of Abel's murder. And that after his brother's murder Cain "went out from the presence of the Lord, and dwelt in the land of Nod, on the east of Eden".[12] Many ancient and modern historians tell us that when the world was first created Egypt was joined to main land Africa by one huge mass of land. In ancient times they say, the whole world was one big land mass. After man sinned we find this land mass breaking up and dividing itself into different bits. We call these bits continents, countries, nations, states and so on. School children, and adults for that matter, have been taught in modern times to see the human race, the world and its geography as a number of bits and pieces scattered across the four corners of the earth. But "in the beginning" it was not so. The earth was one.

Men and women could travel without crossing the seas. Then man sinned and the world split into different bits like a jigsaw puzzle, for example, Africa, Europe, North America and South America. In fact historians say that in ancient times Egypt was in the North of Africa or North Eastern Africa. But in modern times it was changed and many of us know Egypt today as in the "Middle East".[13] Now, imagine the world as a jigsaw puzzle with its many pieces strewn across the four corners of the room like the continents across the four corners of the earth. Think of the little child collecting the pieces of the jigsaw and attempting to fit them together. What the child is trying to do here is to put the world back to the position it would have been in had it not broken up into so many pieces as illustrated by the following parable:

> There was a man who had a little boy that he loved very much. Every day after work the man would come home and play with the little boy. He would always spend all of his extra time playing with the little boy.
>
> One night, while the man was at work, he realised that he had extra work to do for the evening, and that he wouldn't be able to play with his little boy. But, he wanted to be able to give the boy something to keep him busy. So, looking around his office, he saw a magazine with a large map of the world on the cover. He got an idea. He removed the map, and then patiently tore it up into small pieces. Then he put all the pieces in his coat pocket.
>
> When he got home, the little boy came running to him and was ready to play. The man explained that he had extra work to do and couldn't play just now, but he led the little boy into the dining room, and taking out all the pieces of the map, he spread them on the table. He explained that it was a map of the world, and that by the time he could put it back together, his extra work would be finished, and they could both play. Surely this would keep the child busy for hours, he thought. About half an hour later the boy came to the man and said, "Okay, it's finished, Can we play now?"
>
> The man was surprised, saying, "That's impossible. Let's go see." And sure enough, there was the picture of the world; all put together, every piece in its place. The man said, "That's amazing! How did you do that?" The boy said, "It was simple. On

the back of the page was a picture of a man. When I put the man together the whole world fell into place." The man reassuring his son said, "That's right son, when man is together the whole world will be together." [14]

## NIMROD'S CIVILISATION

A careful study of the *Two Babylons* will reveal that Hislop is trying to make the case that the Egyptian god Osiris[15] and the god of Nineveh[16] is Nimrod. I am quite aware that many of Hislop's critics are chronologists who fail to grasp the teleological or scriptural basis on which Hislop's book was written, implying, in my view that the world should continue in apostasy and idolatry; for such critics offer no scriptural basis or solution for their criticism of Hislop's biblical masterpiece. Hislop quotes a number of ancient historians to support his argument. He reminds us that the Bible says that "Cush begat Nimrod", who first built the "kingdom" of Babel and other great cities such as Nineveh and Shinar.[17] In fact Hislop is of the view that it was Nimrod's dad Cush who started the building and construction of Babylon, but it was Nimrod who succeeded in elevating those places to their magnificence and glory to become great nations. Hislop found an ancient historian called Bunsen a source of inspiration. In his book *Philosophy of Ancient History*, Bunsen agrees that Nimrod and his family came from a long line of great men and great builders whose ancestry can be traced to Ham. He declares that the Bible gives the "names of the sons of Ham as Cush, Mizraim, Phut and the race of Canaan. Mizraim peopled Egypt and Canaan the land later possessed by the Hebrews. Phut located in Africa, and Cush extended his colonies over a wide domain".[18]

According to Bunsen:

> Cushite colonies were along the southern shore of Asia and Africa and by archaeological remains, along the southern and eastern coasts of Arabia. That name "Cush" was given to four

great areas, Media, Persia, Susiania and Aria, or the whole
territory between the Indus and the Tigris in prehistoric times.
In Africa, the Ethiopians, the Egyptians, the Libyans, the
Canaanites and Phoenicians were all descendants of Ham. They
were a dark or black coloured race and the pioneers of our
civilization. They were emphatically the monument builders of
the plains of Shinar and the valley of the Nile from Meroe to
Memphis. They were responsible for the monuments that dot
southern Siberia and in America, along the valley of the
Mississippi down to Mexico and in Peru, their images and
monuments stand as voiceless witnesses.[19]

## THE PYRAMIDS OF GIZA

People are still struck by the magnificence and splendour of
the Great Pyramids of Giza, the only remaining of the Seven
Wonders of the Ancient World. Egyptians drew picture
writings or hieroglyphics inside many of their pyramids. They
also left paintings on the inner walls including murals showing Egyptian ways of life, culture and religion. However,
researchers and historians have suggested that there were no
such records or inscriptions on the inside walls or anywhere
on The Great Pyramid or any of the three pyramids on the
Giza plateau. The Great Pyramid is said to have been built by
Enoch from the inspiration and revelation of God before the
flood. The prophet made it absolutely clear that "God wrote in
the pyramids" in stone.[20] And writers such as Joseph Seiss
maintain that The Great Pyramid is the "Bible in Stone".[21]
Moreover, it was not only pyramid building which required
first class knowledge in mathematics, science, astronomy,
astrology, geography and so on that the Egyptians did very
well. They excelled in almost every field. The Bible itself
records that, "Moses was learned in all the wisdom of the
Egyptians."[22] Yet he gave up all this worldly knowledge for
the Word of God. In the words of the Bible, Moses esteemed
the "reproach of Christ greater riches than the treasures of
Egypt".[23]

## GREEK CIVILISATION

We know from the prophet that God wrote three Bibles and that the third Bible is the one we have today which is written on "paper".[24] But what is less well known is that when Ptolemy I, a Macedonian Greek general, commissioned the history of Egypt to be written in Greek, many of the Egyptian words were replaced by Greek words. Nevertheless many Egyptian words found their way into the Bible. And it is in this way that the Egyptian language heavily influenced the text of the Bible which was written in Hebrew or Greek. There are other ways that Egyptian civilisation influenced Greek civilisation. For example authors of Greek literature such as Homer borrowed heavily from Egyptian writings.[25] In fact one writer declared that "the true authors of Greek philosophy were not the Greeks; but ... the Egyptians".[26] "The ancient Egyptian Empire", the author in question continues, "extended to Nubia, Syria, Palestine; Asia Minor, Western Asia and vast areas of Europe".[27] Many "students from Chaldea, Greece, Persia and other countries were educated in Egypt", he said. Once they completed their training in Egypt they returned to their countries of origin to educate their own people. Examples of the scholars educated in Egypt are, "Pythagoras from Samos, who later migrated to Croton, Southern Italy (540.BC), and Herodotus, Plato, Aristotle and Socrates from Greece".[28]

The tradition of Greeks and Romans using Egyptian god and goddesses became part of the Roman Catholic custom and practice. The Egyptian goddess Neit, for example, was known in Greece as Athena, Minerva in Rome and in Europe as St Catherine. Again the Egyptian god Horus became known in Greece as Perseus and in Western Europe as St George whilst the Egyptian Anubis was called Hermes in Greece and St Christopher in Western Christianity.[29] We have already noted in our section on organised religion how the Roman Catholic Church copied the ancient pagan Babylonian and Egyptian practice of idolatry by worshipping the Madonna (Mother) and Child, Ninus and Semiramis in Babylon and Osiris and Isis in Egypt.[30]

## THE RENAISSANCE

Once I read where someone had explained the word renaissance in French as "*ri*", "again", and "*nascere*", meaning "be born". Satan had stolen this idea of being born again from Christianity. Remember the story of Nicodemus when Jesus told him that he must be born again. And he asked whether he had to go back into his mother's womb to be born again? Satan was now using this idea of rebirth to describe a revival of things of the world. Revival as you know means the act of bringing back to life. The renaissance therefore was seen by many as "a cultural movement". Western European historians said that it was a restoration or a re-awakening of the interest in learning, the arts, culture, politics, economics, religion, architecture, science, painting, intellectual and educational pursuits.

The prophet reminds us that since "God made the world's headquarters in the garden of Eden, in Egypt"[31] that Satan or "the deformer" "perverted" or "changed over" or "made" what God said to say something "different". According to the prophet, Satan, who he called, "the deformer" has had "six thousand years of deforming the Seed of God, the Word of God". And he invited the "children of disobedience" to "partake of this wisdom". We see him continuing to tempt the children of God first during the Renaissance in around 1300, and again from the 1500s-1600s. The Renaissance is best known for its great achievements in art with men like Leonardo da Vinci and Michelangelo of the Italian Renaissance. One notable historian noted the influence of Egypt as part of the "whole movement" of the Renaissance "from the beginning".[32] The prophet is clear that:

... it's all right to have wisdom. But if the wisdom is contrary, if the wisdom isn't correct wisdom from God, Divine wisdom, and becomes natural wisdom; I don't care how much science we have, and what more, or education, it's of the Devil ... Civilization is of the Devil .... All culture in the earth, all powers of science, and everything, is of the Devil. It's his gospel he preached, of knowledge, in the Garden of Eden. And he has took that knowledge, perverted knowledge, contrary to the Word and will and plan of God. And now he has had six thousand years to do just exactly what God did, only in a perverted way, and took the same amount of time to bring his own Eden in. Now he has got an Eden here on earth, and it's filled with wisdom, knowledge. That was his gospel at the beginning, knowledge, wisdom, science. Never did God ever cater to such.[33]

The temptation here is for some to suggest that since the philosophy, thinking, knowledge, learning, talents, art or intellectual pursuits and indeed the coomoo are contrary to our very beliefs as Christians on this earth then perhaps we should have nothing at all to do with this world, this earth, which is "Satan's Eden" anyway. Others might wish to walk in the moccasins (shoes) of the American Pentecostal evangelist Frank Bartleman and like him vow to destroy all "my past records of achievements", and "letters of commendation". Bartleman "destroyed" these record of "excellence", "treasured documents", and "false evidences", because he was pursuing his calling as a missionary, evangelist, and preacher. "Nothing but the blood of Jesus",[34] he later cried once he had totally surrendered himself to God and soared like an eagle way beyond the civilisation of natural man.

The prophet is of the view that "before the foundation of the world, when God in His labor pain was bringing forth, bringing forth you, knowing what you would do, He positionally placed you into His Own Body, to be a housewife, to be a farmer, to be a preacher, to be a prophet, to be this, or to be that".[35] The prophet did not, like the Austrian philosopher and Roman Catholic Priest Ivan Illich, advocate the abolition of education;[36] nor that we should embrace "ignorance".[37] echoed in the spirit of rebellion in our age: "we don't need no education, we don't need no thought control ... Teachers leave them kids alone". He accepted that education had its place, but that "education without salvation has no anchor".[38] "I'm trying to tell you that God is not known by education. God is known by faith ... and that alone, and only faith",[39] he continued. Moses, he said, was educated, but without God he was nothing:

> ...Moses went to school, and they schooled him over and over again, because, no doubt, they thought that he would be a great military man. And which history tells us he was a great military man, was able to take the armies of Egypt and become the Pharaoh of Egypt, and set the people free, and send them back to their homeland or let them takeover Egypt ... they trained him, and he could even teach the scholars some wisdom. He was really smart and educated. But that wasn't God's way of doing it. And when he found out it failed, he become bitter.

In fact when Moses came face to face with God the Bible records him as "esteeming the reproach of Christ greater riches that the treasures of Egypt".[40] In *The Masterpiece*, for example, the prophet used Michelangelo, one of the Italian Renaissance artists, to describe how this sculptor by inspiration produced a masterpiece of Moses. "Now, a genuine sculptor is inspired, like a genuine poet, or any genuine singer, musician, whatever it might be."[41] The prophet continued, "I like art, real well. I believe God is in music. I believe God is in nature. God is everywhere. And anything that's contrary to the original is a perversion. God is in dancing; not the kind of dancing you do here. But when the sons and daughters of God are in the Spirit of God, see, that's dancing."[42]

## THE MEANING OF CULTURE

We saw in the previous section that the renaissance was seen by Western historians as "a cultural movement". This prompts us to ask the question, what exactly is the meaning of culture, given that the prophet has already declared that "all culture", "education", and "civilization" "is of the devil". One writer has no doubt that "civilization, culture and society can all mean the same thing".[43] Another source has said that culture is part of "our national heritage", "our national way of life–our national culture".[44] We pass on or transmit our core values through our national culture. And education is defined as "the transmission of our culture". This means that we pass on everything we know, that is our way of life, to our children, and they in turn pass it on to their children. And so our national culture is passed on from one generation to the next either by word of mouth or in writing.

In modern times our culture is also handed down through the internet, emails, DVDs and other electronic devices such as mobiles. This culture, some in our vaunted civilisation suggest, may be "high culture" such as classical music for the elite or well to do or "low culture" such as rock and roll or pop music for the not so cultured and less able members of society such as the lower or underclass.[45] Much of the culture in Britain was handed down in the past from the way in which Christianity was interpreted. One researcher named Jenny Williams who conducted a study of a school in Sparkbrook found that teachers in the education system in Britain saw their role as, "putting over a certain set of values (Christian), [and] a code of behaviour (middle-class)".[46] This way of using Christianity to pass on the culture in Britain is not surprising. For as we have already seen Laslett in *The World We Have Lost* has suggested that by 1675:

> All our ancestors were literal Christian believers, all the time. Not only zealous priests ... not only serious-minded laymen, but also the intellectuals and the publicly responsible looked on the Christian religion as the explanation of life, and on religious

service as its proper end. Not everyone was equally devout, of course ... Much of their devotion must have been formal, and some of it mere conformity. But their world was a Christian world and their religious activity was spontaneous, not forced on them from above.[47]

Another writer declares that the key function of the first British schools which started in the sixth century was to make the scriptures available to the masses.[48] In modern times, however, where Britain is accepted as a multicultural society all cultures are said to be equal. Some people regard Britain as Defender of the "Faiths" because they think that it accepts all faiths and all cultures. One government source objected to the suggestion "that there is no longer any core values to be taught in schools", and that all values are equal.[49] It is no wonder the prophet declared that culture is of the devil given that it appears that anything could be accepted as culture in our modern age.

THE AGE OF ENLIGHTENMENT
The Age of Enlightenment or The Enlightenment was the period in Western Europe during the 1700s when reason and science were used to explain why many of our customs, morals and traditions existed. The Age of Enlightenment was also known as The Age of Reason. It questioned the very existence of God. It really was an age of science, and an increasing move away from the Word of God. The ancients even though they worshipped all kinds of objects as God did not think of a society without God. And as we have already seen even during the seventeenth century in Britain at least then it was unheard of that there could be a civilisation without God in people's lives. But by the middle of the eighteenth century when the industrial revolution started in Britain many people were moving to the industrial towns and cities and attended church less or not at all. According to

Laslett, "when the arrival of industry created huge societies
of persons in the towns with an entirely different outlook
from these Stuart villagers, practically no one went to church,
not if he was working class and was left untouched by
religious emotion".[50] The masses became wiser. They now
knew what it was like to have a hunger for the material things
of the world. They were enlightened. Faith and belief in God
were now replaced by science and reason. The prophet had
no doubt that God gave Adam and Eve the Word "in the
Garden of Eden, to defeat the enemy. And when Eve reasoned
with It, and projected reasons with the Word, it fell apart, and
sin entered".[51] And because "she relied upon her reasonings
instead of her faith in God's Word, she broke the front lines
and the enemy rushed in. And then death struck the world".[52]

## SCIENCE

We saw that it was during the Enlightenment that people
began to replace the knowledge of God with reason which
science embraced. It was from this moment that the idea of
Christianity having anything to do with civilisation was
totally abandoned. For our ancient ancestors Christianity and
civilisation meant more or less the same thing.[53] The prophet
in *The Conflict between God and Satan* (1962), declared that
"Christianity is the grass roots of civilization" in that "civilization come[s] by Christ".[54] However, in *The God of This Evil
Age* (1965) as we have already seen he was clear that
"knowledge and civilization, and true Christianity, has nothing
in common. Civilization, and true Christianity, has not one
thing in common. Civilization is by knowledge. We all know
that. And knowledge is from Eden, proved it, by what he
preached in Eden. And knowledge causes death. Is that right?
What caused death in the Garden of Eden? ... Knowledge,
science, education, is the greatest hindrance that God ever
had. It is of the devil".[55] These two pronouncements on
civilisation takes us back to the two meanings of civilisation

we met at the beginning of the chapter. The first civilisation comes through Christ and therefore has a spiritual meaning.

The second type of civilisation is the one created by natural man which is from the tree of knowledge of good and evil – a civilisation the prophet refers to as "knowledge, science, education", and is of "the devil". By the end of the 1800s science was accepted as a fact so that in modern times writers such as Harris were referring to the belief in God as fiction.[56] Schools in the United Kingdom which have been allowed the freedom to teach whatever they want (free schools) are banned from teaching as a fact that God created the heaven, and earth – recorded as a fact in the Book of Genesis. Moreover, the Department for Education has made it "crystal clear that teaching creationism is at odds with scientific fact".[57]

In an earlier advice to schools the UK government made it quite clear to schools that teaching about God's creation in the account of the Christian Bible has nothing at all to do with the teaching of science in British schools.[58] The prophet has no doubt that man did not come from monkey or ape which is taught as a scientific fact in schools. He does not believe in Charles Darwin's theory of evolution which teaches that man and animals came from the single cell.[59] "We're told", he said, "that we came and by evolution we have grown from a polliwog to a monkey and then to a man. How crazy that is when Genesis the 1st chapter and 11th verse, God said, "Let every seed bring forth of his kind".[60]

## DARWIN'S DEATH BED CONFESSION

If you read the account of Lady Hope on Charles Darwin before he died I think that you will agree with me that on his deathbed he rejected his own ideas on evolution and accepted the Word of God. According to Lady Hope's account Darwin was "almost bedridden" when she visited him. He was "studying" the book of Hebrews, she said. The prophet remarks that in that book Paul "was trying to show to the Hebrews, separating the Old Testament and showing the Old Testament being a shadow or a type of the New".[61] Lady Hope said that when she raised with Darwin the issue of "the strong opinions expressed by many persons on the history of the Creation ... and then their treatment of the earlier chapters of the Book of Genesis", she said: "he seemed greatly distressed, his fingers twitched nervously, and a look of agony came over his face as he said: 'I was a young man with uninformed ideas. I threw out some queries, suggestions, wondering all the time over everything, and to my astonishment, the ideas took like wildfire. People made a religion out of them.'"[62] Darwin's deathbed confession takes us back to the beginning when Satan used reason, man's "uninformed ideas", or intelligence so to speak, to make his own religion, science, and education, to form his own man-made civilisation.

Chapter Six

# MEANING AND ORIGIN OF RIGHTS

*We hold these truths to be self-evident, that all men are created equal,*
*that they are endowed by their Creator with certain unalienable rights*
*that among these are life, liberty and the pursuit of happiness.*
– The American Declaration of Independence, 1776

I hope that you will agree with me that the previous chapter
points to the inescapable fact that "before the foundation of
the earth the purpose of God was to share His Eternal Life
with man",[1] and that knowledge of this plan of God[2] is what
has formed the very foundation, the very basis upon which
an advanced people, an advanced nation, an advanced way of
life, an advanced civilisation for generations, beginning in
Eden. It is an understanding of this plan of God that is at the
heart of the American Declaration of Independence; for it
acknowledges the existence of the "Creator" who has "endowed" His citizens with "certain unalienable rights". There
is evidence that before the *Mayflower* (the ship that trans-
ported English pilgrims to the United States in 1620), there
were earlier French pilgrims, in 1564. A Spanish settlement
in 1565 that destroyed the French pilgrims, "the true first
pilgrims in America",[3] for "scattering odious Lutheran doctrines in these Provinces", does not detract from the fact that
early pilgrims travelled to the United States for religious
freedom.

Whatever one says about the tension between the different
sects when they got to the United States, whether Protestants

and Catholics, or Puritans and non-Puritans, America became the melting pot for many people who fled their country in search of the freedom of religious practice.[4] In the beginning America was principally a Christian nation. Today religious freedom is considered by nations and peoples across the world to be a fundamental human right.

## WHAT DO WE MEAN BY RIGHTS?

For natural man, rights are man-made moral principles which tell us what to do and allow us the freedoms and privileges to exercise our free will in society as long as we do not stop others from exercising their freedom of expression or movement. All of the written laws which set out our rights recognise that first of all we have just one fundamental right, that is, the right to life. Look at the American Declaration of Independence again. You will see that the first right mentioned is the right to life. That is the only right we have. All other rights flow from this basic right. This fundamental right is your right to your own life. If you are a believer, a Christian, you will recognise that you only have one life. And that life is eternal life.

You have the right to live and to do whatever it takes within reason to make sure you keep alive. You have a right to such necessaries as food, shelter and clothing, that is, those things in life without which a person cannot reasonably exist. And you are entitled to do as you see fit to enjoy your own life. This is really what is meant by the right to life, liberty and the pursuit of happiness. These are natural rights. The idea of natural rights comes from the ancients including the Greeks observing the natural laws of nature. In fact the Greeks believed that there is a kind of perfect justice given to man by nature and that the laws made by man must conform to the laws of nature.

Milan Kundera has expressed concern that all human desires have been turned into rights. In this writer's view, "the world has become man's right and everything in it has become a right: the desire for love the right to love, the desire for rest the right to rest, the desire for friendship the right to friendship, the desire to exceed the speed limit to the right to exceed the speed limit, the desire for happiness the right to happiness, the desire to publish a book to the right to publish a book, the desire to shout in the street in the middle of the night the right to shout in the street".[5] This quote demonstrates that some individuals believe that they have the freedom to campaign for a cause which is morally and ethically wrong to be their human right.

Many people do not feel that they are responsible for their actions. You might hear people object to wearing a seat-belt or motor-cycle helmet on the grounds that "it's my body and I have the right to do as I please with it". But this driver or biker may have a child, husband or wife or parent. They do not think about the grief. They do not think about the cost of the medical treatment if they were injured. They do not think of the costs of being put in a care home if their recovery from their accident would take a long time to heal. Many of these modern day claims to individual rights ignore relationships, responsibility and reality. The individual ignore relationship because they more often than not has someone close to him or her such as a husband, wife, brother sister whom they have not thought about would be very distressed about their injury. They ignore responsibility because that individual who has had a spinal injury on a public road becomes the most dependent individual because they rely on members of the public to help them including the ambulance service and nurses and doctors on the ward.

## WHERE DID RIGHTS FIRST COME FROM?
We have already suggested that the idea of rights in the Bible first came from the Garden of Eden when the first man, Adam and the first woman, Eve, were told that they had the freedom

to think and do what they want, but that there would be
consequences if they refused to listen to the Word of God. In
the Bible a picture was painted one time to Eve of how much
brighter and better things would be if she used her powers of
reasoning to disobey the Word of God. In the end both Adam
and Eve disobeyed the Word of God. "There is a difference
between reason and God's Word. God's Word is true; reason
is false",[6] declared the prophet. Our reasoning is not made to
understand the Word of God. "For we walk by faith, not by
sight",[7] says the Scriptures. This means that a person must
believe the Word of God and not use their faculty of reasoning
or logical thinking to accept the Word of God. By the 17th
and 18th centuries more and more intellectuals were suggesting that we should use reason to reform society and challenge
the long held Christian belief that we live by faith alone. These
intellectuals were convinced that society should abandon the
Word of God and choose knowledge and science to make
advances for the benefit of the human race. This period of
history which occurred in the seventeenth and eighteenth
centuries was called by historians "The Age of Enlightenment
(or simply the Enlightenment or Age of Reason)". It started
first in Europe and later spread to the American colonies. It
promoted scientific thought; the idea that God did not exist;
freedom of expression and religious thought; and did not
tolerate abuses of power by the church and the state.

Thus at the time of the Enlightenment we had movements
in such places as America and France where people were
fighting for their freedoms. Moreover, during this period the
people of the huge continent of America were successful in
freeing themselves from the tiny island of England which had
them in bondage for many years. *The American Revolution*
(1765-1783) then and the *American Declaration of Independence*
(1776) led to America's independence from the British Empire.

*The French Declaration of the Rights of Man and of the Citizen*
followed in 1789, declaring that, "Men are born and remain

free and equal in rights" and that "the aim of every political association is the preservation of the natural and inalienable rights of man; these rights are liberty, property, security; and resistance to oppression".[8] It was the idea that we could think and do what we like, even to the extent that men could question and deny the existence of God, which helped to bring about these changes across the Atlantic. The Enlightenment in short played a major part in bringing about these changes. The prophet links the rights enshrined in the *American Declaration of Independence* to our proper God-given rights[9] which have their origin in the Bible. He declared that we are happy to be the children of our fathers today. And "to inherit the rights of being a free American where we can open the Bible and teach, and believe God, and worship Him according to the dictates of our conscience. We're very happy for this privilege".[10]

I like the way the prophet makes the clear distinction between our natural or human rights and our spiritual rights as evident in the following example: "I'm an American citizen and I have a right to do whatever I want to. That's my American privilege. It's your American privilege, but not the Christian privilege. For by Christian, you are a sheep; and a sheep forfeits its rights [natural rights]. It lays still and lets you take away from it all the rights [natural rights] it has. But a goat will kick up a storm about it. That's right. But a sheep forfeits its rights [natural rights]. And a Christian always forfeits their national rights [natural rights] if it's contrary to your Christian rights [spiritual rights]."[11]

## BRITISH CLAIM TO ORIGIN OF RIGHTS

Some British historians suggest that the modern debate on rights first came from a group of English nobles well before America became a British colony. They argue that the people of Britain were able to claim their rights long before the Enlightenment gave birth to the *American Declaration of*

*Independence* and *the French Declaration of the Rights of Man and of the Citizen*. These historians say that *Magna Carta* [Charter] 1215 was the beginning of the first People's Charter in England. It gave certain privileges to a select few of the ruling class. *Magna Carta* was really a piece of paper signed by King John and his barons in 1215. The King agreed in this document that his barons would not be unfairly taxed, arrested, or put into prison for any offence without being tried by a jury.[12]

If anyone from the ruling class was wrongfully arrested and put in prison they could demand to be released. They or their relatives could ask the court for a document called *habeas corpus* which literally means "you may have the body". The people who were guarding them in prison would have to let them go free unless they could show that they had done something wrong against the law. After Charles I was executed in 1642 for being what we would in modern times call a dictator, the *Bill of Rights* in 1689 sought to protect and safeguard the rights of individuals. The *Bill of Rights* was clear that individuals were entitled to a fair trial by jury and their punishment should fit the crime.

*The United Nations Convention against Torture and Other Cruel, Inhuman or Degrading Treatment or Punishment* (1984) seeks to prevent the torture of individuals by different nations. The Convention places a duty on nations to do everything in their power to prevent torture within their borders, and forbids states to transport people to any country where there is reason to believe they will be tortured. It has been suggested that this provision in the United Nations comes from the clause in the 1689 *Bill of Rights* which clearly forbids "cruel and unusual punishments".[13] Neither the *Magna Carta* (1215) nor the *Bill of Rights* (1689) protected the rights of the ordinary individual during these periods of history. The prophet drew our attention to the *Fox's Book of Martyrs*[14] which recorded the torture of Christians across Europe before, during, and after the period of the *Magna Carta* and the *Bill of Rights*. According to the prophet

> ... [You might] ... think that the persecution of the saints had abated. Not so. They were still being destroyed by the devil through the instrumentality of the wicked. They were burned at the stake. They were nailed to logs face down and wild dogs were turned loose upon them, so that the dogs would tear away the flesh and bowels, leaving the victims to die in terrible torture. Babes were ripped from expectant mothers and thrown to the hogs. Women's breasts were cut away, and they were forced to stand erect while each heart throb poured out the blood until they crumpled in death. And the tragedy was even greater to think about when one realizes that this was not solely the work of the heathen, but many times it was caused by so-called Christians who felt that they did God a favor in exterminating these loyal soldiers of the cross who stood for the Word and obedience to the Holy Spirit.[15]

For natural man the torture of an individual violates their human rights. Historians have quite rightly recorded that "there would be widespread outrage in this country [Britain] if the state engaged in the kinds of murder or torture of its citizens that take place in many other parts of the world including Russia, Iran and Sudan".[16] Even in the United States in the twenty-first century a group of more than 250 of America's most experienced legal scholars signed a letter protesting against the treatment of one of its citizens in military prison. They argued that "his 'degrading and in-humane conditions' are illegal, unconstitutional; and could even amount to torture ..."[17] Britain also has not escaped allegations of torture by British troops in combat. It is interesting to note that British historians frequently point to *Magna Carta*, the *Bill of Rights* and some of their earlier writers such as John Locke to remind us that they laid the foundations for the *American Declaration of Independence*. Among other things, Locke's philosophy of "man's natural rights to life, liberty, and estate", and that "men being ... by nature all free, equal, and independent", influenced the *Declaration of Independence*. In fact history records that the then American President Thomas Jefferson incorporated Locke's ideas in the *Declaration of Independence*.[18]

Historians insist that these earliest sources such as the *Magna Carta*, Locke and the *Bill of Rights* are the guarantee of our modern human rights laws and the *United Nations Convention against Torture* (1984). Other historians have suggested that the true source of human rights laws should be traced to the Bible. In fact it is suggested that our God-given rights come from the divine source,[19] namely, the Lord Jesus Christ. Some of our material or historical sources on rights originated in ancient Babylon and can be found in the Code of Hammurabi written about 1780 B.C. Some historians claim that it was incorporated into the laws of the Greeks and Romans which was in turn enshrined in the laws and customs of Western Europe.

**ELECTIVE LOVE**

Whilst the scriptures exhort the believer to "think it not strange concerning the fiery trial which is to try you, as though some strange thing had happened unto you";[20] natural man would think it strange that torture and suffering are linked to the god-given rights of Christians. Torture, inhumane and degrading treatment, "man's inhumanity to man" has no place in a civilised society and is quite rightly outlawed by states and nations. But the sufferings of Christians and the trials they have been through historically, viewed through the eyes of Christians is considered here in light of the Christian walk and the scriptures. The prophet reminds us of the "torture that Jesus went through to prove the Sign of God", that He was the Messiah,[21] because all our rights had been lost by Adam and Eve and went back to God.[22] Moreover, Christ had to come because we needed a Kinsman's Redeemer to pay the price[23] so that we would have "the rights to all the redemptive blessings".[24] But if you are a real Christian, declares the prophet, you must be "willing to forfeit your American rights to be a Christian, cause your nature's changed";[25] and where your "national rights" are "contrary to your Christian rights" you must give these up too.[26]

The prophet has no doubt that the believer must forsake all his rights in order to inherit His rights by way of the cross. "All of our rights of this world, the things that we once cherished and thought was so great; such as treasures of life, such as money and popularity, and, oh, things that the unbeliever seeks after. Then we lay that aside when we find Christ, and He becomes our main stay is Christ, the Son of God."[27] Once we have surrendered all to follow Christ we would be tried and tested[28] in the fiery furnace[29] of life where we are beaten like gold[30] to reflect the very image of Christ, but for a purpose as is evident from the following "exposition" of the prophet:

> Now the Lord God Almighty says, "I KNOW." There He is walking in the midst of His people. There He is, the Chief Shepherd of the flock. But does He hold back the persecution? Does He stem the tribulation? No, He does not. He simply says, "I KNOW your tribulation ... I am not at all unmindful of your suffering." What a stumbling block this is to so many people. Like Israel they wonder if God really loves them. How can God be just and loving if He stands by and watches His people suffer? ... You see, they could not figure out God's love. They thought that love meant no suffering. They thought that love meant a baby with parental care. But God said that His love was "elective" love. The proof of His love is ELECTION ... that no matter what happened, His love was proven truly by the fact they were chosen unto salvation (because God hath chosen you to salvation through sanctification of the Spirit and belief of the truth). He may commit you to death as He did Paul. He may commit you to suffering as He did Job. That is His prerogative. He is sovereign. But it is all with a purpose.

If He did not have a purpose, then He would be the author of frustration and not of peace. His purpose is that after we have suffered awhile we would be made perfect, be established, strengthened and settled. As Job said, "He puts strength in us." (Job 23:6b) You see He, Himself, suffered. He learned obedience by the things that He suffered. He was actually made perfect by the things that He suffered. Hebrews 5:8-9, "Though He were a Son, yet learned He obedience by the things which He suffered; and being made perfect, He became the author of eternal salvation unto all them that obey Him." In plain language, the very character of Jesus was perfected by suffering. And according to Paul He has left His church a measure of suffering that they, too, by their faith in God while suffering for Him, would come to a place of perfection. Why did He want this? ... Unless we suffer with Him we cannot reign with Him. You have to suffer to reign. The reason for this is that character simply is never made without suffering. Character is a VICTORY, not a gift. A man without character can't reign because power apart from character is Satanic. But power with character is fit to rule. And since He wants us to share even His throne on the same basis that He overcame and is set down in His Father's throne, then we have to overcome to sit with Him. And the little temporary suffering we go through now is not worthy to be compared to the tremendous glory that will be revealed in us when He comes. Oh, what treasures are laid up for those who are willing to enter into His kingdom through much tribulation.[31]

So these rights of the Word, eternal life, and our inheritance which were forfeited by Adam and Eve[32] are once again ours because Christ paid the price by his death on the cross at Calvary. But as we have seen it does not end there. In *Images of Christ*, the prophet continues to drive the message home that through suffering we will be shaped and moulded into the image of Christ. He compares the process of bringing the individual to perfection with goldsmiths in the past who was working with gold when it first came out of the ground. It was dross, he said. They, he continues, "beat it with a hammer, and turn it over and over, and beat [it] until all the dross was out of it. And the only way that they knew that it was down to the gold, was when the beater could see his reflection in it. The one who was beating could constantly look until he could almost shave by his own reflection in the gold that he was beating. And when the Holy Spirit of God begins to beat on us with the Gospel hammer, until all of the things of the world is beaten out and we can reflect the image of the Lord God, then I believe we become Christians. For the word 'Christian' means 'Christ-like', and to reflect Him."[33]

He is clear that in order for us to obtain our god-given rights we must be overcomers for "every overcomer has to be put to the test"[34] before he "is heir of all things". As an overcomer we would be given our god-given right to live eternally in that City Abraham sought whose builder and maker is God. It is our right to be in the New Jerusalem! For many believers this is why the notion of *Taking Rights Seriously*[35] should be pursued not only within the human realm, but the spiritual realm – a subject we will explore further in the next chapter.

## Chapter Seven

# PROTECTING HUMAN RIGHTS

*We are happy today to inherit the rights of being free where we can open the Bible and teach, and believe God, and worship Him according to the dictates of our conscience.*[1]
   – William Marrion Branham, The Angel Of The Lord, 1951

### THE RIGHTS AND WRONGS OF RIGHTS

Many times, as we have witnessed in the previous chapter, violence has been used to justify protecting our "rights" to "worship" God. The sixty eight million Christians martyred as recorded in the *Fox's Book of Martyrs* is an example where violence was used by people who believed that they were doing God a service. The arrival of French Pilgrims in America in 1564, forty years before any English settlement, and their massacre by the Spanish Catholics at Fort Caroline, near present day Jacksonville, Florida in the United States in 1565, is another case in point.

In modern times *The Mission*,[2] a top rated religious film by the Vatican, sought to show the Jesuit mission to the South America jungle in the 1750s to convert the Guaraní people to Christianity in a positive light. But the film, "based on true historical events", did not tell the historical truth about the Jesuit involvement in this mission. Critics suggest that the Jesuits were true to their mission of world domination in their conversion of the Guarani people to Roman Catholicism. These people, the critics argue, should never have "Europeanised" the Guarani people; for instead of protecting them the

Jesuits stood back and watched them being slaught-ered in the three year war against the Portuguese slavers. And in any event, declares Andrew Mather in his review of the film: "surprisingly, we are shown the Jesuit missionaries in the light that they intended themselves to be seen in, rather than the subversive, powerful and dangerous image they were contemporarily given."[3] Returning to the French pilgrims at Fort Caroline, it is clear, however, that the 1564 account of the priest who accompanied Admiral Menéndez and his Spanish army to the slaughter of these first pilgrims to set foot on American soil, supports *The Mission's* film review of the savagery of the Jesuits in the past, a theme we will be returning to later:

> ... the greatest victory which I feel for this event is the victory which Our Lord has given us so that his Holy Gospel may be planted and preached in these parts ... The fire and desire he [Admiral Menéndez] has to serve our Lord in throwing down and destroying this Lutheran sect, enemy of our Holy Catholic Faith, does not allow him to feel weary in his work"[4]

Menéndez thought that these inhabitants at Fort Caroline were Lutherans, but he was mistaken. They were French Protestants who followed the teachings of John Calvin, a leading French theologian and minister during the Protestant Reformation. Patrick Henry, the governor of Virginia, was another leading figure to summon the help of God when there was a call to arms in the lead up to *The American Revolutionary War* or as it is sometimes called, *The American War of Independence* (1775-1783). The American War of Independence came about as a result of the thirteen states in North America joining forces to be independent of Britain which held them as a colony for years. You will see from an excerpt of Patrick Henry below how he makes a convincing speech of why the war is necessary for the preservation and protection of the liberty of the individual:

If we wish to be free—if we mean to preserve inviolate those inestimable privileges for which we have been so long contending—if we mean not basely to abandon the noble struggle in which we have been so long engaged, and which we have pledged ourselves never to abandon until the glorious object of our contest shall be obtained, we must fight! I repeat it, sir, we must fight! An appeal to arms and to the God of Hosts is all that is left us! Sir, we are not weak, if we make a proper use of the means which the God of nature hath placed in our power. Three millions of people, armed in the holy cause of liberty, and in such a country as that which we possess, are invincible by any force which our enemy can send against us. Besides, sir, we shall not fight our battles alone. There is a just God who presides over the destinies of nations, and who will raise up friends to fight our battles for us. The battle, sir, is not to the strong alone; it is to the vigilant, the active, the brave. Besides, sir, we have no election. If we were base enough to desire it, it is now too late to retire from the contest. There is no retreat but in submission and slavery! Our chains are forged! Their clanking may be heard on the plains of Boston! The war is inevitable—and let it come! I repeat it, sir, let it come! It is in vain, sir, to extenuate the matter. Gentlemen may cry, "Peace! Peace!"—but there is no peace. The war is actually begun! The next gale that sweeps from the north will bring to our ears the clash of resounding arms! Our brethren are already in the field! Why stand we here idle? What is it that gentlemen wish? What would they have? Is life so dear, or peace so sweet, as to be purchased at the price of chains and slavery? Forbid it, Almighty God! I know not what course others may take; but as for me, give me liberty, or give me death![5]

I do not believe that the three examples of the use of force in the name of God quoted in the cases above in the quest to secure the rights of individuals and nations are in line with the biblical passage: "the Kingdom of God suffereth violence, and the violent taketh it by force".[6] The prophet said that God gave the land of Canaan to the Children of Israel, and that "Joshua had to fight for every inch of ground." This is because God told him that "everywhere that the soles of your feet shall tread is yours",[7] says the prophet; and "footprints is possession", he continues.

Thus when the Children of Israel got to Canaan they had to fight for the land God promised them. It was, the prophet declared, that: "they possessed their rights ... And they could not possess their rights till they got into Canaan. ... When they come into Canaan, then they had rights. And we've got rights. When you receive the Holy Ghost, you're in Canaan. You have to fight for it; every inch of ground you have to fight for it."[8] Now this interpretation of fighting for your rights has a parallel with the reggae artist Bob Marley's lyrics in the natural realm who urges his fans to "Get up, Stand Up: Stand up for your rights"; and "Don't give up the fight." But, if we try to find out what the words "suffereth violence" in Matthew 11:12 mean and compare them with the words "the Kingdom of God is preached, and every man presseth into it" in Luke 16:16 we will get a clearer idea of the biblical meaning of "suffereth violence". When Jesus declares that "the Kingdom of God suffereth violence, and the violent take it by force", he is using a figure of speech. This figure of speech is a signal that the common people are inspired by his teachings and that they desperately want to know what they should do to inherit eternal life. "Suffereth violence" in Greek means, "to force", that is, "to force one's way, presseth"[9] or "to crowd oneself (into)". Luke.16:16 which states that, "the law and the prophets were until John: since that time the kingdom of God is preached, and every man presseth into it" compared with Matthew. 11:12 should give us a better understanding of what Jesus was talking about. Before John the Baptist the message of the hour could be found in "the Law and the Prophets". Since John the message of the teachings of Jesus Christ witnessed the common people fervently and actively clamouring to hear the Word of God. And so by this means doing everything in their power to be Christ-like in order to get to heaven. They were zealously forcing their way into the kingdom with much desperation and great haste. In Shakespearian English the word "suffer" should be interpreted as "allow"; so that people were doing everything they could to be allowed into the Kingdom of God. The word "violence" should be given a wider meaning to include "forceful". Thus Matthew 11:12 conveys the correct meaning of the common people at the time in that they were allowed to hear the Word of God and to make a determined effort to enter into the Kingdom of God.

The twenty first century like the previous century is the age of people's rights. It is also the age of "the lukewarm church". They have a "form of godliness",[10] declares the prophet. The Word of God, he insists, has in our age been eclipsed by our desire to protect our human rights: animal rights; people's rights; children's rights; gay rights; lesbian rights; women's rights; civil rights; moral rights; political rights; constitutional rights; legal rights; property rights; and so on. Universal Rights and religious rights too are on the agenda; so are the rights of sun and moon and stars and cow worshippers and the rights of atheists to have their say and their way. The prophet concluded that this increase in rights for almost everyone and everything is a fulfillment of prophecy.[11] He was particularly critical of the preacher Martin Luther King's involvement in the civil rights movement:

What about the other day when we had this question of segregation, down in the South? When this governor of Alabama... I wish I could talk to that minister, that Martin Luther King. How can the man be a leader, and leading his people into a death trap? If those people were slaves, I'd be down there, my coat off, beating away for them people. They're not slaves. They're citizens. They're citizens of the nation. The question of "going to school". Them people, if they got a hard heart and don't know those things. You can't drive into a people, spiritual things, what is beat in there with political powers. They've got to accept it, be born again, then they'll see these things. But, this man, if I could only speak to him; leading those precious people, under the name of religion, into a death trap where he's going to kill thousands times thousands of them! They don't... They just get the—the natural side.[12]

Here the prophet draws attention to the fact that movements like the civil rights movement is man's way of finding a solution to problems, but that the non-violent civil rights movement was "wrong".[13] Martin Luther King, the civil rights leader, was campaigning against racial segregation in the United States during the nineteen sixties. Segregation in American schools was one of the injustices the civil rights movement was attempting to end at the time. The prophet objected to Martin Luther King's involvement in what he regarded as a political campaign for the rights of individuals. But he was not alone: other preachers held similar views.[14] They were more concerned that he should preach the Word of God which was his calling as a minister of the Gospel, rather than dabbling in politics. But in his "letter from Birmingham jail" King was quite clear as to why he was fighting for equal rights and justice in the United States of America as we can see from his reasons in his letter below:

Before the pilgrims landed at Plymouth, we were here. Before the pen of Jefferson etched the majestic words of the Declaration of Independence across the pages of history, we were here. For more than two centuries our forbears laboured in this country without wages; they made cotton king; they build the homes of their masters while suffering gross injustice and shameful humiliation and yet out of a bottomless vitality they continue to thrive and develop. If the inexpressive cruelties of slavery could not stop us, the opposition we now face will sure fail. We will win our freedom because the sacred heritage of our nation and the eternal will of God are embodied in our echoing demands.[15]

There are many other men apart from Martin Luther King who fought for human rights. I shall give two further examples below of individuals who have made such an attempt in modern times.

## NELSON MANDELA

Mandela (1918-2013), a former South African anti-apartheid hero and President of South Africa from 1994-1999 was involved in a movement similar to that of Martin Luther King in the United States. He fought against segregation in South Africa and campaigned for the civil rights of his people. Mandela's autobiography, *Long Walk to Freedom* (1994) gives some idea of how he fought for those rights even whilst he was in prison. He did many things to achieve some of these basic rights, but time and space would only permit me to talk about one of his main achievements.

Mandela was in a top security "prison within a prison" on Robben Island, a jail that Mandela describes as "without question the harshest, most iron-fisted outpost in the South African penal system". Every day he had to crush stones the size of volley balls into gravel. His work was "tedious" and "strenuous". The temperature on this isolated and remote island caused him to shiver in his light khaki shirt in the winter months of June/July, even though the sun was out, until he felt the cold in his bones. Look at how Mandela demanded his rights in one situation:

> Journeying to the island was like going to another country. Its isolation made it not simply another prison, but a world of its own. ... My dismay was quickly replaced by a sense that a new and difficult fight had begun. From the first day, I had protested about being forced to wear short trousers. I demanded to see the head of the prison and made a list of complaints. The warders ignored my protests, but by the end of the second week, I found a pair of old khaki trousers unceremoniously dumped on the floor of my cell. No pin-striped three-piece suit has ever pleased me so much. But before putting them on I checked to see if my comrades had also been issued with trousers. [16]

Mandela was selfless because he was not only interested in fighting for his own individual rights but the rights of his fellow prisoners. He said that when he discovered that his fellow prisoners had not been issued with trousers he "told the warder to take the trousers back. I insisted all African prisoners must have long trousers".[17] Mandela made demands repeat-edly even in the face of being ignored by the prison authorities time and again. Eventually Mandela and his fellow prisoners got what they demanded. He said that when he and his comrades requested sunglasses "the authorities refused, believing they could ignore us with impunity and that if they turned a deaf ear, we would give up in frustration and the people on the outside would forget about us". In the words of Mandela, "the campaign to improve conditions in prison was part of the apartheid struggle. We fought injustice, no matter how large or how small, wherever we found it; we fought it to preserve our humanity". Eventually the apartheid system was overthrown, segregation ended and the people of South Africa won their human rights, equality and justice.

## POLITICS
Martin Luther King and Nelson Mandela believed that political power would bring about the necessary changes to secure the rights of the people. Whilst the prophet acknowledges that politics is necessary in a democracy he has equally declared "that the devil controls all politics that ever has been or ever will be".[18] And that Satan "through politics ... [had] already got to the White House"[19] which was evident from the support King received from President Kennedy in 1963. For the prophet racial segregation in the Southern States of America[20] and South Africa[21] were the same as existed at the time Jesus met the Samaritan woman.[22] "They were two nationalities of people" he said, "one was a Samaritan; one was a Jew. But Jesus let them know right quick that God had

no colors [colours], or races ... We all are one. We come from Adam, every one of us. All of us are children of God. The country you live in, colored [colour] of our skin... white, brown, yellow, black, whatever it is, we're all one in Christ Jesus".[23] And in the case of south Africa he was clear that in "the south, in Africa, it's got hot down there and turns the skin dark. And I come from up in the Anglo-Saxon country where it's cold and we were bleached out ... We can give one another a blood transfusion. We're the same. God made of all nations, one blood".[24]

King and Mandela were campaigning for the rights of people in nations run by "human government", that is, "politics",[25] to secure the civil and human rights for all. But though the prophet acknowledged that this was "man's day"[26] and that politics was used by man to help solve his earthly problems, he condemned "national politics" as "filth".[27] His conclusion on the question of politics and how we could secure our spiritual god-given rights was that "we are not joined to Christ by politics. We are joined, the Church, to Christ, by the baptism of the Holy Ghost. And the way you know the baptism of the Holy Ghost, is 'cause that Spirit in you identifies every Word of God to be the Truth'".[28]

## VIKTOR FRANKL

Viktor Frankl was a Jewish psychiatrist, born 26 March 1905 in Vienna Austria. He wrote *Man's Search for Meaning* giving an account of the day to day life of his and others personal experiences in concentration camps during World War II. The book is a telling example of how these prisoners fought and attempted to overcome the violation of their human rights. His wife, mother, father and brother died in concentration camps. His sister was his only closest relative who escaped the horrors of the concentration camp, and this was because she went to Australia before the war.

Frankl believed in determinism like Sigmund Freud, one

of the most famous psychologists of the twentieth century whose works he studied. Now, the idea of determinism in psychology is that your very childhood experiences and environment decides what you are for the rest of your life and there is nothing you can do about it. Frankl described how he was tattooed, tortured, and persecuted. He experienced many humiliations and indignations. He was called all sorts of dirty names which affected and hurt him deeply. He did not know from one moment to the next whether he would be thrown into the ovens. He tells of how the prisoners suffered from the "delusion of reprieve"[29] where one moment they thought that they would be thrown into the gas chamber only to find out the next moment that they would be "saved". Confusion, uncertainty, hopelessness, helplessness and fear were their experiences. And when there appeared to be a glimmer of hope by virtue of the fact that they had not been thrown in the ovens, they were faced with the further horror of having to shovel up the bodies or ashes of their fellow prisoners which they were compelled to take to the dump some distance away.

Frankl tells us that one day he made an amazing discovery whilst he was naked on his own in a small room. He called this discovery "the last of the human freedoms". He said that he realised that whilst his Nazi captors could do whatever they wanted to his body they could not affect his mind unless he let them. That was one freedom they had no control over whatsoever. He became an observer of what they were doing to his body whilst they were torturing him. But he could choose within himself whether he would allow the pain and suffering which they inflicted on his body to destroy his peace of mind. Thus between what they did to him and how he reacted he found out that he had the power or freedom to choose how he would respond. In other words, between the stimulus (what they were doing to him), and the response (what he did about what they were doing to him), he was free to choose how he would respond mentally to their actions.[30] He used his imagination and memory to take his mind off his physical torture. He imagined himself in different situations to relieve the mental pain. He recalls that "in my mind I took bus rides, unlocked the front door of my apartment, answered my telephone, switched on the electric lights".[31] He used other strategies in psychology such as seeing himself in his mind's eye talking to students in a lecture theatre about the lessons he learnt of how to respond to a situation where one is tortured. Stephen Covey suggests that this fundamental principle Frankl learnt about human nature and the individual person is that "between stimulus and response, man has the freedom to choose".[32]

## PSYCHOLOGY
There is no doubt that many professionals including psychologists have regarded Frankl's account of his experience as a tool to be used in psychology to help solve man's modern day emotional and mental problems. One hundred printings of the book including its publication in twenty-one different languages with the English edition alone selling more than three million copies is proof enough that man is still trying to search for a meaning in his life. When he was asked on an American TV programme about the book's success as a "bestseller", Frankl remarked that: "I do not at all see in the bestseller status of my book an achievement and accomplishment on my part but rather an expression of the misery of our time ... [especially] ... if hundreds of thousands of people reach out for a book whose very title promises to deal with the question of a meaning to life."[33]

According to the prophet, the psychology of natural man only "changes your thinking".[34] In his view, followers of Buddha and Mohammed "can produce just as much psychology as Christianity". In the words of the prophet, the "Mohammedans can run splinters through their fingers", "lances through their chins", and "sword[s]" through their body without being harmed.[35] Psychology comes from the Greek psyche which the prophet acknowledges means "mind". And "it's the mind of Christ", he says, "that the human being has the privilege to enter in, and know the mind of Christ".[36] Though he acknowledges that natural man's psychology has its place in modern society as long as it is not contrary to the Word of God,[37] he recognises only one text book on psychology, namely the Bible which in his view we need. "It is written by God", he says, "and contains God's psychology. You don't need any doctor to explain it to you. Receive ye the Holy Spirit and let Him do the explaining. He wrote the Book and He can tell you what is in it and what it means."[38] He quotes the following scripture to make his point that for the believer it is not man's psychology like that of Frankl or any other psychology that will secure man's god-given rights but the power of God in man's soul that will give man his true liberty:

"But as it is written, Eye hath not seen, nor ear heard, neither have entered into the heart of man, the things which God hath prepared for them that love Him. But God hath revealed them unto us by His Spirit: for the Spirit searcheth all things, yea, the deep things of God. For what man knoweth the things of a man, save the spirit of man which is in him? even so the things of God knoweth no man, but the Spirit of God. Now we have received not the spirit of the world, but the Spirit which is of God; that we might know the things that are freely given to us of God. Which things also we speak, not in the words which man's wisdom teacheth, but which the Holy Ghost teacheth; comparing spiritual things with spiritual. But the natural man receiveth not the things of the Spirit of God: for they are foolishness unto him: neither can he know them, because they are spiritually discerned. But he that is Spiritual judgeth all things, yet he himself is judged of no man. For who hath known the mind of the Lord, that he may instruct him? But we have the mind of Christ."[39]

I am not in the least suggesting that the prophet was not mindful of having a "sense of balance"[40] when talking about our natural rights or that he was condemning outright the idea of human rights. He was nevertheless coming against, I think, a system of rights which did not have Christ as its central theme whether those rights were human, political, economic, emotional, psychological or religious.

## UNIVERSAL RIGHTS

We have already seen that following the Enlightenment people and nations were becoming more and more concerned about the violation of human rights. When the Second World War ended, human rights again became a continuing concern and the United Nations was formed. One of its main purposes was to promote "respect for human rights and fundamental freedoms for all", irrespective of their race, sex, language or religion. All peoples, nations and tongues were to be responsible for promoting human rights.[41] As a result in 1948 the United Nations passed *The Universal Declaration of Human Rights* and by 2008 it had been translated into some 300 languages with huge numbers of people demanding their human rights across the world. I have included in Annex E at the back of this book the full text of the declaration so that you can have a clearer idea of the kind of human rights covered by the *Universal Declaration*. Article one, for example, was based on the French *Declaration* of 1789: "all human beings are born free and equal in dignity and rights. They are endowed with reason and conscience and should act towards one another in a spirit of brotherhood".

*The Universal Declaration* pays much attention to the fact that everyone has the right to be treated as human beings and with dignity no matter where they come from or whatever their colour, creed, culture or gender. One of the key messages that the *Universal Declaration* attempts to get across to everyone in the world is that every individual has the right to be valued and respected. It reaffirmed its "faith in fundamental human rights ... the dignity and worth of the human ... recognition of the inherent dignity and of the equal and inalienable rights"[42] which should be protected by all states and nations. As the word "universal" means "the whole world", *The Universal Declaration* is expected to be observed by every nation and every one of us in every country in every generation throughout the earth. We are all responsible for promoting and protecting the human rights laid down by the United Nations.

## THE LAODICEAN AGE

The prophet has referred to our age as "The Laodicean Age", that is, the age of "people's rights" because there was never an age where there were so many people all over the world demanding their rights. And he identified the United Nations with the one-world government. In closing this Chapter I have quoted extensively below from the *Church Ages* so that you can capture the essence of the point the prophet has made on the United Nations and its connection with "people's rights" and the "one-world government":

> The name, Laodicea, which means, "people's rights" was very common and was given to several cities in honor of royal ladies so named. This city was one of the most politically important and financially flourishing cities in Asia Minor. Enormous amounts of property were bequeathed to the city by prominent citizens. It was the seat of a great medical school. Its people were distinguished in the arts and sciences. It was often called the 'metropolis' as it was the county seat for twenty-five other cities. The pagan god worshipped there was Zeus. In fact this city was once called Diopolis (City of Zeus) in honor of their god. In the fourth century an important church council was held there. Frequent earthquakes finally caused its complete abandonment.
>
> How fitting were the characteristics of this last age to represent the age in which we now live. For example, they worshipped one god, Zeus, who was the chief and father of the gods. This

forecast the twentieth century 'one God, father-of-us-all' religious premise that sets forth the brotherhood of man, and is even now bringing together the Protestants, Catholics, Jews, Hindus, etc. with the intent that a mutual form of worship will increase our love, understanding, and care of each other. The Catholics and Protestants are even now striving for, and actually gaining ground in this union with the avowed intent that all others will follow. This very attitude was seen in the United Nations Organization when the world leaders refused to recognize any one individual concept of spiritual worship but recommended putting aside all those separate concepts with the hopes that all religions become leveled into one, for all desire the same goals, all have the same purposes and all are basically right.

Notice the name, Laodicea, 'the people's rights', or 'justice of the peoples.' Was there ever an age like the twentieth century church age that has seen ALL nations rising up and demanding equality, socially and financially? This is the age of the communists where all men are supposedly equal, though it is only so in theory. This is the age of political parties who call themselves Christian Democrats, and Christian Socialists, Christian Commonwealth Federation, etc. According to our liberal theologians Jesus was a socialist and the early church under the guidance of the Spirit practiced socialism, and thus we ought to do so today.

When the ancients called Laodicea the metropolis it was looking forward to the one-world government that we are now setting up. As we think of that city being the location of a great church council we see foreshadowed the ecumenical move taking place today, wherein very soon we will see all the 'so-called' Christians come together. Indeed, the church and state, religion and politics are coming together. The tares are being bound. The wheat will soon be ready for the garner.

It was a city of earthquakes, such earthquakes as finally destroyed it. This age will end in God shaking the whole world that has gone off to make love with the old harlot. Not only will world systems crumble, but the very earth will be shaken and then renovated for the millennial reign of Christ.[43]

Now, it's significant that the prophet has chosen the ancient

city of Laodicea, Peoples Rights, to tell that this is a sign of
things to come in our generation; for example a one world
government, ecumenism, the destruction of the cosmos and
in the end the total destruction of the world order. "We're at
the end of every natural thing",[44] he said. For example, in
1956 he warned that: "our great America and our great
economy that we have is rottening under the foundations,
and someday, I see it in the making right now, she'll lay in the
ruins".[45] But his warning of the collapse of the economy is
not levelled at America alone in the end time, but to the
world's crumbling economic and other systems at the closing
of the age: "We're in the Laodicean church age, the consummation of all ages. We're at the consummation of the
political world ... We're at the consummation of all things",[46]
he proclaimed. The prophet has said time and again that at
the end of this age, God is going to send the Elijah of Malachi
4, the end-time prophet-messenger of Revelation 10:7, "who
will reveal the mysteries as contained in the Word, and who
has the ministry to turn the hearts of the children to the
fathers".[47]

# Chapter Eight

# A NEW DAWN

*There cannot be true peace if everyone is his own criterion, if everyone can always claim exclusively his own rights, without at the same time caring for the good of others, of everyone, on the basis of the nature that unites every human being on this earth.*
  – Address of Pope Francis to Diplomatic Corps 22 March 2013[1]

"Very soon", declared the prophet in 1963, "we will see all the 'so-called' Christians come together", including "the church, and state, religion and politics".[2] Bringing all religions together in the name of world peace was one of the centre pieces of Pope John Paul II's reforms. He was head of the Roman Catholic Church from 1978 to 2005. He strongly believed in the cooperation of the state and the church. During his papacy John Paul II improved relations with Communist Russia. He did much to support the move to bring down the Berlin wall, and to reunite East and West. The Iron Curtain[3] came down in 1989 when the Berlin Wall was demolished. Mikhail Gorbachev, leader of the Soviet Union from 1985-1991, remarked that: "the collapse of the Iron Curtain would have been impossible without John Paul II". In 1963 the prophet noted that should there be a reuniting of East and West, then such a reunion, "puts the Roman Empire ... just exactly in the old circle it was in the time of Jesus".[4] This meant that the whole world would roughly be in the same position it was in at the time when Rome ruled the world and all nations were under its control. It was therefore necessary for the Roman Catholic Church to help to end the Cold War under the pretext of universal peace. This move was seen as a powerful incentive to all nations to agree to "the establishment of some universal public authority acknowledged by all".[5] In the eyes of the prophet "(the pagan Roman Empire) came back to life and power as the 'Holy Roman Empire'." "Rome", he continued, "as a material nation had suffered much depletion and soon would suffer it completely; but it mattered not now, for her religious empire would keep her on top of the world governing from the inside where she would not appear to do so from the outside."[6]

## THE DARK AGES AND OUR AGE

In many ways, declared the prophet in 1960, our age was similar to the Dark Ages or the Thyatirean Church Age which he said occurred between 606-1520 [7] Larkin (1850-1924), stepping out of the nineteenth century into the twentieth century noted in 1918 that "the Church at Thyatira" could be viewed as an epoch in Church history which demonstrates that: "this period extended from A.D.606 to the Reformation A.D.1520",[8] the same period that the prophet refers to as the "Dark Ages". This period was the same like our age, proclaims the prophet – a period where many people did not want to know about God. The Gospel Light, he said, was almost blacked out when the Church raised up a man to take the place of God.[9]

In our age, declares the prophet, "instead of light it was the blackness of apostasy".[10] This meant, he said, people did not believe God exists. And therefore by the end of the age "Christ was now outside the door."[11] The Dark Ages, he said, was also an age of Papal Schism. This resulted in two men within the Catholic Church being "legitimately elected" as pope by the College of Cardinals. They both claimed that they had the right to be pope. One ruled from Avignon in France, Benedict III; the other Pope Gregory XII from Rome in Italy, elected 30 November, 1406. In our time we also have two popes. In 2013 Pope Francis, the first Jesuit pope, was elected as the Bishop of Rome, and sovereign Pontiff of the Vatican City. The Vatican has in the past appointed a second pope. In our time Pope Emeritus Benedict XVI is our second Pope. He was the first pope to have resigned for six hundred years since Pope Gregory XII in 1415.[12]

## THE FIRST JESUIT POPE: A MAN OF PEACE

Though it is claimed that pope Benedict XVI has given a pledge of "unconditional reverence and obedience" to Pope Francis, many church leaders fear that he will still exercise some considerable influence over the new Pope Francis behind the scenes. When Pope Gregory XII in 1406 became the Head of the Roman Catholic Church it was an attempt to bring peace and end the fighting over which pope should rule. In our time Pope Francis like Pope Gregory XII is striving for world peace. He claims that he wants to tackle natural and spiritual global poverty and to unite all nations and religions.[13] In his 2013 Easter message to the world, Pope Francis called for peace in Africa, Asia, and the Middle East and across the globe. The pope said that he wanted to create, develop, and engage a world in: "building bridges with God and between people", "religions", "non-believers", and "cultures" including "civil and religious leaders of the Islamic world"[14] where we would all "learn to grow in love".[15]

We can see here that what the prophet saw over fifty years ago as the coming together of Christians of all denominations to form a union between "the church and state, religion and politics",[16] is now taking place in our generation. He described the pope at the helm of a one-world religion, promising to "bring world peace".[17] "Notice", warns the prophet, "his plans to build a super denominational church, the World Council of Churches, see, a super denominate [denomination], so that all the world will worship ... under the name of united Christianity ... It's a modern Tower of Babel."[18] In the words of Hislop, it is "Mystery Babylon ... derived from ancient Babylon".[19] Pope Francis said that he called himself Francis after Francis of Assisi (1181-1226). Assisi, he continued, championed the cause of the poor and "tells us we should work to build peace".[20] Christ is the only "Author of peace",[21] "Prince of Peace",[22] and "King of Peace",[23] declares the prophet. It has been disputed that the so called "Saint Francis of Assisi Prayer of Peace" ever appeared in any of his writings. There is, however, evidence to suggest that the Assisi prayer was originally written at the turn of the twentieth century.[24] But Pope Francis said that he wanted to apply Assisi's approach of working towards world peace to our generation. It would help him reach out to people from all walks of life, he said. In this way he was confident that it would help him win hearts and minds in spreading the dogmas of Roman Catholicism.

Assisi, however, was not a Jesuit. The Jesuits were formed over three hundred years after Assisi died. Nevertheless, Pope Francis said he intended to work harder to "promote a New Evangelisation". This "New Evangelisation" was introduced by Pope Benedict XVI in 2010. It was seen as a way of returning the Christian backslider to the Catholic fold and bringing new converts to Roman Catholicism. Evangelisation is the practice of taking the doctrine of Roman Catholicism to places in the world where it has not been taught or preached. It also means taking Roman Catholicism to places where people have stopped going to the Roman Catholic Church or where the masses rarely attend Church.

## A MODERN APPROACH FOR A MODERN AGE

There is compelling evidence to suggest that the Roman Catholic Church has sought not only "another way", but new ways to achieve their ancient goal of world domination in modern times.[25] Such an aim can be traced to its secret Code of Practice called *The Secret Instructions of The Jesuits (1723)*[26] which consolidates and records its most ancient doctrine's custom and practice. Chapter XVII. Rule VII of *The Secret Instructions* states that: "our political schemes must be cunningly varied, according to the different postures of the times".[27] According to Chapter XVII. Rule VII:

> Wherefore, let no methods be untried, with cunning and privacy, by degrees, to increase the worldly interests of the Society, and then, no doubt, a golden age will go hand in hand with an universal and lasting peace ...[28]

Thus the secret Code, a copy of which is in the British Library, demonstrates that choosing a pope to suit the spirit of the age has been Vatican policy and practice from the first time the organisation titled the "universal Catholic Church" or Roman Catholic Church was founded in the first century after the birth of Christ. Thus the twenty first century meeting of the College of Cardinals to elect the first Jesuit pope with a leadership style that reflects the age in which we live is not new. In the eyes of the Vatican what the people of the twenty first century need is a people's pope,[29] one who gives the appearance of a humble man of peace, and one who ostensibly consults the laity on the affairs of church and state, and seems to care for the poor and oppressed. Thus throughout this book reference to the pope in any century whether they are called Pope Innocent, Pope John or Pope Paul should be deemed to be reference to the institution of the office of the pope irrespective of the leader of the organisation of the Roman Catholic Church who occupies the office. The Pope and his office are inseparable – they are one, the Roman Catholic Church or Roman Catholicism. The Jesuits too are part and parcel of the same institution and are therefore one and the same thing, namely, the Roman Catholic Church. Indeed they have since ancient times made sure that the doctrine of Roman Catholicism has been carried out. But, in the final analysis the pope reigns supreme. Historically he is the very symbol and embodiment of Roman Catholicism.

Like many modern day political leaders or heads of state the hierarchy of the Holy See or central government of the Roman Catholic Church is anxious that a modern day pope gives the appearance of being in favour of democracy and modern-isation. This line of thinking is in keeping with the Church's ancient custom and practice to give at least the semblance of democracy. In reality, however, it has no intention of giving way to any changes in its doctrine. Thus though its leaders in the past may have been elected because of their unique styles of leadership it was merely the form rather than the nature and substance of the doctrine that has changed. Its doctrine per se has remained intact up to this day. And so these hidden rules in *The Secret Instructions* make it clear that like politicians the Roman Catholic Church should lie to the people. They should tell them that what the Roman Catholic Church really wants to achieve is world peace.

Only the highest ranks of the Jesuits, called the "professed Jesuits" knew about *The Secret Instructions*. Such men gave the appearance of being saints, humble men of God. However, they were cunning and crafty. The rest of its members were men of high moral and academic standing in society. They knew nothing about the secret code. They were recruited to give the Society the appearance of respectability. Some historians claim that the Vatican denies that the secret code ever existed. The appalling history of the Roman Catholic Church in its treatment of believers over time ties in with the mission of *The Secret Instructions*. Lie and deny was the Roman Catholic Church's policy. This policy is penned in the Jesuits' Latin maxim "jura, perjura, veritatem que denega", "swear forswear and the truth deny!" Members of the inner circle [the Professed Jesuits] of the Jesuit Secret Order were sworn to secrecy under oath.

On discovery of the *The Secret Instructions* by "strangers", "Let it be positively denied that these are principles of the Society",[30] the Rules warned members of its Secret Order. The Jesuits vowed "always to act with "unanimity"; or at least to have the outward appearance of doing so".[31] They were encouraged to present themselves as acting for the "common good of mankind"[32], and "diligently to seek occasions of doing good to their neighbours as to themselves".[33] These principles were to be "cautiously and with cunning instilled into the people"[34] so "that they may be ready at our beck, even to sacrifice their nearest relations, and most intimate friends, when we say it is for our interest and advantage".[35] Moreover, they were instructed to "slyly"[36] and with great humility and "reverence"[37] gain the respect and confidence of princes, kings, and men of renown; so that they may draw them into their "clutches".[38] And "with caution and secrecy ... foment and heighten the animosities that arise among princes and great men, even to such a degree, that they may weaken each other".[39] "But this must be cloaked with such cunning and management, as to avoid giving the least suspicion of our intending to usurp the prince's [take over their] ... authority."[40] Furthermore the masses were to be wholly dependent on the Roman Catholic Church.[41]

Historically Roman Catholicism has ordered its foot soldiers, the Jesuits, to different nations to convert, chastise and control them. This is very evident after the Reformation which started in 1520. The main aim of Roman Catholicism was to put down Protestantism. It attempted to overthrow heads of protestant nations. Next it tried to replace them with its own leaders. A few of these attempts listed below are from W.C. Brownlee's book:[42]

- Spanish Armada sailed from Spain in 1588 to overthrow protestant England led by Queen Elizabeth I, but failed.
- The Gunpowder Plot 1605 [known as the Jesuit Treason

Plot] to assassinate the protestant King James I of England (who was also King James VI of Scotland) by Roman Catholics in England led by Robert Catesby, failed to replace James with his nine-year-old daughter princess Elizabeth as Catholic Head of State.

- Henry IV King of France from 1572-1610, baptised a Catholic converted to Protestantism, was assassinated by the Roman Catholic François Ravaillac.
- William I, Prince of Orange or William of Orange (1533-1584), Dutch protestant, shot twice and killed by the Roman Catholic Balthasar Gérard.

The very controversial work titled *Vatican Assassins* (2001) made some damning claims that the Jesuits had "absolute – unlimited power". It is emphatic that the "absolutist" power exercised by "the Jesuit General" "is supreme – even over the pope".[43] But such an assertion goes against the prophet's interpretation of Revelation 6:1-8. The prophet makes it abundantly clear that it is the pope in the name of the Roman Catholic Church who has assumed absolute power. "He [the pope]", continues the prophet, "was a triple crowned pope who sat as God in his temple, calling himself the Vicar of Christ."[44]

Therefore from this interpretation, it is the pope, not the Jesuit General who has wrongly taken the place of God on this earth. To be fair to *Vatican Assassins* it highlighted Roman Catholicism's alleged corruption and abuse of power in all departments of American government, businesses and institutions. This is not surprising since large numbers of Roman Catholics live in the Americas. For example, there were some 78 million Roman Catholics in the United States out of a population of 313 million people in 2013. Moreover, Latin America represents 42 per cent of the 1.2 billion total Catholic populations worldwide.

So, if we use a broad definition of Latin America it includes: North America, Central America, the Caribbean and South

America, This shows us how successful the Roman Catholic Church has been in working towards taking control of the Americas. And the Vatican's election of a new Pope from Latin America in 2013 is its reward for the rapid conversion of its people to Roman Catholicism. *Vatican Assassins* view is that the influence of Roman Catholicism in America was the reason why four of its presidents were "murdered by Jesuit-controlled assassins".[45] These four presidents, it says, were: President Abraham Lincoln (1809-1865),[46] President James Garfield (1831-1881), President William McKinley (1843-1901), and President John F. Kennedy (1917-1963). According to some authorities the allegation in *Vatican Assassins* is just another one of those "conspiracy theories". But some of these claims may be plausible on account of Roman Catholicism's cover-up of its history of the mass killing of people who resisted conversion to Roman Catholicism.

We have already seen that Roman Catholicism massacred the first Pilgrim Fathers [French] to set foot on American soil. *Vatican Assassins'* preoccupation with the Jesuits does not invalidate the questions it raises about the assassinations and other abuses allegedly committed by the Roman Catholic Church. Some sources say that heads of states including presidents of the United States, and others were "removed" or "dismissed" over time for disobeying Roman Catholicism's orders whether or not they were Roman Catholic.

In an attempt to nail down the absolute power of the pope the prophet proclaimed that: "There's an iron curtain; there's a bamboo curtain; and there's a purple curtain. Brother, don't you fear none of the rest of them, but watch that purple curtain. She's setting right here on the throne today in this country ... Wait till she gets wormed into the Cabinet [Cabinet of U.S. government] and everywhere she can, then watch what happens. Look what it done in other nations; look what it's always done."[47] The prophet was commenting here on "a Catholic President ruling"[48] the United States whilst at the same time drawing our attention to its past and present activities in other nations and their government administration. As early as 1962 when John F. Kennedy became the first Catholic President of the United States the prophet observed that Roman Catholicism's influence was spreading across the United States like wildfire: "In the last six months", observed the prophet, "since he's been elected [President John F Kennedy], in the state of Kentucky about three hundred and ten thousand people have turned from Protestant to Catholic in the state of Kentucky".[49] He felt that this was a signal of Roman Catholic domination in the United States. He saw it as a sign of his 1933 vision coming to pass. Thus modern talk of Roman Catholicism getting into the highest offices in the governments of nations, schools, churches, and business administration fits in with this picture the prophet has painted of its influence in all aspects of government in the United States.

## ROMAN CATHOLICISM'S CONTINUING RISE TO POWER
In the sixth of his seven visions of 1933 the prophet felt that the Roman Catholic Church would rule the United States. In the vision, he said, he saw "a most beautiful, but cruel woman". She "held the people in her complete power". He "believed that this was the rise of the Roman Catholic Church".[50] In his view the woman represented the Roman Catholic Church that will conquer the world. In *The Laodicean Church Age* (1960) he reiterated that this "powerful woman, great woman", will " ... either be President, or it'll be a woman representing the Catholic Church (which I think it is) will take over here someday and she'll rule this country".[51] It is conceivable that the election of Hilary Clinton, American politician, diplomat, and United States Secretary of State from 2009 to 2013 as President could signal the fulfilment of the prophet's sixth vision. This would definitely be the case if she succeeds in her quest to become the first woman President in

the 2016 United States Presidential Election.[52] The prophet consistently portrays a woman as representing or symbolising the church.[53] And he therefore concludes that "this great church, great woman"[54] is an "unholy woman",[55] which is "'the church setting on the seven hills', the Roman Church".[56]

Thus according to the prophet's sixth vision his interpretation is that the United States "President ... will be a woman representing the Catholic Church".[57] His belief is, whether in fact the United States elects a female President to the White House or not America will be controlled by the Roman Catholic Church before she is "annihilated".[58] For in his "last and seventh vision", he said, "I heard a most terrible explosion. As I turned to look I saw nothing but debris, craters, and smoke all over the land of America."[59]

The prophet had no doubt that it is neither "Russia" nor "Communism" that will "conquer the world", but "Romanism",[60] or the "Purple Curtain" as he describes the "Roman Catholic Church". The spread of Roman Catholicism's influence can be seen in the 21st century with the election of the new pope. In 2013, for example, the United States, except Italy, was the only country to send the largest number of Cardinals to vote for the new pope since the Roman Catholic Church was established in 325.[61] In 1954 the prophet prophesied that one day when the "united confederation of churches" is established, a new pope from the United States of America will be elected to head this united Church from his headquarters.[62] The prophet is referring here to the one-world government headed by the pope which he prophesied will one day rule over the earth.

In our current global climate, however, where everyone is clamouring for peace, it is not suggested that the Roman Catholic Church would use its military might at present in the same way that it did in the past. As we have already seen it has vowed to use "another way" to achieve its "ancient goals". But this "other way" it has chosen is the road to peace. It is an approach it used from the beginning when it first broke away from the True Christian Church. This is evident in Revelation 6. Here the Church at Rome is represented as innocence. It is symbolised as a white horse when it first started out on its journey, declares the prophet. The white horse is "the beast" which "is a power",[63] he says. Furthermore, he continues, Bible commentators and historians have suggested that the man who sat on the white horse was "the Holy Spirit". They are of the view this rider went out in the early age conquering and winning souls for the Kingdom of God. The bow in the hand of the white horse rider is like that of "Cupid", it has been suggested. For Cupid "shot the arrow of love into the hearts of the people, the love of God, and He conquered".[64] This is what the prophet has indicated was the belief of some biblical scholars. But we will explore later his reasons for rejecting this interpretation of scriptures.

Chapter Nine

# THE CHANGING FACE OF ROMAN CATHOLICISM

*This changing face of Roman Catholicism is consistent with how Scripture describes the last days. "Some will fall away from the faith, paying attention to deceitful spirits ..." (1 Tim. 4:1). They appear to be godly men but they have chosen to believe another gospel ... a gospel of works, sacraments and indulgences, [which] will continue to deceive others without resistance unless the Body of Christ takes a stand to earnestly contend for the faith*
— Ankerberg Theological Research Institute

**THE JESUIT WAY**
Once Pope Paul III permanently established the Roman Inquisition in 1542 as the Congregation of the Holy Office of the Inquisition, the Church's outward appearance as "innocent" and "saintly" entered a new phase. The Inquisition's role was to investigate, and take action against Protestantism and heresy. In many cases the agents of the Roman Catholic Church set up Kangaroo Courts to try the accused. This meant that the accused were brought before the court, sentenced and executed without being allowed to put their side of the case.

Although the persecution of Christians under the Roman Emperor Diocletian (284-305) has been held to be the bloodiest in the history of Christianity, the atrocities committed against protestant Christians after the Reformation were said to be far worse than those carried out during the early Roman Empire.

According to Frederick Tupper Saussy, the Congregation of the Holy Office of the Inquisition has been administered by the Jesuits since the time it was set up.[1] In 1908 Pope Pius X changed its name to the Holy Office. And in 1965 it was again renamed by Pope Paul VI as the Congregation for the Doctrine of the Faith.[2] It has kept that name to the present. Cardinal Josef Ratzinger became Prefect of the Congregation in 1981 before he held the office of Pope Benedict XVI from 2005-2013. In fact it was the Roman Catholic Church that used their "foot soldiers", the Jesuits, to start the "Counter Reformation". "Counter" means "against" or to oppose. The Counter Reformation was the Catholic Reformation. Its main aim was to hunt down and destroy any individual or nation that protested against the Catholic doctrine. Now, if you were a protestant during the Dark Ages you would not be hearing the following words of peace from the reigning pope in the name of the Roman Catholic hierarchy: "My wish is that the dialogue between us should help to build bridges connecting all people, in such a way that everyone can see in the other not an enemy, not a rival, but a brother or sister to be welcomed and embraced."[3]

The Language of peace, humility and reconciliation used by the Roman Catholic hierarchy in the above quote is the Language of the Jesuit Order in the name of the Roman Catholic Church. This is clearly evident in the words which follow from the Jesuits Superior General, Adolfo Nicolás Pachón in the first half of the twenty first century. He was elected by the Order as its head in 2008. His position was confirmed by Pope Benedict XVI in the same year he was elected. Nicolás said that it was the Jesuits' intention: "to build bridges between our lives, our faith, the Christian tradition and other cultures, traditions and religions".[4]

Here he was merely restating Roman Catholic policy which the first Jesuit pope, Pope Francis, repeated almost word for word after his election as Pope in 2013. The letter and spirit of these words can be traced to the shear dedication and commitment of its founder, Ignatius Loyola (1491-1556). Loyola, a former "military man"[5] together with Francis Xavier (1506-1552) and four other members of the "Company of Jesuits", founded the Order, that is, the Society of Jesus or Jesuits on the 15th August 1534. The Order was later approved by Pope Paul III in 1540.

It would appear that the name of Francis of Assisi was more appealing to the Roman Catholic hierarchy for the first Jesuit Pope to adopt than that of Francis Xavier, that is, the "great Roman Catholic missionary" and co-founder of the Society of Jesus or Jesuits. One rather suspects that this is because Xavier had shed too much blood of countless numbers of "Protestants and heretics" over time which forced Pope Clement XIV to abolish the Jesuits in 1773. They were guilty of the mass murder of millions of people in every country they visited. The Jesuits had shed too much blood. This led to their expulsion from most countries in Europe and South America. They were, however, restored by Pope Piux XVII in 1814. Perhaps adopting the name of Francis of Assisi (1182-1226), a non-Jesuit, and unquestionably a saintly figure and a man of peace who had shed no blood would gain the support of more people in the eyes of the Roman Catholic hierarchy.

Francis Xavier and his company of Jesuits not only slaughtered, but forcefully converted to Roman Catholicism those victims they kept alive. There are many examples in history, says the prophet, where the Jesuits shed innocent blood. He recounts how in 1640 in Ireland the "Roman Jesuits" army and "priests" had "one hundred thousand of Saint Patrick's converts ... killed" including ordinary factory workers.[6] Ignatius, history reminds us, turned his attention from "military enthusiasm to ghostly fanaticism".[7] This observation appears to be supported by the following Jesuit Oath:

I declare from my heart, without mental reservation, that the
Pope is Christ's Vicar General and ... He hath power to depose
Heretical Kings, Princes, and States ... that they may safely be
destroyed. Therefore, to the utmost of my power I will defend
this doctrine ... I do further declare the doctrine of the Church of
England, of the Calvinists [sic], the Huguenots, and other
Protestants to be damnable and those to be damned who will
not forsake same.[8]

The Fox's Book of Martyrs provide ample evidence of the
Jesuits in the name of Roman Catholicism's determination to
stick to its promises under oath to obey its Secret Instructions.
In addition, the prophet's statement that: "from the time of
Saint Augustine of Hippo until 1586 on the Roman martyrology, the Roman Catholic church put sixty-eight million
Protestants to death"[9] provides further proof of its crimes
against humanity. Jesuits committed such acts because they
pledged their "absolute subservience to the pope". They
vowed that whatever "His Holiness", the Pope, wanted them
to do they would do[10] to promote the dogmas of the Roman
Catholic Church. Some of these "unscriptural" dogmas
identified by the prophet include: "believing and practicing
the Catechism";[11] celebration of "Christmas"[12] on the 25th
December; "Maryolatry";[13] paying homage to the "Madonna
or Mother and Child";[14] "saying the Apostle's Creed";[15]
"sprinkling"[16] infants at birth; a belief that "the communion
is the literal body of Christ";[17] the practice of "trinitarian
baptism";[18] and celebration of the Feast of Assumption on
the 15 August each year – the day Catholics believe that Mary
was taken up into heaven body and soul.[19] It was these
doctrines of Roman Catholicism which Martin Luther in his
book Babylonian Captivity of the Church (1520)[20] came against
which started the Protestant Reformation. The Roman
Catholic Church excommunicated him, that is, they threw
him out of the Church for saying that Roman Catholicism
was nothing more than the pagan practices in ancient

Babylon. Nevertheless, Roman Catholicism was determined to get into all aspects of human life and institutions to spread its doctrine by fair or foul means: education, trade, schools, hospitals, universities, agriculture, government. Its aim was to make every man, woman and child on the earth a Roman Catholic.

## THE POPE CAN DO NO WRONG

In education the Jesuit maxims were: "Give us the education of the children of this day – and the next generation will be ours"; and Francis Xavier's motto was, "give me a child for his first seven years and I'll give you the man". Its "education" was "indoctrination" into the doctrine of the Roman Catholic Church as part of the Church's policy of world domination. Mass mind control was the key to Roman Catholicism. It is no wonder that with such a policy of mind control that Ignatius, one of the Jesuits founding fathers was fully persuaded in his heart that the doctrine of the "infallibility of the pope" as "the Vicar of Christ on earth" was absolutely the truth and nothing but the truth. "I will believe that the white that I see is black if the hierarchical Church so defines it",[21] he cried. The teaching of this doctrine of "infallibility" (the pope rules by divine right and therefore can do no wrong) is known as the *Magisterium* of the Church, as explained below.

> The task of giving an authentic interpretation of the Word of God, whether in its written form or in the form of Tradition, has been entrusted to the living, teaching office of the Church alone. Its authority in this matter is exercised in the name of Lord Jesus Christ. This means that the task of the interpretation has been entrusted to the bishops in communion with the successor of Peter, the Bishop of Rome.[22]

We learn from the *Magesterium* that only the pope and or the Roman Catholic Church has the divine right to interpret the Word of God whether it is in the Bible or not.[23] In *God Is His*

*Own Interpreter (1964)* the prophet makes it absolutely clear that God needs no man-made interpreter to vindicate His Word.[24] The pope's claim to be the only man of God with the right to tell us what the Word of God says is evident from the 1540 Jesuit constitution as follows:

> [L]et whoever desires to fight under the sacred banner of the Cross, and to serve only God and the Roman pontiff, His vicar on earth, after a solemn vow of perpetual chastity,- let him keep in mind that he is part of a society, instituted for the purpose of perfecting souls in life and in Christian doctrine, for the propagation of the faith . . . Let all members know, and let it be not only at the beginning of their profession, but let them think over it daily as long as they live, that the society as a whole, and each of them, owes obedience to our most holy lord, the pope, and the other Roman pontiffs, his successors, and to fight with faithful obedience for God. And however much he may be learned in the Gospel, and however we may be taught in the orthodox faith, let all Christians profess themselves under the Roman pontiff as leader, and vicar of *Jesus Christ*.[25]

Roman Catholicism believes that "if the dead voice of God [the written Word of God in the Bible] ...seems to conflict with the living voice [the words of the living pope] ... the living voice must prevail".[26] The words in brackets are my emphasis. Although this quote was used to refer to the power of the head of the Jesuits it is really in essence an example of the absolute power of the pope. Thus if what he says is different from what the Bible says then Roman Catholics must reject the Word of God given by inspiration and revelation in the Bible. They must ignore the Bible and do what the pope tells them to do. We have seen that historically it would have been considered heresy to obey the Bible and ignore the words of the pope. This is because Roman Catholicism claims that he is God on earth.

The divine right of the pope to reign on earth by the command of God, declares the prophet, started with Pope

Innocent III (1160-1216). According to the prophet, Pope Innocent III declared he was the "vicar of Christ – supreme sovereign over the church and the world".[27] Moreover, continues the prophet, the Inquisition was firmly established by Pope Innocent III under whose leadership was "shed more blood than at any other time except in the Reformation".[28] At this period of history the churches in all nations were controlled by the pope. And so powerful was Pope Innocent III in 1208 that he decreed the Roman Catholic Church in England would not be allowed to marry, baptise, or bury the dead. This was because King John rejected outright the archbishop of Canterbury appointed by the Pope. When John threw out the bishops in response to Pope Innocent III's actions, the pope immediately excommunicated him, and declared the English throne vacant. Realising that the Pope was the most powerful man on earth, John in 1213 accepted that the authority of the pope was sovereign. No sooner was John on good terms with Innocent III than they fell out again. Pope Innocent III declared Magna Carta (1215) to be null and void (invalid) because King John did not seek his consent before he agreed the Charter of Rights with the barons.

Where did the pope get the idea that he had such absolute power? Some historians like Hislop suggest that the idea of the Sovereign Pontiff was borrowed from the Chaldeans or Babylonians and Egyptians. They believed that their kings were God's representatives on earth. Hislop, for example, states that the idea of the Pontiff was based on the "original Council of Pontiffs at Babylon".[29] It was later used as a title to represent the pagan high priest of Rome before the office was passed on to the pope.

On the other hand, John Julius Norwich in *The Popes: A History* (2011), drawing on speculative history supports the Roman Catholic hierarchy's view in asserting its false claim that the pope derives his origin and authority from the Bible. They allege that the first pope of Rome was Peter.[30] But there is no doubt that the Scriptures record Peter as having both a wife and a mother living with him.[31] In fact, like other Bible commentators the prophet sought to demolish the attempt of the Roman Catholic Church to discredit the fact that Peter had a wife. He was categorical that "Peter never founded the Catholic Church", that "Saint Peter was a married man"; and that there is no historical evidence to suggest that Peter ever visited Rome.[32]

The prophet therefore supports the view that, "when pagan Rome was converted to make papal Rome ... it had ... a pope in the stead of a king, and the pope is the spiritual king. That's the reason he's a crowned spiritual king, claims to be the vicar of Jesus Christ".[33] Moreover, says the prophet, "If vicar of Christ means 'instead of Christ' or 'in place of' or 'on behalf of God' then the pope was calling himself the Holy Ghost or deposing the Holy Ghost, acting for Him."[34] In other words, emphasises the prophet, the Church "made him [the pope] a god" and gave "him a triple crown: the jurisdiction over heaven, purgatory, and hell".[35] In fact, the pope was seen as the only mediator between God and man, thus contradicting the Bible which clearly states that "...there is one God, and one mediator between God and men, the man Christ Jesus".[36] Mediation is just another one of the variety of "political schemes"[37] Roman Catholicism has made up to achieve a "universal and lasting peace".[38]

## MYSTICISM

"Mysticism" is yet another modern day political ploy borrowed from the East[39] to achieve Roman Catholicism's goal of world peace. Writers like Hislop believe that mysticism was first practiced by the ancient people of Babylon, Chaldea and Egypt. It is claimed that Roman Catholicism has filtered it into evangelical and protestant movements to win back many protestant believers and pastors to the "one true Church". In the case of Islam it is seen as the only way to achieve world peace: "Beyond these models of reconciliation, a theology of mysticism provides some hope for common ground between Christianity and Islam",[40] writes Anthony Campolo. It is feared that mysticism is used to trap all religions into the Ecumenical Council.[41] "There are all kinds of mysticism ...all kinds of different theories, sensations, and everything in the world today", declared the prophet in 1961.[42] But he warned "preachers" of the Gospel that the practice of "mysticism" was against the Word of God and contrary to "the Scriptures".[43]

Mysticism, peace, innocence, evangelisation, are the changing masks of Roman Catholicism. Roman Catholicism since it started has been like Biàn liăn, to borrow a Chinese expression. It has had many faces. Biàn liăn is the art of Chinese face mask changing. We use the term here to mean the ability to suddenly switch from one thing to the next. We saw, for example, that at the beginning of its journey Roman Catholicism started out as innocent, peaceful. Suddenly there was a dramatic change in its attitude. The ones it appeared to love, suddenly became its victims. Roman Catholicism is now renewing its efforts to penetrate into Africa, Asia, America, Central and Eastern Europe. Decent, friendly, moral, religious and serious men are being trained as Jesuits to bring the gospel of peace to the world and to convert humanity. But, could it be that these nationals, like their brethren in the past, are not let into "the secret of certain instructions"? If they are not, "they could, with an honest conscience, deny and even swear on the cross, that no such *Secret Instructions* were ever given, or ever received".[44] Could we then be witnessing once more the changing face of Roman Catholicism now wearing the mask of world peace?[45] Is history repeating itself?

Chapter Ten

# THE COUNTDOWN

*Now, we know the Thyatira age has come and gone, and the Ephesian age has come and gone, the Philadelphian age has come and gone. And we are in the seventh church age, at the end of it, the Laodicean age. And that is the countdown.* – William Marrion Branham, Countdown (1962)

### THE SEALS
In *The Revelation of the Seven Seals* (1963) the prophet introduces us to four horse riders, one we have already met, namely the white horse rider. He tells us that in fact there were not four horse riders, but one. He said that it was the same horse rider on the same horse at different stages and ages. In the First Seal he said that the white horse rider started out as "righteous" and "innocent". The rider is "a super religious hero", he said; an "impersonator of Christ", because he has no arrows; no name, and only a bow, the prophet continues. Christ has a name which is the Word of God, he reminds us. The white horse rider who starts out in the first church age as "a Man of Peace" goes forth to conquer the laity.

Moreover, the prophet tells us, that at the opening of the first church age the Holy Spirit was against the "the deeds of the Nicolaitanes". "Nico", he says, means "to conquer" and "Laity" means "the church, the laity". Thus "Nicolaitanes" means, "to conquer the laity", that "is to take the Holy Spirit out of the church and give it all to one holy man, let him be the boss of all of it". And this boss is Rome; the hierarchy of the Roman Church which started out as a saying, an innocent doctrine, he says, which impersonates Christ coming on a white horse, Rome.[1] In the Second Seal the prophet states that "the same system [the Roman Catholic Church] riding ... from the innocent white to a bloody red, signalled an event that took place during the Dark Ages". The sword in the man's hand represents "church political war", he said, "as is evident by the horse being a beast which in biblical terms is a symbol that represents a power", he explains. For example, he continues, "a red horse and his rider goes forth; power given to him to slay with a great sword" thus resulting in the death of millions, he said. "From the time of Saint Augustine of Hippo until 1586 on the Roman martyrology, the Roman Catholic church put sixty-eight million Protestants to death", the prophet reminds us. He said that it was very important for us to remember that this man's sword was red with the blood of the saints. And that "during the dark ages there were millions fed to lions and slaughtered in every way, because they wouldn't bow down to that Catholic dogma". He describes this "superman" going forth with a sword in his hand, riding a red horse, and "wading through the blood of everybody that disagrees with him".[2]

In the third seal in Revelation 6:5-7 the voice said: "Come and see." A "black horse" appeared. Its rider "had a pair of balances in his hand". The voice called out: "A measure of wheat for a penny, and three measures of barley for a penny, but see that thou hurt not the oil and the wine." The prophet said that this meant that the believers had fallen on hard times. They could barely make ends meet. "All hope's gone no hope at all; everything looked dark for the little believers", he said. "That's the reason it's called" or "represented" as a dark horse. He was weighed in the balances and found wanting of natural and spiritual food. Hence "his balances or his scales in his hand", calling out "a measure of wheat for a penny, and three measures of barley for a penny", because wheat and barley is natural staff of life".

It was their staple diet, the poorer man's daily diet – the food he eats daily.[3] Poor people depended on barley and wheat every day for their daily bread to give them life and hope. But says the prophet, Roman Catholicism was charging them for their spiritual food. They were hungering and thirsting daily for the Word of God. "What it means", the prophet says, is that the rider which represented the Roman Catholic Church was "charging his subjects for the kind of the hope of life that he was sending out to them by making ... them pay for prayer, charging for prayer. They still do it ... novenas. Cause, what was he doing? Capturing the wealth of the world because he had the scales in his hand weighing out a measure of wheat for a penny and three measures of barley for a penny", to increase the riches of the "hierarchical church". "The rider on a black horse", he concludes, is "stripping his subjects of their money", as "the Bible predicts that he holds ... the wealth of the world ... they just take all the money and just stripped the people for everything they've got, everything".[4] This superman in Revelation 6:7-8 is now riding on a pale horse: "and his name that sat on him was Death, and Hell followed him. And power was given unto them over the four parts of the earth, to kill with sword, and with hunger; and with death, and with the beasts of the field".

The "power was given unto them", "them", says the prophet, is the "antichrist called death". He explains death here first began with the white horse which kills by the spirit, a spiritual death; then the second horse comes along, the red horse which kills by the sword, using political power when the church and state united. The third sign of death was when the black horse rider came on the scene. He spread his false doctrine to the saints. They paid dearly for their spiritual food. The food sold to them was weighed in the balances. They then had to give the little monies they had, the meagre pennies they had in their possession to the Roman Catholic Church. They had to pay big money to be prayed for by the priests and to hear the Word of God.

And finally the horse rider changed. He was the fourth horse rider. It was the final stage of death. He was sitting on a pale horse. It represented eternal separation from God. When the first four Seals were opened we can clearly see that each of the four horse riders was represented under each of the four seals. The First seal reveals the first horse rider, the white; the second seal, the red; the third seal, the black; and the fourth seal, the pale. "Actually", says the prophet, the pale horse rider becomes "the three in one thing", namely: anti-christ, first, white; second, false prophet, red; third, vicar of heavens and earth and purgatory, black; fourth, the beast, pale horse, Satan being kicked out of heaven".[5]

## THE ANTICHRIST

Thus, this antichrist riding on a beast symbolises power because "a horse is a beast that represents a power", declares the prophet. His power is political power; national power; religious power; demon power. "Satan's Superman" possesses "all kinds of powers mixed together ... mixed with creeds, denominations, man-made doctrines", declares the prophet, and "from the four corners of the earth, they [the antichrist] gather them; gathers them to Armageddon ... Gathers them together, on this mixed coloured, worldly, pale, sick horse...". Each one of those horses was a stage of his ministry, a stage of the early church that had formed into a denomination at Nicaea, 325. The original Pentecostal church upon whom the Holy Ghost was poured was copied by the antichrist spirit of the Roman Catholic Church.

The prophet traces the entry of this antichrist spirit to the time when the apostles Junius and Andronicus of the True Church were thrown out of Rome around 44. They first went to Rome in 36 to spread the gospel. He said that when they left Rome a splinter group broke away from the True Church. This other group, he said, became "hopelessly backslidden, and began to introduce pagan ceremonies under Christian titles."[6] He said that it was this splinter group that called itself the First Church or Roman Catholic Church. It was in that Church, he continued, that "the spirit of the antichrist" went into to live. Moreover, declared the prophet, it "formed an organisation"[7] that "gave birth to some daughters". Both the Mother Church and her daughters joined together into one big organisation called "Death",[8] he said. One of its daughters publicly confessed in 2005 that they had agreed to get together again on the issue of the veneration of Mary.

In their "continuing journey toward full communion, the Roman Catholic Church and the Churches of the Anglican Communion", announced that: "Our Agreed Statement concerning the Blessed Virgin Mary as pattern of grace and hope is a powerful reflection of our efforts to seek out what we hold in common ... [as] Our two traditions share many of the same feasts associated with Mary. From our experience we have found that it is in the realm of worship that we realise our deepest convergence as we give thanks to God for the Mother of the Lord who is one with us in that vast community of love and prayer we call the Communion of saints."[9] This "continuing journey toward full Communion", is part of the ecumenical vision and mission of unity with all religions confirmed by the sovereign Pontiff Francis in his address to the nations' diplomats in 2013. One rather suspects that some of the most powerful and zealous champions of the English Reformation like William Tyndale (1494-1536), and perhaps Thomas Cromwell (1532-1540), Henry VIII's chief minister, would be shocked to hear of the Church of England's return to Rome. It was Cromwell who advised Henry VIII to make a complete break with Rome and to place himself at the head of the Church of England. In fact Henry was not really a leader of the English Protestant Reformation and many of the Roman Catholic ordinances, custom and practice remained in place in the Church of England. His reason for splitting up with the Roman Catholic Church was because the Pope refused to annul his marriage to Catherine of Aragon so that he could marry Anne Boleyn.

Finally, in one of its most blatant acts of apostasy in 2013 the Church of England has caused outrage over its declaration that the biblical requirement of repentance for one's sins is no longer a requirement for baptism in its Church.[10] Essentially the interpretation of Scripture like the one the Anglican Church has undertaken over baptism is a key feature of the World Council of Churches, that is, the ecumenical movement. For such a movement is of the view that it has the power to interpret Scripture. It believes that it can add to and or take out of the Bible fundamental biblical teachings. To be quite blunt, ecumenicalism is nothing less than a one world government that believes that it is infallible.

## WHAT THE FOUR HORSE RIDERS REPRESENT
Historically we know that the Roman Catholic Church symbolises the four horse riders, beginning with the white horse or innocence before 325. But after 325 the Roman Emperor Constantine called the First Ecumenical Council at Nicaea "to bring all groups together where they could iron out their differences, and come to a common understanding, and all be one".[11] But this symbolism which is rolled into all four powers of white, red, black, and pale to form one superpower will continue its ride into Armageddon. There it will once again unleash its deadly powers resulting in physical death. In our generation, that is, the twenty-first century, Roman Catholicism gives the appearance of innocence, "peace". It is a sign that we are now approaching the count-down of the age captured in the prophet's summary of the end of the gentile age below:

> Seven is God's perfect number. And now, He has given us the correct countdown, and His countdown is not ten, but seven.

We've just been through it in the Seven Church Ages. Now, we find out that over in Revelations, the first countdown was the first age. The second countdown, the second age and on to the seventh countdown. And here visible before us, as the picture's drawed, that we had this countdown. The first number counted was Ephesus. The second number counted was Smyrna ... then Pergamos, Thyatira. Fifth was Sardis. Sixth was Philadelphia. And seventh was the Laodicean, the last church age. Then it's the zero time for the church to leave, after the church ages have served their term. Now, we know the Thyatira age has come and gone, and the Ephesian age has come and gone, the Philadelphian age has come and gone. And we are in the seventh church age, at the end of it, the Laodicean age. And that is the countdown.[12]

## Chapter Eleven

# SIGNS OF THE TIMES

*And they asked him, saying, Master, but when shall these things be? ...
Then said He unto them ... Nation shall rise against nation ... and fearful
sights and great signs shall there be from heaven.*
— Luke 21:7-11, King James Version

### THE FULLNESS OF TIME

If we look at how the prophet has placed the seven church
ages within Larkin's "Seven Church Periods"[1] chronological
time structure, that is to say, in date order, signifying the period
of time within which each church age occurred, we would
see how he came to the conclusion that we are now living in
the dispensation of the fullness of time. Some people call the
fullness of time the end time: first Church age, Ephesian (53-
170); second church age, Smyrnaean (170-312); third
church age, Pergamean (312-606); fourth church age,
Thyatirean (606-1520); fifth church age, Sardisean (1520-
1750); sixth church age, Philadelphian (1750-1906); and
seventh church age, Laodicean (1906-present).

At the end time the civilisation of natural man will cease.
All that man can do in terms of improving the earth and
harnessing the natural resources in the world would have
failed. This would leave man in a state of misery and frustration because having done everything in his power to
perfect his world he would have seen the futility in all that he
has done. The monetary system, the political system, the
military system and even the religious system will all fail.
Natural man will find that there is no satisfaction in any of

these things.

## THE WORLD ECONOMY

We have already seen that in trying to solve the problems man faces, nations will unite to find a common solution to deal with the world's existing crisis. Bodies such as the United Nations, European Union, and the North Atlantic Treaty Organisation (NATO) already exist for this purpose. They are examples of the extent to which world leaders intend to form themselves into an alliance to resolve the problems facing our world and the global economy. We have already noted the prophet saying that nations uniting in this way are bound to lead to the creation of a one world government. A world where each individual country or state governs itself singlehanded would be a thing of the past. People would be demanding that the crisis facing the world should be solved by one United Nation. Some fifty years ago the prophet stated that "this nation [United States] is going to be busted, and the rest of the world that's on the gold standard is busted".[2] The global economic recession the world is now experiencing in the 21st century saw the collapse in the economies of Greece, Portugal, Spain, Ireland, Italy and Cyprus. This has prompted the Vatican to call for an "overhaul of the world's financial systems". It proposes the setting up of a "supranational authority to oversee the global economy".[3] On the 7th July 2011, the then Pope Benedict XVI said that there was an "urgent need of a true world political authority" with "real teeth". He was clear that:

> In the face of the unrelenting growth of global independence, there is a strongly felt need, even in the midst of a global recession, for a reform of the United Nations Organisation, and likewise of economic institutions and international finance, so that the concept of the family of nations can acquire real teeth.[4]

In my view talk of "a reform of the United Nations Organisation" is nothing short of a call for a one world government. I rather suspect that the proposed new look United Nations would be committed to the kind of principles in the mission statement of the World Economic Forum. It is the "independent international organisation". Its members are committed "to improving the state of the world by engaging business, political, academic" and other leaders" to shape society's "global agendas".[5] But their annual meeting of 4, 000 elite global, political and business leaders at their 2014 Davos summit up the mountain in the Swiss Alps failed to put the world to rights. No wonder the Vatican has consistently and persistently seized the opportunity to call for a new "authority" (reformed UN) on the grounds that such a body is "needed to bring more democratic and ethical principles to a market place run amok",[6] that is, out of control. It is clear that such a statement by the Vatican sets the scene for the Roman Catholic Church to finally emerge as the only force that can unite everybody, mainly because of the mode of exchange, which is money. The prophet had no doubt that "the wealth of the world ... was found in her",[7] namely, the Roman Catholic Church. He made it clear that the Vatican was the richest state in the world. When our monetary system as a mode of exchange fail, declares the prophet, Rome [the Pope heading the new look UN] which " has acquired nearly all the supplies of gold ... at the right time ... will destroy the present day money system by calling in all the paper [bonds], and demanding gold. With no gold, the system falls".[8]

What the prophet is saying here is that because "the Catholic church (the hierarchy) owns the gold of the world",[9] it will be at liberty to buy into every venture. And will have a stake in every venture, own every venture and give the pope the power to control these ventures and our mode of exchange.[10] His power to control money and resources could extend to ventures already in existence in the Middle East. The Middle East produces approximately two thirds of the world's oil. It has been said that if the Middle East supply of the world's oil to Europe and the Western World was cut off, it would not be long before the lights in whole continents such as the United States go out. Though the United States is eager to describe oil as a fuel of the past, despite its fracking revolution, it appears to be hav-ing some difficulty in finding real alternatives in sufficient quantity to limit its dependency on oil from foreign countries such as Saudi Arabia. The situation in the Middle East today is threatening the supply of oil to places like the United States. It is as bad as it was when the prophet made the following comment in 1956 when talking about places like Iran and India on the rise: "... And to see in the Middle East all these things rising up", he thundered. He continues:

> '... these troubles. Little nations up there who has not been thought of or even spoke of for many, many hundreds, yes, thousands of years' ... maybe two thousand years or twenty-five hundred, nothing has been said much about those little countries, until just these last days.'[11]

Economic historians such as Martin Jacques have observed that in the twenty-first century the developing countries together "account for the overwhelming majority of the world's population", and its "economic growth rate has been greater than that of the developed world".

He suggests that by 2050 the developing world, par-ticularly eastern Asian countries like China, would be the largest economic power in the world outstripping the United States.[12] Jacques' observation in his book *When China Rules the World* confirms what the prophet was saying about China. The prophet said in his view China, one of the world's oldest civilisations[13] will be on the rise again.[14] Eastern nations, proclaimed the prophet, will, according to the Bible, "blossom like a rose and would bring forth her abundance".[15]

But the growth in the economy of these nations will be controlled by the one-world government. The prophet is clear that: "it is in this age that the churches are going to come together. And as they are even now controlling world politics, they will soon control the finances of the world".[16] Statements by the Vatican in 2011 leave no room for doubt that it considers politics to be the most important single factor in putting things right in the world. It is clear that, "politics – which is responsible for the common good" instead of the economy finance must be used first to solve the world's problems. And "that existing multinational institutions like the International Monetary Fund has not been responding adequately to global economic problems".[17]

Thus in the words of the Vatican's 2011 proposal: "we should not be afraid to propose new ideas, even if they might destabilise pre-existing balances of power that prevail over the weakest".[18] This kind of thinking appears to be in line with the prophet's statement that Rome will take control of politics and the economy worldwide as it did under the Roman Empire. At the time of the Roman Empire the whole world came under the rule of Rome. The Vatican had responsibility for matters of religion. But it was not too long before it became a state in its own right. It therefore became responsible not only for matters of state but also for Roman Catholicism. Roman Catholicism was the main religion in each nation throughout its empire, Europe and the rest of the world.

In the film *Left Behind* it is the president of the United Nations, Nicolae Carpathia, who appears as the "global icon" or "world leader". "Nicolae" means "victory of the people". It has a similar sound to "Nicolaitane" which means, "to conquer the laity". Both names are used to refer to the leader of the one-world government. In the film the United Nations is housed in a modern state-of-the arts building with up to the minute scientific equipment and new technologies. It is world leaders like Nicolae and the Pharaohs and Caesars[19] before him who could legitimately claim the right to watch their citizens' every move. In our day new technologies are used to monitor our activities. But under a one-world government whistleblowers who once could seek asylum under international law[20] may not be able to escape persecution.[21] Internet traffic; fibre optic cables; mastery of cyberspace are the tools of the new world order. Scientific advance would make it possible for the United Nation's leader to create "a system of total surveillance" in the name of world peace. It could then get hold of our personal details from our telephone calls, emails and internet trafficking. The idea of the Pope having absolute power in the affairs of men small and great as we have seen is not new. Burke McCarty reminds us that in the early history of the Roman Catholic Church before modern technology every parish priest acted as spies, and knew "the most intimate details and conduct" of the "private life" of every person in his area:

> The priest of every parish in this country [America] is the king-pin in this web of spying, and reports regularly to his bishop every item of interest, directly or indirectly and in turn, the bishop to his archbishop, the archbishop to the cardinal and the cardinal to the pope. The confessional box is the Roman clearing house, whereby the pope keeps his finger on the pulse of the world.[22]

According to a recent PewResearch (2013) most American people as we have already noted who have grown up with a history of spying[23] are still in favour of surveillance. They were becoming increasingly concerned in the twenty first century about their government's collection of their personal details in the name of peace and to fight terrorism. Such concerns have been raised because of the fear of United States

Agencies such as the National Security Agency spying activities to monitor US citizens. Moreover, it has been suggested that many people have been conditioned by Hollywood to accept spying as the normal way of life they have seen on the big screen.

## PALESTINE (ISRAEL) GOD'S TIMEPIECE

The prophet has said that "if you want to see what day you're living in, look where the Jews are"[24] today, beginning with them becoming a nation after the Second World War. Palestine (Israel) is God's timepiece,[25] because she is returning to her homeland, he said. Her relationship with the Vatican is another sign of the times. "For the first time in history, the pope [Pope John Paul VI] from Rome, which has been the Church's greatest enemy ... leaves ... from Rome to Palestine, Jerusalem",[26] declared the prophet in 1964. This was a clear sign of things to come. For the time will come, says the prophet, when the Jews and the Pope will enter into an agreement which will result in the Pope taking control of the Holy Land. After his election Pope Francis received an invitation from the President of Israel following their discussions at the Vatican on important issues relating to the Middle East. These issues included the war in Syria, and relations between Israel and the Palestinians. The President said the Pope's visit to Israel "could contribute significantly to increasing the trust and belief in peace".[27]

The Vatican welcomed the invitation. It recognised the importance of the Pope taking control of Jerusalem. It therefore stressed that his visit would help to begin talks again between Israelis and Palestinians. And in the end will "decidedly" contribute "to the peace and stability of the region".[28] Reports then began to circulate about the Vatican and Israel entering into an agreement in June 2013 giving the Pope "an official seat" and "special authority" of the Last Supper Room ("Upper Room").[29] The Upper Room is built on top of the traditional Tomb of David on the grounds of Mount Zion. Should such an agreement be entered into, it would be the beginning of a much longer term arrangement between the Jews and the Vatican. Some fear, however, that "this strategic move by the Vatican will be used to openly promote their [Roman Catholicism's] agenda"[30] of universal and lasting peace and world domination.

## SIGNS IN THE SKY

Again, warns the prophet, these last days would be marked by "signs in the heaven above (flying saucers where even the Pentagon and all don't know what to think of it), fearful sights in the skies, men's heart failing, fear, perplexed of times, distress between the nations, the sea roaring – tidal waves, earthquakes in divers places, and men shall be heady, high-minded, lovers of pleasure more than lovers of God, trucebreakers, false accusers, incontinent, and despisers of those that are good".[31] It is alleged that the Vatican entered into an agreement with the United States to monitor these "signs in the heavens" in preparation "for the Arrival of an Alien Savior", to quote from Tom Horn and Chris Putnam in their book Exo-Vaticana (2013).[32] They claim that it has now set up the Vatican Observatory Research Group (VOR) on top of the 10, 700ft "high peak" in Arizona called Mount Graham. The Observatory is called Mount Graham International Observatory. They further claim that it is a gigantic multibillion dollar observatory covering a huge area of land.

The Vatican Advanced Technology Telescope[33] on Mount Graham, Arizona, is owned by the Vatican says Horn and Putnam. And it has launched Project L.U.C.I.F.E.R (Large Binocular Telescope Near-infrared Utility with Camera and Integral Field Unit for Extragalactic Research) in order to investigate visitations from outer space, they said. Its powerful light-gathering capacity will make it possible to collect "the faintest and most distant objects in the universe", it has been suggested. For the Vatican to come up with the name of Lucifer (Satan), meaning the "harbinger of light", must have required some stretching of the imagination and "manipulation of language" for the Vatican to code name their Project L.U.C.I.F.E.R. Horn and Putnam are at pains to point out that "while the Catholic apologists will object that there is no official church teachings on Extraterrestrial Intelligence (ETI)", it is possible to say that such an official policy exists from books, materials and other documentation the Roman Catholic Church has authorised such as Kenneth J. Delano's *Many Worlds, One God* (1977) which "is described on its dust jacket as 'an intelligent discussion of the existence of extraterrestrial life and its impact upon mankind'".[34] Reports of unusual "signs in the heavens" in Arizona or indeed the universe are not new. In 1963 the prophet reported having been caught up in an unusually large cloud of seven angels appearing over Arizona in the shape of a pyramid.[35] Ex followers of the teachings of Branham have joined atheists, agnostics, naysayers, and chronologists to deny that the prophet's personal experience of being caught up in the cloud was supernatural, and condemned many of his accounts as spurious and inconsistent.[36]

These sceptics could not effectively challenge the authenticity of the image of a light photographed appearing over the prophet's head. As he pointed out the photographer who shot the image over his head commented that "it was the first time in all human history that a supernatural Being was ever photographed ... It surely must have been there, for that optical lens – mechanical lens of a camera won't take psychology ... It was there".[37] This light, said the prophet, was the same Pillar of Cloud by day and Pillar of Fire by night that followed the Children of Israel in the Wilderness.[38]

Moreover, in 1965 he talked about seeing the "Angel of the Lord" coming down, "and a great Light flying like a comet".[39] "These great signs and wonders", declared the prophet, "would appear in the sky, and people call them flying saucers."[40] They are prophesied in the Bible to take place in the last days, he said. He believed that these signs in the sky are Investigating Angels and that the scriptural explanation of them is as follows:

> Jesus said, "As it was in the days of Sodom, so shall it be in the coming of the Son of man." And before the destruction of Sodom, and fire fell and burned the city and the plains up; there was *Angels sent from heaven who looked in and searched out to find out if these things were true or not.* And would it not be just like God to send back His Angels to investigate and to find out just before the great destruction comes.[41]

The prophet reminds us that during the time of the collapse of the world economies there would be Investigating Angels [called UFOs by some government officials) visiting our planet before the destruction of the cosmos (kosmos) prophesied by Daniel 2:31-45. In these scriptures Daniel records the rise and fall of each of the following empires, beginning with Babylon, the kingdom of gold; then the Median-Persian, silver; Grecian, brass; Roman, iron and clay. In our generation he prophesies the total destruction of our world by a "stone ... cut out of the mountain without hands, and ... it brake in pieces the iron, the brass, the clay, the silver, and the gold". These metals, he records, represent all the nations of the earth over time including our existing kingdoms.[42]

*Exo-Vaticana* refers to government and other reports of thousands of newspapers, eyewitness testimonies, photographs, and radar tracking giving accounts of unusual sightings in the sky. They focus on eye-witness, newspaper and other accounts of Unidentified Flying Objects (UFOs) circling above Rome in 1978 and an unusual light appearing over the Vatican in 2005.[43] Now, what would have been thought of as "science fiction" in 1933 when the prophet prophesied in his fourth vision that there would be new technological developments and "great advances in science that would come after the Second World War",[44] has today caught the attention of the Vatican. For it has now used technological advances to install project L.U.C.I.F.E.R on Mount Graham, USA. Horn and Putnam refer to this as the "Vatican's Astonishing Plan" for the visitation of "an Alien Serpent Savior". With Roman Catholicism dabbling in "occultism" and "Babylonian mysteries" it is not surprising that the prophet reminds us that "God said He'd give them over to strong delusions to believe a lie and be damned by it."[45]

On the other hand, the prophet does not dismiss outright how advanced science was in the days of Noah nor does he dismiss its advancement today. What he says about the signs in the sky is contrary to Horn and Putnam's suggestion that these visitations from space are "demonic".[46] We have already seen that the prophet likened these signs in the heavens in the last days to the visitation of the angels who went to Sodom before its destruction. "Science", declared, the prophet, "was far more advanced", in the days of Noah than in our day.[47] Scientists, he said, would shoot things to the moon to prove that there is no rain in the sky.[48] "Atomic energy ... might've been the same thing that caused the antediluvian destruction, that [threw] the world ... away from the sun pushed it backwards and caused the rain."[49] The earth remains tilted and out of kilter to this day. As we have already seen the prophet is convinced that before its final destruction by fire the earth will be visited again by Investigating Angels which some people call "UFOs" or "flying saucers". Their visitation should act as a final warning that these signs signal the end of the gentile age. But before the destruction of this world of chaos, declares the prophet, the Bride of Christ will be raptured,[50] a scenario captured in the film *Left Behind*:

'in one chaotic moment, millions of people around the world suddenly disappear leaving their clothes, wedding rings, eye glasses and shoes in crumpled piles. Mass confusion hits while vehicles suddenly unmanned veer out of control, fires erupt and hysteria breaks out as the living stare in disbelief and fear at the empty places where their loved ones were just seconds before.'[51]

This biblical interpretation of the Bride of Christ meeting "the Lord in the air" is the view of the film makers but it gives us one worldview of the following verses in I Thessalonians about the "rapture", although the word rapture is not in the Bible:

> For if we believe that Jesus died and rose again, even so them also which sleep in Jesus will God bring with him. [15]For this we say unto you by the word of the Lord, that we which are alive and remain unto the coming of the Lord shall not prevent them which are asleep. [16]For the Lord himself shall descend from heaven with a shout, with the voice of the archangel, and with the trump of God: and the dead in Christ shall rise first: [17]Then we which are alive and remain shall be caught up together with them in the clouds, to meet the Lord in the air: and so shall we ever be with the Lord.[52]

Following the rapture the tribulation period will set in, that is, the time where those believers who are left behind will be persecuted for their Christian beliefs. And the Pope as religious leader will in the name of Roman Catholicism take over Jerusalem, the "ancient seat of all of our religion".[53]

Chapter Twelve

# CLOSING OF THE AGE

*For when they shall say, Peace and safety; then sudden destruction cometh upon them, as travail upon a woman with child; and they shall not escape.* — 1 Thessalonians 5:3, King James Version

## THE TRIBULATION

The tribulation period is a clear sign that we are at the end of the age. Let us hear briefly from the prophet again about the world in which we will be living just before the tribulation:

> Rome ... will take over absolute authority by the World Council of Churches. This may seem farfetched to some but actually ... this ecumenical move will end up with Rome at the head even though the people did not envision it that way ... With the world church system under her Rome will be controlling, and this image (church system) will be obedient to Rome because Rome controls the gold of the world. Thus all the people have to belong to the world church system or be at the mercy of the elements for they cannot buy or sell without the mark of the beast in the hand or head. This mark in the head means that they will have to take the doctrine of the world church system which is trinitarianism, etc., and the mark in the hand which means to do the will of the world church. With this great power the church systems will persecute the true bride. This image will try to keep the bride from preaching and teaching, etc. Her ministers will be forbidden to give comfort and truth to the people who need it. But before the antichrist (in person) takes over this complete world system of churches the true church will be taken away from this world to be with the Lord. God will catch away His bride for the great Marriage Supper of the Lamb.[1]

The prophet keeps emphasising that the Bride of Christ does not go into the tribulation.[2] Those saints who are left behind and the one hundred and forty four thousand Jews in Israel will go through the tribulation, he said.[3] This will take place "for three and one-half years while the retributive wrath of God is poured out",[4] he warns. Rome will then "make a covenant [agreement]"[5] with the Jews after which it would take control of "the government of the Jews for the remaining "three and a half years of the tribulation".[6] During this peace agreement the Pope is now the supreme "head" of this "scientific church".[7] He will be challenged by some Jews led by the resurrected Moses and Elijah. They would have come on the scene in Jerusalem.[8] The Pope will then come against these two witnesses. This is because they will be seen as terrorists trying to oppose the man of peace. These two prophets are sent of God to gather the 144,000 Jews.[9] They will "preach the same message of Pentecost, to those Jews when they rejected their Messiah",[10] says the prophet. These prophets and their followers will be killed by the Roman military by order of the Pope,[11] declares the prophet. Also, those Christians who were left behind after the rapture of the Bride will be hated and killed by the Roman military in the same way; then there will be weeping, and "wailing and gnashing of teeth".[12]

The world will celebrate their death. In the midst of that celebration when Moses and Elijah are slain in the streets of Jerusalem and their death is viewed on CNN, BBC News – 24 hours, Al Jazeera and other international media, many nations will also witness their resurrection[13] after three days in the same way as the Lord Jesus Christ rose from the dead. People will not only see them rise, but translated and ascending into heaven, confirming Acts 1 when the Lord Jesus Christ was taken to heaven. This event will now expose the pope as a false prophet and cause disenchantment amongst the nations of the world because the only force that appears to be holding the world and its people together has proven to be false.[14] We are still in time and the earth will be going through its cleansing process because sin is still on the earth. The world as we know it has to be thoroughly purged by fire. The elements will "burn with a fervent heat" and there will be volcanic eruptions thousands of miles in the air. "It's not altogether just a literal fire, it's also a holy fire", which aims to take away "all the germs, insects, and all natural and polluted life which will change the whole face of the earth from the condition it is in now to a perfect earth free from sin". In this continuous purging, the purpose is for heavens and earth to pass away in the sense of "passing from one form to another", or "one condition to another". It is the *kosmos*, or "world order that will pass away", declares the prophet. "The politics, the sinners, the systems, sin, disease, germs, and everything that is evil will be done away."[15] It "doesn't mean that the earth, the planet, is going to pass away",[16] declares the prophet. Moreover, this cleansing process through the baptism of the earth with fire, in the words of the prophet, "will push up a pyramid-like mountain" fulfilling Isaiah 65:25 prophecy that "they shall not hurt nor destroy in all my holy mountain", saith the LORD.

## THE GREAT MILLENNIAL REIGN

In the midst of this upheaval the Lord Jesus Christ will come down from heaven to the earth with "ten thousand times ten thousand and thousands of thousands"[17] of His saints which will be the start of the Great Millennial Reign. The saints who went into the rapture have now come back with the Lord Jesus Christ into Jerusalem. The nations will recognise the deity of God. They will come to Jerusalem to worship and it will go on for a thousand years. The "Millennium is merely the Honeymoon"[18] for the Bridegroom and His Bride on their way to that Eternal City.[19] There will be peace for a thousand years and this will be witnessed by some people who will still be alive because when the Lord comes there will be immediate peace and serenity and healing. At the same time the Kingdom of God established on our planet will transform the earth.

Thus in the Millennium: "The old will be young ... forever. Sickness will fade away and death will be no more. They shall build houses, they will inhabit them. They'll plant vineyards and eat the fruit thereof. They'll not plant and another inhabit ... He'll not plant and another eats, die off and somebody else take it; but he'll live there ... The wolf and the lamb shall feed together. And the lion shall eat straw like the bullock, and a child shall lead them around ... We'll be changed from what we are now, to that glorious image of the Son of God which is immortal."[20] This is the plan God had in mind: "That from before the foundation of the earth the purpose of God was to share His Eternal Life with man "[21]

## THE GREAT WHITE THRONE JUDGMENT

According to the scriptures, "it doth not yet appear what we shall be: but we know that, when he shall appear, we shall be like him; for we shall see him as he is".[22] And after the thousand years is over "Satan is loosed out of his prison" and he gathers his armies "to go out to deceive the nations" and to make war again with the saints, "just exactly as he did in glory" when he was cast out of heaven in the beginning. He was able to deceive the nations because they did not have eternal life. And then God rained fire and brimstone out of the heaven which "devoured them" and the "devil was cast into the lake of fire and brimstone".[23] Thus the purpose for which God created the devil is complete for he was created to bring overcomers to Christ. After he is cast into the lake of fire there is the great white throne judgment where the dead, both right and wrong, are raised. And the books are opened, and the Book of Life was open; and the saints, the Wife and the Husband, set and judge the world. And there it comes to pass the saying: "All nations shall stand before Him there, and He'll judge them with the rod of iron."[24]

In the closing hours of the judgment, "the sea gave up the dead which were in it; and death and hell delivered up the dead which were in them: and hell and they were judged everyman according to their works. And death and hell were cast into the lake of fire. This is the second death. And whosoever was not found written in the book of life was cast into the lake of fire".[25] There is now time no longer. No more heartache. No more pain. No more sorrow. No more strain. No more sea. All the lands separated by the seas have now come together into one land mass. Heaven and earth have kissed each other. And the natural age of the prophet has melted into that grand old age of eternity.

**THE ETERNAL CITY: A NEW HEAVEN AND A NEW EARTH**
Once there has been the purging of the earth "with a fervent heat" and the dissolution of the heavens by fire; we are now ready for the establishment of "a new heaven and a new earth"[26] as the eternal habitation of the redeemed which John proceeds to describe in Revelation Chapter 21, when he proclaims: "And I saw a new heaven and a new earth: for the first heaven and the first earth were passed away; and there was no more sea. And I John saw the holy city, the New Jerusalem, coming down from God out of heaven, prepared as a bride adorned for her husband. And I heard a great voice out of heaven saying, Behold, the tabernacle of God is with men, and he shall dwell with them, and they shall be his people, and God himself shall be with them, and be their God."[27] The encounter earlier with the mighty explosion beneath the earth's crust, triggering a violent and fervent activity from within its interior, thus causing the upward thrust or movement of a pyramid-like mountain to rise some fifteen hundred miles above the earth's surface, was in preparation for the descent of the New Jerusalem coming

down to earth from heaven ready to receive the Holy City. The dimensions and measurements of the Holy City are described in Revelation 21: 15-17.

> And he that talked with me had a golden reed to measure the city, and the gates thereof, and the wall thereof. And the city lieth foursquare, and the length is as large as the breadth: and he measured the city with the reed, twelve thousand furlongs. The length, the breadth, and the height of it are equal. And he measured the wall thereof, an hundred and forty and four cubits, according to the measure of a man, that is, of the angel.[28]

The prophet makes it clear that the measurements are not those of "a square or cube", but that of "the pyramid" which "lieth foursquare", because "the dimension of this angle is exactly the same", "the length by the breadth by the height",[29] including the wall as in the squared based pyramid below.[30] In line with Scripture the prophet's standard of measurement for each side of the Pyramid-like City is 1500 miles.[31] It has been conjectured that the Great Pyramid is 1/10,000 of the New Jerusalem in microcosm and that the reverse is true of the New Jerusalem which is a 10,000

## Square Based Pyramid

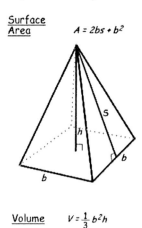

Surface
Area          $A = 2bs + b^2$

Volume        $V = \frac{1}{3} b^2 h$

magnification of the Great Pyramid in macrocosm.

This revelation of the geographical measurements, he says, indubitably unlocks the secrets of the Great Pyramid in ancient Egypt, which he declares is a testimony of "Enoch's sign in Egypt." The prophet says that he has no doubt that "before the antediluvian destruction" Enoch brought forth this sign, namely, the Great Pyramid.[32] In his description of this geographical mountain, he insists that its dimensions are equal in length, breadth and height with remarkable precision both in orientation towards the four cardinal points and in keeping with the base square and sloping sides.

According to the prophet, if the walls on each side were straight then the Holy City would not be visible to the whole world. The Holy City or New Jerusalem is in a place Rosenmueller in his *Biblical Geography* regards as "the middle of the earth",[33] and identified by the prophet as present day Israel or Palestine. The New Jerusalem, says the prophet, will be at the pinnacle of the Mount of Olives; and there "in the middle of the earth" the whole world will see the Light of the world – Jesus, "the Headstone"[34] on the Throne, right at the top of the pyramid-like mountain, fifteen hundred miles high.

The Great Pyramid in Egypt was never capped, the prophet insists, and there is no doubt that he regards this spectacular event as a supernatural fulfilment of what the Egyptians were trying to achieve in the natural world by building "the greatest wonder in ancient Egypt", namely, The Great Pyramid, to create heaven on earth as evidence of the cradle of civilisation.[35] The redeemed in the Holy City was proof of what the prophet was referring to in Chapter V when he said that "God will set up His own kind of civilisation on earth, when He takes it over." Here in this civilisation will be the redeemed. Here will be the Seed of God. Here will be Jew and Gentile, all of God's children, from every tongue, and language and nation who were always eternal in God's thoughts when He first spoke the Word.

The redeemed here in the new earth, are the ones who recognise that they are an expression of the attributes in Christ before the foundation of the world. Here with hindsight, they identify with Abraham's seed, the adopted sons of God, and all those whose names are written in the Lamb's Book of Life before the foundation of the world. Here, they identify themselves with "God, *en morphe*, masked in the Pillar of Fire. God, *en morphe*, in a Man called Jesus. God, *en morphe*, in His Church, God above us and God with us. God in us"[36] and now God in the Bride of Christ. Here, they know that just as God changes His form, so too do they because they now live in this new civilisation, in their glorified bodies. Here they live immortal. Here they are part of that perfect human race God planned to establish on this earth. Here they know they have finally arrived at the "city" Abraham was looking for "which hath foundations, whose builder and maker is God",

# Summary and Conclusion

*The moving finger writes and having writ moves on nor all your piety or wit shall lure it back to cancel half neither a line, nor all your tears wash out a word of it.* — Omar Khayyam, *Rubáiyát*[1]

The conclusion of this work is not only a summation of our journey through these pages but it brings us full circle to the beginning when the Word of God was first writ large in the heavens before the foundation of the world. The Bible uses the words "write", "writing" and "written" as symbols to describe how God recorded His "will". For example, on Mount Sinai Moses was given "two tables of testimony, tables of stone, written with the finger of God";[2] and in Hebrew 8:10 He said: "I will put my laws into their mind, and write them on their hearts." Thus, His will express the "thoughts" He had in His mind when the Lamb was slain before the foundation of the world. It was at the time He wrote His will that your name was written in heaven and placed in the Lamb's Book of Life. In my view "the moving finger" in the above quotation symbolises "the finger of God" that wrote His will. The Bible or "Biblos" in Greek and "Book" in most English speaking nations is the will of God. We know that in law the person who makes a will (the testator) must die before the beneficiary who may be a son or daughter receives their inheritance. The Bible is God's last Will or Testament. Like the law the Bible is emphatic that "where a testament is, there must also of necessity be the death of the testator. For a testament is of force after men are dead: otherwise it is of no strength at all while the testator liveth".[3] And since Christ died for us we are now joint heirs with Him. We are his beneficiaries.

We have already seen that "apocalypse" means "the unveiling of what has previously been hidden". Therefore we "are written epistles read of all men". In developing this theme a little further we will use what historians call historical imagination to crystallise and reflect on what we have read throughout this work. Imagine, for example, that you are the redeemed residing in the New Jerusalem in that city where the Lamb is the light. You are reflecting on the prophet's words that the "apocalypse" or "unveiling" "is perfectly described in the example of a sculptor unveiling his work of statuary, exposing it to the onlooker". You recall that "it is an uncovering, revealing what was previously hidden". You recollect that "the uncovering is not only the revelation of the Person of Jesus Christ but it is the revelation of His future works".[4] And no doubt whilst you are in that City you are thinking that it is now clear that you are a beneficiary of His will. You now understand what was meant when it was said that He knew the end from the beginning and that you were always joint heirs with Him. In that Pyramid-like City, time does not exist; neither does the notion of conclusion or end. You ruminate on the words in TS Eliot's poem which state that: "there will be time, there will be time to prepare a face to meet the faces that you meet ...time for you and time for me, and time yet for a hundred indecisions, and time for a hundred visions and revisions".[5]

In fact you realise that here in this Eternal City there is "time no longer"[6] for this age has been swallowed up into eternity. You now know that the notion of "conclusion" which suggests the end or finality only signals a new beginning in the eternal realm of God. Your inner voice brings home to your mind the truth of the prophet's words that we only have to watch nature to grasp the truth of this reality

that the "natural types the spiritual". You begin to think of
what he said thus: "He sees it in the sun. The sun raises in the
morning, like a baby, its weak; then at noon it's in its strength;
then in the evening it gets weak again and dies. But, that's
not the end of the sun; it comes up again the next morning to
testify to another generation, that there is a life, death, burial,
and resurrection."[7] Again he said, "We find the trees, the
leaves go off the trees, and the life in the tree goes down into
the ground, like the grave, and stays there until the wrath of
the winter is past, then comes back again, bringing forth new
life. It's a testimony that we live again."[8]

As you emerge from this historical imagination you know
that you have gained a panoramic view of the entire history
of our Biblical heritage from the standpoint of the redeemed.
They have been changed from mortality to immortality. The
redeemed from this age have melted into that Grand Age in
that City where the Lamb is the Light. It is here in the City of
God, that Eternal City, one can truly reflect on God's master-
plan. It is here you truly begin to reflect on the fact that we
were always in Christ before the foundation of the world. It is
here that you know for sure that we are joint heirs with Him
in the New Jerusalem on this planet earth. You reflect again
on the prophet's words. It is historical hindsight at its best. It
is what historians call reflective history. In fact this is what
this conclusion is about. Here we have the opportunity to
approach the task teleologically with our own spirit, that is,
with the Spirit of Christ because the Bible says that we know
not what we will be like when He appears, but when He does
appear we will be like Him. We will have glorified bodies like
Him! When He has completed the Masterpiece, namely, His
Bride, He will reveal it at the uncovering of the statuary. Thus
when we reflect on *The Age of The Prophet Branham* in the
remaining pages of this book it has no farther aim than to
present our heritage complete in that it will be the final
summation of this book. Or that Book of which it is said in

Hebrews 10:7 "Lo I come in the volume of the Book."

Viewing this work through the eyes of the redeemed in the New Jerusalem leads to the perfect realisation that in Biblical history, especially from a teleological perspective, the conclusion or end signals a new beginning. The process of death, burial and resurrection is now a reality as captured in the age old maxim, "we come from eternity and we go back to eternity". The prophet uses drama to illuminate our minds on Biblical history. In fact some historians suggest that in attempting to reflect historical truths and to understand what has gone on in the thinking of the author, actor or main character in history we should re-enact in thought what has taken place in the mind of the *dramatis personae,* that is, the person who figures prominently in some historical event. The prophet endeavours to do this when giving an exposition of the first scene in Genesis, The Book of Beginnings. Here, it is God who features in the opening sentence: "In the beginning God created the heavens and earth." This is the history of our roots. The prophet says that the main character in this scene is really Elohim, the Self-existing One. He is convinced that the use of the word God in this opening sentence is misleading. This is because, he said, God is an object of worship. And there was no one to worship Him before the beginning until He created angels to do so. His perfect will was to create man to worship Him in spirit and in truth.

We have witnessed *in The Age of the Prophet Branham* that God's purpose for creating us was to share His Eternal Life with us. He wanted a family. Remember that according to the prophet, God had a threefold purpose in the creation of man: First, God wanted to express Himself fully in Christ. Second, He wanted to have the pre-eminence in His Church, the Body of Christ, that is, the Bride to express Himself through Her. And finally He wanted to restore the Kingdom "back to where He walked in the cool of the evening, with His people, talked with them, and fellowshipped with them".[9]

Let us again look at the way in which the prophet dramatised the scene before the beginning. There was no light in the skies. No moon. No stars. Not even a speck of dust. God alone existed with His attributes in all that great space of eternity. Out of God came the Logos, that is, the Word, a little light which projected from Him out of His infinite Being. This light was "like a little child playing before the father's house". He knew then "what would be at the end from the beginning".[10] He was God above us writing the zodiac in the sky. He's writing His first Bible confirming that "the Word of God is forever settled in heaven". He first created the sun, moon, stars and other planets. He then turns His attention to the creation of the earth and man. He said, "Let Us", plural, make man in "Our", plural, "own image".[11] The "Us" in Genesis is both Father and Son confirming that He is "one God, one Person with three major titles, with three offices manifesting those titles".[12] "Now, if God is unseen, if the Logos was in the form of a Halo, then It's supernatural. Then He had to make a man in His own image. John 4 says that God is a Spirit. And He had to make a spirit man .... He brings It down from a sacred Halo to a little white cloud, something that's more visible; that's man. He gives him the rulership over the Kingdom. And he governed the beasts like the Holy Spirit leads the church today."[13] So you now reflect on the fact that this reference to the creation of man in Genesis 1:26 is a reference to the creation of spirit man.

No wonder you can pause for a moment and cast your mind back to the redeemed we met in the New Jerusalem in the previous chapter. No doubt you would consider yourself to be one of them. You now stop for a while in your imagination to admire the avenues, big freeways, parks, and the River of Life running right through the park where the Redeemed live. You see in your mind's eye every street made of transparent gold. You observe the trees of Life bearing twelve kinds of fruit and the kings and the honoured men of the earth bringing their honour and glory into the gates.[14]

Your mind quickly beholds what God was doing after He created spirit man. You marvel at the prophet's words seeping in your consciousness again: "But there was no man to till the soil," you think. "Then He put man in the image of man on earth, created him out of the dust of the earth."[15] God put a soul in a man. This white cloud, Deity, came down, not in the animal, but in the man. Then here's this man. And now the man sinned. And when he sinned and fell, then that little cloud in there became marred and black. Then the Logos came down and was made flesh and dwelt among us to redeem this man back to the love of the Father. "And He came in by the baptism of the Holy Spirit and chased sin out of the human and brings man back again in fellowship with God."[16] Oh how glorious you think. How wonderful it is to come to the unveiling of Almighty God. How sublime it is to witness the mystery of God in Christ reconciling the world to Himself as the Age continues to unfold.

The reality of the prophet's exposition of the extent to which God changes His form but not His nature explodes again unto the screen of your mind. The Greek expression *en morphe* he chooses to explain the many manifestations of God fires your historical imagination. You hear his voice thundering in your inner being giving an exposition of the term *en morphe*: "God, *en morphe*, masked in the Pillar of Fire. God, *en morphe*, in a Man called Jesus. God, *en morphe*, in His Church. God above us, God with us, God in us; the condescending of God. Up There, holy, no one could touch Him, He settled upon the mountain; and even if an animal touched the mountain, had to die."[17] "And then God come down and changed His tent, and come down and lived with us, become one of us. 'And we held Him', the Bible said. First Timothy 3:16, 'Without controversy great is the mystery of godliness; for God was manifested in the flesh, handled with hands.' God eat meat. God drank water. God slept. God cried. He was one of us. Beautiful, typed in the Bible! That was God above us; God with us; now it's God in us, the Holy Spirit. Not the third Person; the same Person!"[18]

An example of how a teacher sought to explain to a class in a Religious lesson the idea of Elohim and the notion of *en morphe* comes to mind. The objective of that lesson was to explore Genesis Chapter I and to enable the pupils to gain an understanding of the purpose of God for our lives before the foundation of the world. The teacher asked the class to close their eyes. Imagine a very small dot. That's the Intelligence, God. In your mind draw a small circle round that small dot. That small circle is the soul. Then round that small circle draw in your mind's eye another slightly bigger circle. That's the Spirit. Finally, round the circle representing the Spirit, the teacher told the class to draw a much bigger circle which was the Body. And in *Things That Are To Be* (1965) the prophet crystallises this exercise thus:

> There's three people of you. The outside is the body. You got five senses, that you contact your earthly home with that. The inside is a spirit. There's five senses there, love and conscience, and so forth, you contact. But the inside of that is the soul.[19]

We now know that this exercise was an attempt to demonstrate how God was projecting; manifesting, unfolding and revealing His threefold Being – a trinity. Here you think that God is sovereign. He changes His form not His nature. This is a clear example of Him changing His mask (*en morphe*). At one point He appeared as Father. At another point He appeared as Son. At another point He appeared in the form of the Holy Spirit. Your historical imagination kicks in and reminds you that: man is triune. Thus when the LaFontaines, a Christian family gospel music group in their song to the Bride titled *I Feel The Pull*, reached down within their very being to sing about "the deep that call to the deep like a great magnet pulling me" it touches the very core of your being. The mellifluous expression of their words that "the Spirit's groanings deep within must be God here in my soul", connects with the seed in your soul. Indeed, you think, this is a veritable fact which you identify with the truism in Christendom: "I come from God and I go back to God" or "I come from eternity and go back to eternity." This experience confirms beyond a shadow of a doubt that you were part of God before the foundation of the world.

The LaFontaines' lyric touches your emotions and affects your mind. You are aware that their words uncompromisingly echo the words of Christ, "no one cometh to me except my father draws him". Their words resonate in your soul like those verses from the old negro spirituals sung by African slaves in the Caribbean and the Americas; for these negro spirituals capture the thirst in the soul of those in bondage reflected in the poem of Aimé Césaire titled *Cahier d'un retour au pays natal* or *Return to My Native Land*. You begin to repeat the words of the LaFontaines: "Oh He was drawing me." Then you remembered that these were the words they echoed when they were nearing a crescendo, until they knew for sure that the Spirit was moving them to give their all to "reach the goal" because "I feel the pull".[20]

You then think of how they turned to the live audience as though they and the audience were one, a kindred spirit or collective will as it were, just like "the traditional performers and audiences in Africa were one".[21] And in this live show where the LaFontaines' family and audience appeared to be in unison, in one spirit, as it were, you remember them asking a captivated audience, "Do you feel the pull tonight?" Perhaps, you thought, there is that one in a million predestinated seed in the audience who feels the pull and might answer His call. It is no wonder, you think, that in Christendom the unbeliever is urged to "repent and be baptised in the name of Jesus Christ for the remission of sins, and ye shall receive the gift of the

Holy Ghost".[22] This is because it is the spoken Word of God that touches the seed in the soul that is calling out to the individual to return to their spiritual native land. You emerge from your ponderings knowing that your historical reflections were more than a reverie. In fact the prophet's message *Lifting Him Up Out Of History* is the very epitome, the crowning glory of *The Age of the Prophet Branham*. Like this book *Lifting Him Up Out Of History* provides a historical perspective which demonstrates quite clearly the extent to which the seed of God within the soul has caused His children to be affected by the supernatural. The prophet has no doubt that the supernatural rumblings in a person's soul comes from the very depth of their heart because science has declared that there is a tiny compartment in the heart where the soul resides. Thus this discovery gives expression to the Biblical truth that "As a man thinketh in his heart so is he", because "there are faculties in the heart to think", says the prophet. Contrary to conventional wisdom therefore the prophet concludes that "man really thinks with his heart, not with his head".[23]

The manifestation of Christ through His children in the annals of history has eclipsed or surpassed all other natural or secular historical events borne out in the pages of this book. In fact, *The Age of the Prophet Branham* holds no certain mystery. It has sought to correctly reproduce the highlights of the prophet's message on modern events made clear by prophecy with its inherent power to ignite and set fire in the soul of the predestinated. They are already the called and elected before the foundation of the world. If you have the seed of God within your soul you must have felt the pull to repent and be baptised in the name of Jesus Christ for the remission of sins. If you have already repented and are baptised for the remission of sins you must have felt the pull that "He is drawing you to give a higher praise", to use the words of the LaFontaines once more. Only the predestinated will feel the pull and will know whether they are elected or not because you would have most definitely connected with what is written herein to enable you to "Know Thyself" and claim your Biblical heritage which is "Christ in you the hope of glory."

You will know that to be like Jesus means that you must have His "potentials". He was able to walk on water. He was glorified. He appeared, disappeared, and reappeared. He could be touched and handled after His death, burial and resurrection. He ate and had a three course meal with His disciples after He rose from the dead. He came through the wall and appeared to them to the extent that they thought He was a Spirit until He challenged them to handle Him. They were affected by the supernatural because the "entrance of His words" into their souls which "giveth light and understanding unto the simple" who feel the pull and answer His call was manifested in their lives. The whole creation is groaning and waiting for the manifestation of the sons and daughters of God, namely, the predestinated, the elect of God, those who feel the pull and answer His call in this age – the age in which God is in His Bride, in us, in you. It is an age where God speaks to the individual "lip to ear" – an age where you have the ability to hear from God. "God", the Bible declares, "who at sundry times and in divers manners spake in time past unto the fathers by the prophets hath in these last days spoken unto us by his Son"; or "in His Son", according to the prophet.

In these last days He is God in us. Because His Spirit was sent back at Pentecost to live in His children [The Bride of Christ] who feel the pull and answer the call to manifest Him before they are raptured. You know that Christ will not physically return to the earth in these last days. He will only manifest Himself through you His Bride at the end time. That's why He is continually unfolding His Word to you. It is you and Christ as persons together. This junction of time or breach is sometimes compared to the time when Christ after the resurrection appeared to the two men on their way to Emmaus. They did not recognise Him. The Scriptures declare that they only recognised Him when He broke bread with them: "And beginning at Moses and all the prophets, He expounded unto them in all the Scriptures the things concerning Himself".[24]

You have already seen that He appeared to His disciples again when they were eating. He was then raptured. Then His Spirit was sent back to live in His disciples at Pentecost where there was a manifestation of supernatural power with signs wonders and miracles being wrought through the apostles. The Bride will display the same supernatural manifestations in these last days before she is raptured. Right now Christ in her the hope of glory is revealing Himself in His Bride. This epoch in the Bride Age is sometimes referred to as the third pull – a term the prophet uses to describe this period where Christ in you the hope of glory is opening up your understanding of His Word by constantly revealing His Word to you. And in the fullness of the dispensation of time, which is now, you will be powered up with His Word to go after the lost sheep with the spoken Word. You saw that the spoken Word is the original seed which thundered in the beginning "Let there be" and there was. But you may now be aware that the revelation of the Son of Man in the Bride in the twenty first century takes place in the midst of the era where the Bible reminds us that the conditions were similar to the time of Lot.

We are therefore witnessing these signs of the times in the closing hours spoken of by the prophet as it was in the days of Lot: They ate. They drank. They married. They were given in marriage. They bought. They sold. They planted. They builded. Again the Bible warns us that in the last days there will be wars and rumours of wars. Man's heart failing for fear. Diseases. Tsunamis. Earthquakes. Storms. Arrogance. Men will be lovers of pleasure more than lovers of God. Disobedient children. Terrorists and terrorism. Sexual perversion. A godless generation. In the United Kingdom the first atheist church with a "godless congregation" and an avowed vision and commitment to set up "satellite congregations in more than 20 cities across Britain and the world" was erected in the first half of the year 2013.[25] Its minister declared that his pastor is the Devil. The same nation which heard that minister's call to serve Satan was urged to answer a further call for it to be a Defender of Faiths.

Thus in light of the time and season in which we live, it behoves me to say again what I have already said at the beginning in the preface, that is to say that, this book has attempted to show that the end-time prophet messenger William Marrion Branham, the seventh angel came to tell us and show us the mysteries that are in the Bible. There is nothing William Branham said about the Lord that is not in the Bible. He came to tell us our position in relation to God, to Jesus Christ His Son and what will happen until the establishment of His Kingdom on the face of this earth. This was described to Daniel in the middle of the Bible. It was described to him in several ways in Daniel Chapters 9, 10, 11, 12, for example: in the image that Nebuchadnezzar saw; in the beasts, the different four beasts that he saw, showing the type of kingdoms and power that will be upon the face of the earth; then in the movement of civilisation from the east to the west; how the end will come, and especially in Daniel 12 when he describes the interplay of politics, religion and civilisation.

The King of the North referred to in Daniel 12 is politics, money, the economy, government and so on. And the King of the South is talking about religion trying to get people from all the different religions back to God. All this was described in symbolic form because Daniel was told to seal up all these things until their true meaning will be revealed in the end time, thus prophesying the coming of the seventh angel in Revelation 10:7 which declares that: "in the days of the voice of the seventh angel when he shall begin to sound the mystery of God should be finished". He is Elijah of Malachi 4, the end-time prophet-messenger God promised to send "who will reveal the mysteries as contained in the Word, and who has the ministry to turn the hearts of the children to the fathers".[26] This is what we are trying to show you in this book, namely, that the prophet was fulfilling what was written in the Scriptures and making the Scriptures plain and known to us. For it is clear that there is much confusion and uncertainty in the world. And that man's abandonment of the power of God in his soul for hedonism, pleasure, profligacy and greed; and his excesses and overindulgence in wealth, popularity, immorality, eating, drinking, new technologies, environmental pollution, and nuclear arms and so on has resulted in the collapse of the economy.

Everything has a price. And the price one pays for gaining the whole world is losing one's own soul and a busted economy which will be rescued by a One World Government with the Vatican in control in the name of world peace. But before the squeeze and tribulation sets in there will be the third pull. The Bride of Christ will be manifested on this earth and finally raptured. So what is the solution? I hope that *The Age of the Prophet Branham* will inspire you to go to the angel as described in Revelation 10 and take the Book and eat it. And that you yourself will become a new person. Nevertheless, I believe that the prophet should have the last word on the matter which he proclaimed unwaveringly in *The Seven Church Ages*: "If you have not already given your life to Him, may you turn your heart to God this moment, and kneel down right where you are, and ask His forgiveness for your sins, and surrender your life to Him."[27] I concur.

# APPENDIX A

## BRANHAM'S ORIGINAL SOURCES

I have looked at two main sources referred to by the prophet in his works. The first source is what the Voice of God Recordings [VGR] calls the "Association Books" because they were written or spoken directly by the prophet or in collaboration with the prophet and that of another writer. The second source used by the prophet is a selection of other books he consulted and copied by the Voice of God Recordings unto their books infobase in The Table 2005 Version 2.0 and other recent versions. I have painstakingly checked the British Library for these books, and I have included these references below. I found in the British Library archives that many of these ancient books the prophet consulted date back from the fifteenth century to the beginning of the twentieth century. They were written by believers and writers of impeccable reputation. There are a number of editions of many of these books and I have endeavoured to select the oldest editions for reference which are listed in the following pages. Most of these books are available in the British Library. Where I have not been able to trace a very small number of them I have indicated "not listed in the British Library" against the title and author in the references below. However, as a historian I agree with the Voice of God Recordings that a great deal of caution must be exercised by individuals when making references to other sources; and that it is up to the reader to be fully persuaded that what they have read and heard is the truth. A useful approach to ascertaining that you are satisfied with what has been written by others is to consider first and foremost what the prophet has said in the light of Scriptures and your own leading by the Holy Spirit, the Divine Source of history.

In "A word of caution concerning the other 39 books" they have copied unto their books infobase VGR has made it abundantly clear, to use their own words, that: "The Voice of God Recordings does not guarantee the text in this Book infobase to be accurate, complete, or consistent with the printed books from which Brother Branham read and quoted. These books reflect the beliefs of the various authors whose works are included, and do not necessarily represent the teachings of the message. The fact that Bro Branham was led by the Holy Spirit to quote certain portions from a book does not authenticate the entire contents of that book. What Bro Branham quoted from these various books is vindicated; the rest is not necessarily vindicated. Please take everything these books say with guarded caution, remembering the Absolute is the taped Message of William Branham, not what some author or historians stated."

## VOICE OF GOD RECORDINGS

### ASSOCIATION BOOKS

Branham, *Do You Fear Cancer* [book] & on The Table 2005 Version 2.0 DVD, Jeffersonville, Indiana: Voice of God Recordings

Branham, *Operations of Church Offices*, The Table 2005 Version 2.0 DVD, Jeffersonville, Indiana: Voice of God Recordings

Branham, *Personal Testimony of the Coming of the Gift*, The Table 2005 Version 2.0 DVD, Jeffersonville, Indiana: Voice of God Recordings

Gordon Lindsay, *Divine Healing in the Branham Campaigns*, The Table 2005 Version 2.0 DVD, Jeffersonville, Indiana: Voice of God Recordings

Branham, *As the Eagle Stirreth Her Nest* (1960), [book] & on The Table 2005 Version 2.0 DVD, Jeffersonville, Indiana: Voice of God Recordings

Branham, *The Eleventh Commandment* [book] & on The Table 2005 Version 2.0 DVD, Jeffersonville, Indiana: Voice of God Recordings

Branham, *Foot Prints On The Sands Of Time: The Autobiography of William Marrion Branham*, The Table 2005 Version 2.0 DVD, Jeffersonville, Indiana: Voice of God Recordings

Gordon Lindsay, *William Branham, A Man Sent From God* [book] & on The Table 2005 Version 2.0 DVD, Jeffersonville, Indiana: Voice of God Recordings

Billy Paul Branham, *Memorial Service*, The Table 2005 Version 2.0 DVD, Jeffersonville, Indiana: Voice of God Recordings

Branham, *I Was Not Disobedient to the Heavenly Vision* (1949), The

Table 2005 Version 2.0 DVD, Jeffersonville, Indiana: Voice of God Recordings

Branham, *Jesus Christ The Same Yesterday, Today And Forever,* The Table 2005 Version 2.0 DVD, Jeffersonville, Indiana: Voice of God Recordings

Branham, *He Ascended Up On High And Gave Gifts Unto Men,* The Table 2005 Version 2.0 DVD, Jeffersonville, Indiana: Voice of God Recordings

Branham, *Sermons of William M. Branham,* The Table 2005 Version 2.0 DVD, Jeffersonville, Indiana: Voice of God Recordings

Julius Stadklev, *A Prophet Visits South Africa,* The Table 2005 Version 2.0 DVD, Jeffersonville, Indiana: Voice of God Recordings

Branham, *The Supernatural Gospel,* The Table 2005 Version 2.0 DVD, Jeffersonville, Indiana: Voice of God Recordings

Lee Vayle, *Twentieth Century Prophet, The Messenger to the Laodicean Church Age,* The Table 2005 Version 2.0 DVD, Jeffersonville, Indiana: Voice of God Recordings

## BRITISH LIBRARY AND VOICE OF GOD RECORDINGS

### EARLY CHURCH FATHERS
ANTE NICENE FATHERS
**Title:** The Ante-Nicene fathers: translations of the writings of the fathers down to A.D. 325 / Alexander Roberts and James Donaldson, editors.
**Contributor:** Alexander Roberts 1826-1901. ;
James Donaldson 1831-1915. ;
A Coxe (Arthur Cleveland), 1818-1896. ;
Allan Menzies 1845-1916. ;
Ernest C Richardson (Ernest Cushing), 1860-1939. ;
Bernard Pick 1842-1917.
**Publication Details:** Grand Rapids : Eerdmans, 1979-1986.
**Language:** English
**Uniform Title:** Ante-Nicene Christian library.
**Edition:** American reprint of the Edinburgh ed. / revised and chronologically arranged, with brief prefaces and occasional notes, by A. Cleveland Coxe, photolithoprinted..
**Identifier:** System number 011275769
**Notes:** Vol. 1-8 originally published: Buffalo: Christian literature company, 1885-1896. _ Vol. 9 is a reprint of the original

supplement to the American ed. I. Bibliographical synopsis/by Ernest C. Richardson. II. General index/by Bernhard Pick. _ Buffalo : Christian Literature Company, 1896. _ Vol. 10 is a reprint of: Ante-Nicene Christian library. Additional volume/edited by Allan Menzies. _ 5th ed. _ New York : Scribner, 1913. These volumes were originally issued as v. 10 and 9 respectively. Vols. 4 and 10 bear the additional imprint: Edinburgh : T. & T. Clark.

**Physical Description:** 10 v.

**Shelfmark(s):** General Reference Collection YC.1990.b.3038

**UIN:** BLL01011275769

[See also: The Table 2005 Version 2.0 DVD, Jeffersonville, Indiana: Voice of God Recordings – Section titled Books where the Ante Nicene Fathers is printed )

NICENE FATHERS &POST NICENE FATHERS

**Title:** A Select Library of the Nicene and Post-Nicene Fathers of the Christian Church. Edited by P. Schaff.

**Author:** Philipp SCHAFF

**Publication Details:** 14 vol. Christian Literature Co.: New York, 1892-87-90.

**Identifier:** System number 003268390

**Creation Date:** 1892

**Physical Description:** 8°.

**Shelfmark(s):** General Reference Collection 3624.c.5.

**UIN:** BLL01003268390

(http://explore.bl.uk/primo_library/libweb/action/search.do?ct=Pr evious+Page&pag=prv&dscnt=0&ublrpp=10&vl(174399379UI0) =any&scp.scps=scope%3A(BLCONTENT)&frbg=&tab=local_tab&d stmp=1363767077242&srt=rank&ct=Next Page&mode=Basic&dum=true&indx=11&tb=t&vl(freeText0)=Nic ene and post Nicene fathers&fn=search&vid=BLVU1&ublrpp=10)

[See also: The Table 2005 Version 2.0 DVD, Jeffersonville, Indiana: Voice of God Recordings – Section titled Books where the whole Nicene and post Fathers is printed)

## BOOKS FOR REFERENCE AND STUDY

ENCYCLOPEDIA OF MORMONISM

**Title:** Encyclopaedia of Mormonism : the history, scripture, doctrine, and procedure of The Church of Jesus Christ of Latter-day Saints /

edited by Daniel H. Ludlow.
**Contributor:** Daniel H Ludlow
**Subjects:** Church of Jesus Christ of Latter-day Saints – Encyclopaedias;
Mormon Church – Encyclopaedias; Mormons – Encyclopaedias;
Dewey: 289.303
**Publication Details:** New York : Macmillan ; New York ; Oxford :
Maxwell Macmillan International, c1992.
**Language:** English
**Description:** Contents: v. 1. A-D – v. 2. E-M – v. 3. N-S – v. 4. T-Z,
appendixes, index.
**Identifier:** ISBN 002904040X (set) : No price; ISBN 0028796004
(v. 1) : No price; ISBN 0028796012 (v. 2) : No
http://explore.bl.uk/primo_library/libweb/action/search.do?dscnt
=0&vl(174399379UI0)=any&frbg=&scp.scps=scope%3A%28BLC
ONTENT%29&tab=local_tab&dstmp=1363768488630&srt=rank
&ct=search&mode=Basic&dum=true&tb=t&indx=1&vl(freeText0)
=encyclopedia+of+mormonism+&vid=BLVU1&fn=search
"That Mormon doctrine of the pre-existence of souls" printed in,
The Table 2005 Version 2.0 DVD. Jeffersonville, Indiana: Voice of
God Recordings – Section titled Books). These excerpts were taken
from an earlier edition of the *Encyclopaedia of Mormonism* to the one
referred to in the British Library Catalogue listed above.

EASTON'S BIBLE DICTIONARY
**Title:** Illustrated Bible Dictionary and Treasury of Biblical history,
biography, geography, doctrine and literature. With numerous
illustrations and ... maps.
**Author:**M. G. EASTON
**Publication Details:** London : T. Nelson & Sons, 1893.
**Identifier:** System number 001028148
**Physical Description:** xi, 724 p. ; 8°.
**Related Work:** Bible. Appendix. Miscellaneous
**Shelfmark(s):** General Reference Collection 3125.df.15.
UIN: BLL01001028148
http://explore.bl.uk/primo_library/libweb/action/search.do?dscnt
=0&vl(174399379UI0)=any&frbg=&scp.scps=scope%3A%28BLC
ONTENT%29&tab=local_tab&dstmp=1363785514408&srt=rank
&ct=search&mode=Basic&dum=true&tb=t&indx=1&vl(freeText0)
=easton+
[See also: The Table 2005 Version 2.0 DVD. Jeffersonville, Indiana:
Voice of God Recordings – Section titled Books where the Easton's

Bible Dictionary is printed)
HITCHCOCK'S BIBLE NAMES DICTIONARY
**Title:** Wilmore's New Analytical Reference Bible. Containing ...
Comprehensive Bible Helps ... revised and edited by Philip Schaff ...
A complete analysis of the Holy Bible ... Edited by Rosewll D.
Hitchcock ... Cruden's Concordance ... revised by John Eadie ...
Illustrated with maps and engravings.
**Contributor:** John EADIE LL.D. ;
Roswell Dwight HITCHCOCK ;
Philipp SCHAFF ;
J. A WILMORE
**Publication Details:** New York ; London : Funk & Wagnalls Co.,
[1921]
**Uniform Title:** Bible. English
**Identifier:** System number 000314796
**Notes:** Version of 1611.
**Physical Description:** 3 pt. ; 4°.
**Shelfmark(s):** General Reference Collection 3052.dd.19.
UIN: BLL01000314796
http://explore.bl.uk/primo_library/libweb/action/search.do?dscnt
=0&vl(174399379UI0)=any&frbg=&scp.scps=scope%3A%28BLC
ONTENT%29&tab=local_tab&dstmp=1363790175628&srt=rank
&ct=search&mode=Basic&dum=true&tb=t&indx=1&vl(freeText0)
=a+complete+analysis+of+the+holy+bible%2C+hitchcock&vid=
BLVU1&fn=search
(See also: The Table 2005 Version 2.0 DVD, Jeffersonville, Indiana:
Voice of God Recordings – Section titled Books where Hitchcock's
Bible names are printed from an earlier 1800 edition of *A Complete
Analysis of the Holy Bible.*


THE TWO BABYLONS – ALEXANDER HISLOP
**Title:** [The Two Babylons; or the Papal worship proved to be the
worship of Nimrod and his wife. ... Second edition.]
**Author:** Alexander HISLOP, Rev., Minister of the East Free Church,
Arbroath.
**Publication Details:** London, Glasgow [printed], 1871.
**Edition:** Fourth edition..
**Identifier:** System number 001693138
**Related Titles:** The Two Babylons; or the Papal worship proved to be
the worship of Nimrod and his wife. ... Second edition. pp. xv. 478.

W. White and Co.: Edinburgh, 1858. 8°. (Uk)MP1.0001785211
**Physical Description:** 8°.
**Shelfmark(s):** General Reference Collection 3939.bb.41.
UIN: BLL01001693138
http://explore.bl.uk/primo_library/libweb/action/search.do?dscnt
=0&vl(174399379UI0)=any&frbg=&scp.scps=scope%3A%28BLC
ONTENT%29&tab=local_tab&dstmp=1363789920055&srt=rank
&ct=search&mode=Basic&dum=true&tb=t&indx=1&vl(freeText0)
=the+two+babylons+alexander+hislop&vid=BLVU1&fn=search
[See also: The Table 2005 Version 2.0 DVD, Jeffersonville, Indiana:
Voice of God Recordings – Section titled Books where The Two
Babylons – Alexander Hislop's book is printed)

LIFE AND TIMES OF JESUS THE MESSIAH – ALFRED EDERSHEIM.
**Title:** [The life and times of Jesus the Messiah.]
**Author:** Alfred EDERSHEIM
**Publication Details:** London: Longmans & Co., 1884.
**Edition:** Second edition..
**Identifier:** System number 001034785
**Related Titles:** The life and times of Jesus the Messiah. 2 vol.
Longmans & Co.: London, 1883. 8°. (Uk)MP1.0001090500
**Physical Description:** 2 vol. ; 8°.
**Shelfmark(s):** General Reference Collection 4808.h.10.
UIN: BLL01001034785
http://explore.bl.uk/primo_library/libweb/action/search.do?dscnt
=0&vl(174399379UI0)=any&frbg=&scp.scps=scope%3A%28BLC
ONTENT%29&tab=local_tab&dstmp=1363789659411&srt=rank
&ct=search&mode=Basic&dum=true&tb=t&indx=1&vl(freeText0)
=life+and+times+of+jesus+the+messiah%2C+alfred+edersheim&
vid=BLVU1&fn=search
[See also: The Table 2005 Version 2.0 DVD, Jeffersonville, Indiana:
Voice of God Recordings – Section titled Books where The Life and
Times of Jesus the Messiah – Alfred Edersheim, Volume 1 , New
York: Green & Co; London & Bombay, 1906 is printed)

SKETCHES OF JEWISH SOCIAL LIFE IN THE DAYS OF CHRIST
 – ALFRED EDERSHEIM
**Title:** Sketches of Jewish Social Life in the Days of Christ.
**Author:** Alfred EDERSHEIM
**Publication Details:** pp. vii. 342. Pickering & Inglis: London;

[printed in U.S.A.,] 1960.
**Identifier:** System number 001034796
**Creation Date:** 1960
**Physical Description:** 8°.
**Shelfmark(s):** General Reference Collection 4857.ff.10.
Document Supply W9/7497
**UIN:** BLL01001034796
http://explore.bl.uk/primo_library/libweb/action/search.do?dscnt
=0&vl(174399379UI0)=any&frbg=&scp.scps=scope%3A%28BLC
ONTENT%29&tab=local_tab&dstmp=1363789183883&srt=rank
&ct=search&mode=Basic&dum=true&tb=t&indx=1&vl(freeText0)
=sketches+of+the+jewish+social+life+in+the+day+of+christ+AL
FRED+EDERSHEIM&vid=BLVU1&fn=search
[See also: The Table 2005 Version 2.0 DVD, Jeffersonville, Indiana:
Voice of God Recordings – Section titled Books where Sketches of
the Jewish Social Life in the Day of Christ – Alfred Edersheim, is
printed)

THE TEMPLE ITS MINISTRY AND SERVICES – ALFRED EDERSHEIM
**Title:** The Temple: its ministry and services as they were at the time
of Jesus Christ.
**Author:** Alfred EDERSHEIM
**Publication Details:** London : Religious Tract Society, [1900]
**Language:** English
**Identifier:** System number 001034798
**Related Titles:** The Temple: etc. London, [1909.] 8°. (Uk)
MP1.0001090513.1
The Temple, etc. James Clark & Co.: London, 1959. 8°. (Uk)
MP1.0001090513.2
The Temple, etc. London, 1960. 8°. (Uk)MP1.0001090513.3
**Physical Description:** 414 p. ; 8°.
**Shelfmark(s):** General Reference Collection 04034.ee.34.
**UIN:** BLL01001034798
http://explore.bl.uk/primo_library/libweb/action/search.do?dscnt
=0&vl(174399379UI0)=any&frbg=&scp.scps=scope%3A%28BLC
ONTENT%29&tab=local_tab&dstmp=1363790478967&srt=rank
&ct=search&mode=Basic&dum=true&tb=t&indx=1&vl(freeText0)
=the+temple+its+ministry+and+services%2C+alfred+edersheim
&vid=BLVU1&fn=search
[See also: The Table 2005 Version 2.0 DVD, Jeffersonville, Indiana:

Voice of God Recordings – Section titled Books where The Temple Its Ministry \and Services – Alfred Edersheim is printed)

THE WORKS OF FLAVIUS JOSEPHUS
**Title:** The works of Flavius Josephus
**Publication Details:** London
**Language:** English
**Creation Date:** 1702
http://explore.bl.uk/primo_library/libweb/action/search.do?dscnt
=0&vl(174399379UI0)=any&frbg=&scp.scps=scope%3A%28BLC
ONTENT%29&tab=local_tab&dstmp=1363839196113&srt=rank
&ct=search&mode=Basic&dum=true&tb=t&indx=1&vl(freeText0)
=the+works+of+flavius+josephus&vid=BLVU1&fn=search
[See also: The Table 2005 Version 2.0 DVD, Jeffersonville, Indiana: Voice of God Recordings – Section titled Books where The works of Flavius Josephus is printed)

LECTURES ON SYSTEMATIC THEOLOGY – Charles Finney
**Title:** Finney's systematic theology / Charles Finney ; edited by J. H. Fairchild.
**Author:** Charles
**Subjects:** Theology ; Christian ethics — Addresses, essays, lectures; Dewey: 230
**Publication Details:** Minneapolis : Bethany Fellowship, 1976.
**Language:** English
**Uniform Title:** Lectures on systematic theology
**Edition:** Abridged..
**Identifier:** ISBN 0871231530; System number 013840332
**Notes:** First published in 1846 under title: Finney's Lectures on systematic theology.
**Physical Description:** xx, 435 p. ; 22 cm.
**Shelfmark(s):** Document Supply 85/09243
UIN: BLL01013840332
http://explore.bl.uk/primo_library/libweb/action/search.do?dscnt
=0&vl(174399379UI0)=any&frbg=&scp.scps=scope%3A%28BLC
ONTENT%29&tab=local_tab&dstmp=1363839747466&srt=rank
&ct=search&mode=Basic&dum=true&tb=t&indx=1&vl(freeText0)
=LECTURES+ON+SYSTEMATIC+THEOLOGY+-
+Charles+Finney&vid=BLVU1&fn=search
[See also: The Table 2005 Version 2.0 DVD, Jeffersonville, Indiana:

Voice of God Recordings – Section titled Books where Lectures on systematic theology –Charles Finney is printed).

REVIVAL OF RELIGION – CHARLES FINNEY
**Title:** Revivals of religion: lectures/Newly revised and edited with introduction and original notes by William Henry Harding.
**Author: Charles G. Finney,** 1972-1875
**Contributor:** William
**Publication Details:** London : Morgan and Scott Ltd, 1910.
**Language:** English
**Identifier:** System number 010229106
**Shelfmark(s):** Document Supply X13/0416
**UIN:** BLL01010229106
http://explore.bl.uk/primo_library/libweb/action/search.do?dscnt
=0&vl(174399379UI0)=any&frbg=&scp.scps=scope%3A%28BLC
ONTENT%29&tab=local_tab&dstmp=1363840368805&srt=rank
&ct=search&mode=Basic&dum=true&tb=t&indx=1&vl(freeText0)
=REVIVAL+OF+RELIGION+-
+CHARLES+FINNEY&vid=BLVU1&fn=search
[See also: The Table 2005 Version 2.0 DVD, Jeffersonville, Indiana: Voice of God Recordings – Section titled Books where Revival of Religion –Charles Finney is printed).

A COMMENTARY CRITICAL AND EXPLANATORY ON THE WHOLE BIBLE – JAMIESON, FAUSSETT, & BROWN
**Not listed in the British Library Catalogue** [See The Table 2005 Version 2.0 DVD, Jeffersonville, Indiana: Voice of God Recordings – Section titled Books where it is printed).

THE DIDACHE
**Title:** The Didache [and other texts]/trans. by James A. Kleist.
**Publication Details:** New York : Newman Press, 1948.
**Language:** English
**Identifier:** ISBN 0809102471; System number 012155268
**Series:** Ancient Christian Writers ; no 6
**Shelfmark(s):** Document Supply 0900.316000 v 6
**UIN:** BLL01012155268
http://explore.bl.uk/primo_library/libweb/action/search.do?ct=Ne
xt+Page&pag=nxt&dscnt=1&vl(174399379UI0)=any&scp.scps=s
cope%3A(BLCONTENT)&frbg=&tab=local_tab&dstmp=13638417

03883&srt=rank&ct=search&mode=Basic&dum=true&tb=t&indx
=1&vl(freeText0)=THE
DIDACHE&fn=search&vid=BLVU1&ublrpp=10
[See also: The Table 2005 Version 2.0 DVD, Jeffersonville, Indiana:
Voice of God Recordings – Section titled Books where The Didache
is printed).

## OTHER BIBLE TRANSLATIONS

AMERICAN STANDARD VERSION
**Not listed in the British Library Catalogue** [See The Table 2005
Version 2.0 DVD, Jeffersonville, Indiana: Voice of God Recordings –
Section titled Books where it is printed).

YOUNG'S LITERAL TRANSLATION
**Title:** Young's literal translation of the holy bible
**Author:** Robert
**Publication Details:** Baker Book House, [1984]
**Edition:** Rev ed.,
**Identifier:** ISBN 0801099102 (pbk); System number 012324037
**Shelfmark(s):** Document Supply 85/07682
**UIN:** BLL01012324037
http://explore.bl.uk/primo_library/libweb/action/search.do?dscnt
=0&vl(174399379UI0)=any&frbg=&scp.scps=scope%3A%28BLC
ONTENT%29&tab=local_tab&dstmp=1363842633506&srt=rank
&ct=search&mode=Basic&dum=true&tb=t&indx=1&vl(freeText0)
=YOUNG%27S+LITERAL+TRANSLATION+OF+THE+BIBLE&vid
=BLVU1&fn=search
[See also: The Table 2005 Version 2.0 DVD, Jeffersonville, Indiana:
Voice of God Recordings – Section titled Books where Young's Literal
Translation is printed).

## BOOKS BY AND ABOUT PEOPLE

50 YEARS IN THE CHURCH OF ROME – CHARLES CHINIQUY
**Not listed in the British Library Catalogue** [See The Table 2005
Version 2.0 DVD, Jeffersonville, Indiana: Voice of God Recordings –
Section titled Books where it is printed).
SUNSHINE AND SMILES – BUDDY ROBINSON
**Not listed in the British Library Catalogue** [See The Table 2005

Version 2.0 DVD, Jeffersonville, Indiana: Voice of God Recordings –
Section titled Books where it is printed).

"THIRTY YEARS IN HELL" – FRESENBORG
**Title:** "Thirty Years in Hell"; or, "From Darkness to Light." [An
attack on Roman Catholicism.]
**Author:** Bernard FRESENBORG
**Publication Details:** pp. 328. North-American Book House: St.
Louis, Mo., [1904.]
**Identifier:** System number 001324864
**Creation Date:** 1904
**Physical Description:** 8°.
**Shelfmark(s):** General Reference Collection 3940.i.18.
**UIN:** BLL01001324864
http://explore.bl.uk/primo_library/libweb/action/search.do?dscnt
=0&vl(174399379UI0)=any&frbg=&scp.scps=scope%3A%28BLC
ONTENT%29&tab=local_tab&dstmp=1363843459555&srt=rank
&ct=search&mode=Basic&dum=true&tb=t&indx=1&vl(freeText0)
=%22THIRTY+YEARS+IN+HELL%22+%E2%80%93+FRESENB
ORG&vid=BLVU1&fn=search
[See also: The Table 2005 Version 2.0 DVD, Jeffersonville, Indiana:
Voice of God Recordings – Section titled Books where Thirty Years
in Hell is printed).

HOW DID IT HAPPEN? – R. HAZELTINE
**Not listed in the British Library Catalogue** [See The Table 2005
Version 2.0 DVD, Jeffersonville, Indiana: Voice of God Recordings –
Section titled Books where it is printed).

NUN'S TESTIMONY – CHARLOTTE KECKLER
**Not listed in the British Library Catalogue** [See The Table 2005
Version 2.0 DVD, Jeffersonville, Indiana: Voice of God Recordings –
Section titled Books where it is printed).

LIFE STORY – CHARLES H. SPURGEON
**Title:** Charles H. Spurgeon. The Essex lad who became the prince of
preachers. [With plates, including a portrait.]
**Author:** James T. ALLEN, Author of "Briergate.".
**Contributor:** C. H Spurgeon (Charles Haddon), 1834-1892
**Publication Details:** London ; Glasgow : Pickering & Inglis, [1931]

**Identifier:** System number 000055995
**Related Titles:** without the title page.] [Charles H. Spurgeon.] In Jesus Christ. Mighty Messengers of Christ, etc. [1933.] 8°. (Uk)MP1.0000061902.1 without the title page.] [Charles H. Spurgeon, etc.] In Vision. Vision and Victory, etc. [1932.] 8°. (Uk)MP1.0000061902.2
**Physical Description:** 64 p. ; 8°. **Related Work:** Appendix
**Shelfmark(s):** General Reference Collection 4907.aa.42.
**UIN:** BLL01000055995
http://explore.bl.uk/primo_library/libweb/action/search.do?dscnt
=0&vl(174399379UI0)=any&frbg=&scp.scps=scope%3A%28BLC
ONTENT%29&tab=local_tab&dstmp=1363844293583&srt=rank
&ct=search&mode=Basic&dum=true&tb=t&indx=1&vl(freeText0)
=Charles+h.+Spurgeon%2C+the+essex+lad+who+became+the+
prince+of+preachers+by+james+t.+Allen&vid=BLVU1&fn=searc
h
[See also: The Table 2005 Version 2.0 DVD, Jeffersonville, Indiana: Voice of God Recordings – Section titled Books where Young's Literal Translation is printed),

"TILL HE COME." – C. H. SPURGEON
**Title:** "Till He Come Communion meditations and addresses", etc.
**Author: C.H. Spurgeon** (Charles Haddon), 1834-1892
**Publication Details:** London : Passmore & Alabaster, 1894.
**Uniform Title:** Single Works
**Identifier:** System number 003469296
**Physical Description:** 358 p. ; 8°.
**Shelfmark(s):** General Reference Collection 4324.cc.25.
**UIN:** BLL01003469296
http://explore.bl.uk/primo_library/libweb/action/search.do?dscnt
=0&vl(174399379UI0)=any&frbg=&scp.scps=scope%3A%28BLC
ONTENT%29&tab=local_tab&dstmp=1363845237666&srt=rank
&ct=search&mode=Basic&dum=true&tb=t&indx=1&vl(freeText0)
=%22TILL+HE+COME.%22+-
+C.+H.+Spurgeon&vid=BLVU1&fn=search
[See also: The Table 2005 Version 2.0 DVD, Jeffersonville, Indiana: Voice of God Recordings – Section titled Books where "Till He Come" – C.H. Spurgeon is printed].
THE NEW PARK STREET PULPIT. – C. H. SPURGEON
**Title:** The New Park Street Pulpit: containing sermons preached and

revised by C. H. Spurgeon. vol. 1-7.
**Contributor:** C. H Spurgeon (Charles Haddon), 1834-1892
**Subjects:** Periodical
**Publication Details:** London, 1856-62.
**Language:** English
**Identifier:** System number 002849879
**Related Titles:** The Metropolitan Tabernacle Pulpit, etc. vol. 8-63.
London, 1863, 1917. 8°. (Uk)MP1.0003035058.1
**Physical Description:** 8°.
**Related Work:** Single Works
Works edited or with prefaces by Spurgeon
**Shelfmark(s):** General Reference Collection P.P.790.ga.
UIN: BLL01002849879
http://explore.bl.uk/primo_library/libweb/action/search.do?dscnt
=0&vl(174399379UI0)=any&frbg=&scp.scps=scope%3A%28BLC
ONTENT%29&tab=local_tab&dstmp=1363845902284&srt=rank
&ct=search&mode=Basic&dum=true&tb=t&indx=1&vl(freeText0)
=THE+NEW+PARK+STREET+PULPIT.+-
+C.+H.+SPURGEON&vid=BLVU1&fn=search
[See also: The Table 2005 Version 2.0 DVD, Jeffersonville, Indiana:
Voice of God Recordings – Section titled Books where The New Park
Street Pulpit – C.H. Spurgeon is printed].

A COLLECTION OF SERMONS BY GEORGE WHITEFIELD
**Title:** [A Collection of 23 sermons , printed separately].
**Author:** George
**Subjects:** Sermons, English ; Presbyterian church—Sermons
**Publication Details:** London : Printed for James Hutton [etc.], 1738-
40.
**Language:** English
**Identifier:** System number 014455624
**Notes:** Binder's title. Some Sermons have individual title pages.
Reproduction note: Microfilm, Ann Arbor, Mich., University
Microfilms Int'l., 1976. 35 mm.
**Physical Description:** 1 v. (various pagings).
**Series:** Amer. Culture Ser., Philosophy, Psych. & Religion collection
; reel 55:5
**Shelfmark(s):** Document Supply MFR/3008 *1* reel 55:5
UIN: BLL01014455624
http://explore.bl.uk/primo_library/libweb/action/search.do?dscnt

=0&vl(174399379UIO)=any&frbg=&scp.scps=scope%3A%28BLC
ONTENT%29&tab=local_tab&dstmp=1363846329292&srt=rank
&ct=search&mode=Basic&dum=true&tb=t&indx=1&vl(freeText0)
=A+COLLECTION+OF+SERMONS+BY+GEORGE+WHITEFIELD&
vid=BLVU1&fn=search
[See also: The Table 2005 Version 2.0 DVD, Jeffersonville, Indiana:
Voice of God Recordings – Section titled Books where A Collection
of Sermons by George Whitefield is printed].

THE LIFE OF MARTIN LUTHER
**Title: The life,** deeds and opinions Dr. Martin Luther: with an
appendix/faithfully translated from the German of John Frederick
William Tischer by John Kortz.
**Author:** John Frederick William Tischer
**Subjects:** Luther, Martin, 1483-1546 : Reformation – Germany –
Biography
**Publication Details:** Hudson, [N.Y.] : Samuel W. Clark, 1818.
**Language:** English
**Identifier:** System number 008587087
**Physical Description:** vii,259p. ; 18cm.
**Shelfmark(s):** General Reference Collection RB.23.b.2992
**UIN:** BLL01008587087
http://explore.bl.uk/primo_library/libweb/action/search.do?dscnt
=0&vl(174399379UIO)=any&frbg=&scp.scps=scope%3A%28BLC
ONTENT%29&tab=local_tab&dstmp=1363847297035&srt=rank
&ct=search&mode=Basic&dum=true&tb=t&indx=1&vl(freeText0)
=The+Life+of+Martin+Luther+by+John+Frederick+William+Tis
cher.&vid=BLVU1&fn=search
[See also: The Table 2005 Version 2.0 DVD, Jeffersonville, Indiana:
Voice of God Recordings – Section titled Books where The Life of
Martin Luther is printed].

HUS THE HERITIC
**Not listed in the British Library Catalogue** [See The Table 2005
Version 2.0 DVD, Jeffersonville, Indiana: Voice of God Recordings –
Section titled Books where it is printed).

MISCELLANEOUS BOOKS
ELIJAH THE TISHBITE
**Title:** [Elijah the Tishbite: translated from the German.]

**Author:** Friedrich Wilhelm KRUMMACHER
**Publication Details:** London, 1854.
**Uniform Title:** Single Works
**Edition:** [Another edition.].
**Identifier:** System number 002028025
**Related Titles:** Elijah the Tishbite: translated from the German. pp. 195. Aylott & Jones: London, [1852.] 8°. (Uk)MP1.0002149669
**Physical Description:** 8°.
**Shelfmark(s):** General Reference Collection 1126.k.18.
UIN: BLL01002028025
http://explore.bl.uk/primo_library/libweb/action/search.do?dscnt
=0&vl(174399379UI0)=any&frbg=&scp.scps=scope%3A%28BLC
ONTENT%29&tab=local_tab&dstmp=1363882795921&srt=rank
&ct=search&mode=Basic&dum=true&tb=t&indx=1&vl(freeText0)
=Elijah+the+Tishbite&vid=BLVU1&fn=search
[See also: The Table 2005 Version 2.0 DVD, Jeffersonville, Indiana: Voice of God Recordings – Section titled Books where Elijah the Tishbite is printed].

THE FACTS OF OUR FAITH
**Not listed in the British Library Catalogue** [See The Table 2005 Version 2.0 DVD, Jeffersonville, Indiana: Voice of God Recordings – Section titled Books where The Facts of Our Faith or Our Faith and The Facts are printed].
See also http://archive.org/details/ourfaithandfacts00donouoft which makes reference to the book.

THE GLORIOUS REFORMATION – SCHMUCKER
**Title:** Discourse in commemoration of the glorious Reformation of the sixteenth century ... Third edition, with additions.
**Author:** Samuel Simon SCHMUCKER
**Publication Details:** New York, 1838.
**Identifier:** System number 003287569
**Physical Description:** 12°.
**Shelfmark(s):** General Reference Collection 4650.a.12.
UIN: BLL01003287569
http://catalogue.bl.uk/primo_library/libweb/action/search.do?dsc
nt=0&vl(174399379UI0)=any&frbg=&scp.scps=scope%3A%28B
LCONTENT%29&tab=local_tab&dstmp=1363911425990&srt=ra
nk&ct=search&mode=Basic&dum=true&tb=t&indx=1&vl(freeText

0)=THE+GLORIOUS+REFORMATION+-
+SCHMUCKER&vid=BLVU1&fn=search
[See also: The Table 2005 Version 2.0 DVD, Jeffersonville, Indiana:
Voice of God Recordings – Section titled Books where The Glorious
Reformation – Schmucker is printed].

GRACE ABOUNDING TO THE CHIEF OF SINNERS
**Title:** Grace abounding to the chief of sinners in A Faithful Account
of the Life and Death of John Bunyan
**Publication Details:** London
**Language:** English
**Creation Date:** 1716
http://catalogue.bl.uk/primo_library/libweb/action/search.do?ct=
Next+Page&pag=nxt&dscnt=0&ublrpp=10&vl(174399379UI0)=
any&scp.scps=scope%3A(BLCONTENT)&frbg=&tab=local_tab&dst
mp=1363911935439&srt=rank&ct=Next
Page&mode=Basic&dum=true&indx=11&tb=t&vl(freeText0)=Joh
n Bunyan%2C Grace Abounding to the Chief of Sinners&fn-
search&vid=BLVU1&ublpp=10
[See also: The Table 2005 Version 2.0 DVD, Jeffersonville, Indiana:
Voice of God Recordings – Section titled Books where Grace
Abounding to the Chief of Sinners is printed].

THE HOLY WAR
**Title:** The holy was: made by Shaddai upon Diabolus, ... By Mr. John
Bunyan, ...
**Author:** John Bunyan, 1628-1688.
**Subjects:** 1701-1800
**Publication Details:** London : printed for Alex. Hogg, [1790?]
**Language:** English
**Place Name:** Great Britain England London.
**Edition:** An entire new and complete edition, illustrated with notes,
.. by an able friend to the Gospel..
**Identifier:** System number 015311114
**Physical Description:** viii, 343[5], 32p., plates; 8°.
**Shelfmark(s):** General Reference Collection RB.23.a.6678
**UIN:** BLL01015311114
http://catalogue.bl.uk/primo_library/libweb/action/search.do?dsc
nt=0&vl(174399379UI0)=any&frbg=&scp.scps=scope%3A%28B
LCONTENT%29&tab=local_tab&dstmp=1363912654683&srt=ra

nk&ct=search&mode=Basic&dum=true&tb=t&indx=21&vl(freeTe
xt0)=John+Bunyan%2C+The+Holy+War&vid=BLVU1&fn=search
[See also: The Table 2005 Version 2.0 DVD, Jeffersonville, Indiana:
Voice of God Recordings – Section titled Books where The Holy War
is printed].

FOXES BOOK OF MARTYRS
**Title:** Foxe's Book of Martyrs/ edited by the Rev John Kennedy.
**Author:** Fox
**Contributor:** John Kennedy
**Publication Details:** London : John Tallis, [n.d.]
**Language:** English
**Identifier:** System number 010230814
**Shelfmark(s):** Document Supply Wq6/0371
**UIN:** BLL01010230814
http://catalogue.bl.uk/primo_library/libweb/action/search.do?dsc
nt=0&vl(174399379UI0)=any&frbg=&scp.scps=scope%3A%28B
LCONTENT%29&tab=local_tab&dstmp=1363913732878&srt=ra
nk&ct=search&mode=Basic&dum=true&tb=t&indx=1&vl(freeText
0)=FOXES+BOOK+OF+MARTYRS&vid=BLVU1&fn=search
[See also: The Table 2005 Version 2.0 DVD, Jeffersonville, Indiana:
Voice of God Recordings – Section titled Books where The Foxes
Book of Martyrs is printed].

EARTH'S EARLIEST AGES – PEMBER
**Not listed in the British Library Catalogue** [See The Table 2005
Version 2.0 DVD, Jeffersonville, Indiana: Voice of God Recordings –
Section titled Books where The Earth's Earliest Ages – C.H. Pember
is printed].

THE PILGRIM'S PROGRESS
**Title:** The pilgrim's progress,
**Publication Details:** London
**Language:** English
**Creation Date:** 1702
http://catalogue.bl.uk/primo_library/libweb/action/search.do?dsc
nt=0&vl(174399379UI0)=any&frbg=&scp.scps=scope%3A%28B
LCONTENT%29&tab=local_tab&dstmp=1363914919655&srt=ra
nk&ct=search&mode=Basic&dum=true&tb=t&indx=21&vl(freeTe
xt0)=THE+PILGRIM%27S+PROGRESS&vid=BLVU1&fn=search

[See also: The Table 2005 Version 2.0 DVD, Jeffersonville, Indiana: Voice of God Recordings – Section titled Books where The Pilgrim's Progress is printed].

THE PILLAR OF FIRE
**Title: The Pillar of Fire;** or, Israel in bondage. Illustrated, etc.
**Author:** Joseph Holt INGRAHAM
**Publication Details:** London, 1865.
**Language:** English
**Identifier:** System number 001800997
**Physical Description:** 8°.
**Shelfmark(s):** General Reference Collection 4415.cc.18.
**UIN:** BLL01001800997
http://catalogue.bl.uk/primo_library/libweb/action/search.do?dsc
nt=0&vl(174399379UI0)=any&frbg=&scp.scps=scope%3A%28B
LCONTENT%29&tab=local_tab&dstmp=1363916022047&srt=ra
nk&ct=search&mode=Basic&dum=true&tb=t&indx=1&vl(freeText
0)=Joseph+Holt+Ingraham%2C+The+Pillar+of+Fire&vid=BLVU
1&fn=search
[See The Table 2005 Version 2.0 DVD, Jeffersonville, Indiana: Voice of God Recordings – Section titled Books where The Pillar of Fire is printed].

THE PRINCE OF THE HOUSE OF DAVID
**Title:** The Prince of the House of David, etc.
**Author:** Joseph
**Language:** English
**Identifier:** System number 001801009
**Related Titles:** [The Prince of the House of David, etc.] In Lily Series. The Lily Series. [1870, etc.] 8°. (Uk)MP1.0001900392.1
**Notes:** In : Adina, pseud.The Prince, etc. 1859. 8°.
**Creation Date:** 1859
**Shelfmark(s):** General Reference Collection 4414.d.2.
**UIN:** BLL01001801009
http://catalogue.bl.uk/primo_library/libweb/action/search.do?dsc
nt=0&vl(174399379UI0)=any&frbg=&scp.scps=scope%3A%28B
LCONTENT%29&tab=local_tab&dstmp=1363915401478&srt=ra
nk&ct=search&mode=Basic&dum=true&tb=t&indx=1&vl(freeText
0)=The+Prince+of+the+House+of+David&vid=BLVU1&fn=search
[See also: The Table 2005 Version 2.0 DVD, Jeffersonville, Indiana:

Voice of God Recordings – Section titled Books where The Prince of
the House of David is printed].

THE THRONE OF DAVID
**Title:** [The Throne of David; from the consecration of the Shepherd
of Bethlehem to the rebellion of Prince Absolom. [A tale.]]
**Author:** Joseph Holt INGRAHAM
**Publication Details:** London, [1875]
**Edition:** [Another edition.] The Throne of David, etc..
**Identifier:** System number 001801038
**Related Titles:** The Throne of David; from the consecration of the
Shepherd of Bethlehem to the rebellion of Prince Absolom. [A tale.]
London, 1866. 8°. (Uk)MP1.0001900413
**Notes:** Part of the "Home Treasure Library.".
**Physical Description:** 8°.
http://catalogue.bl.uk/primo_library/libweb/action/search.do?dsc
nt=0&vl(174399379UI0)=any&frbg=&scp.scps=scope%3A%28B
LCONTENT%29&tab=local_tab&dstmp=1363916349287&srt=ra
nk&ct=search&mode=Basic&dum=true&tb=t&indx=1&vl(freeText
0)=Joseph+Holt+Ingraham%2C+The+Throne+of+David&vid=BL
VU1&fn=search
[See also: The Table 2005 Version 2.0 DVD, Jeffersonville, Indiana:
Voice of God Recordings – Section titled Books where he Throne of
David is printed].

# APPENDIX B

Henry Wadsworth Longfellow. 1807–1882

## A Psalm of Life

### What the Heart of the Young Man Said to the Psalmist

TELL me not, in mournful numbers,
Life is but an empty dream!—
For the soul is dead that slumbers,
And things are not what they seem.

Life is real! Life is earnest!                    5
And the grave is not its goal;
Dust thou art, to dust returnest,
Was not spoken of the soul.

Not enjoyment, and not sorrow,
Is our destined end or way;                       10
But to act, that each to-morrow
Find us farther than to-day.

Art is long, and Time is fleeting,
And our hearts, though stout and brave,
Still, like muffled drums, are beating             15
Funeral marches to the grave.

In the world's broad field of battle,
In the bivouac of Life,
Be not like dumb, driven cattle!
Be a hero in the strife!                           20

Trust no Future, howe'er pleasant!
Let the dead Past bury its dead!
Act,—act in the living Present!
Heart within, and God o'erhead!

Lives of great men all remind us                    *25*
We can make our lives sublime,
And, departing, leave behind us
Footprints on the sands of time;

Footprints, that perhaps another,
Sailing o'er life's solemn main,                    *30*
A forlorn and shipwrecked brother,
Seeing, shall take heart again.

Let us, then, be up and doing,
With a heart for any fate;
Still achieving, still pursuing,                    *35*
Learn to labor and to wait.

# APPENDIX C

The LaFontaines'

**I Feel The Pull**

At night I lay in
Bed and begin to
Cry

And my mind just
Fails to know
Exactly why

I can't explain
With tongue or pen

The Spirit's
groanings Deep
within

It must be God
Here in my soul

'Cause I feel the
Pull

I feel the pull

I hear the call

And I know His
Spirit's moving
me
to give my all

He speaks to me

And I agree

Lord, please come
And take control

I feel the pull

I went to hear the
Word

And with each line
and phrase

Oh, he was
drawing me to
give an higher
praise

There's a deep
call to the deep

Like a great
Magnet pulling
Me

I know for sure
That I'll reach the
Goal

'Cause I feel the
Pull

I feel the pull

I hear the call

And I know His
Spirit's moving me
to give my all

He speaks to me
And I agree

Lord, please come
And take control
I feel the pull

Lord, please come
And take control

# APPENDIX D

WORLDWIDE CONTACTS & HOSTS OF BRANAHAM'S
BOOKS & TAPES*

| COUNTRY | EMAIL | TELEPHONE NO |
|---|---|---|
| Angola | angola@vgroffice.org | 244 (923) 52 19 83 |
| Argentina | argentina@vgroffice.org | 54-11-4750-1523 |
| Benin | benin@vgroffice.org | 229-95-86-20-83 |
| Bolivia | bolivia@vgroffice.org | (591) 2-223-0531 |
| Brazil | brazil@vgroffice.org | 55 13 3921 8777 |
| Cameroon | cameroon@vgroffice.org | 237-99-64-70-10 |
| Canada | canada@vgroffice.org | 450 627 1686 |
| Chile | chile@vgroffice.org | 56-41-245 4002 |
| Colombia | colombia@vgroffice.org | 57 (1) 292-0867 |
| Costa Rica | costarica@vgroffice.org | (506) 2245-3932 |
| Democratic Rep of Congo | | |
| | congo@vgroffice.org | 243 810 34 24 67 |
| Ecuador | ecuador@vgroffice.org | 593 (4) 243-7193 |
| Finland | finland@vgroffice.org | 358-9-855 8509 |
| Ghana | ghana@vgroffice.org | +233 244 23 8452 |
| Honduras | honduras@vgroffice.org | (504) 2239-242 |
| India | india@vgroffice.org | 44 28274560 |
| Ivory Coast | ivorycoast@vgroffice.org | +225 07 91 0987 |
| Kenya | kenya@vgroffice.org | 254-202-244702 |
| Malawi | malawi@vgroffice.org | 265-187-7188 |
| Mexico (City) | mexico@vgroffice.org | 52 (55) 5544-1813 |
| Mexico (Central) | Guadalajara@vgroffice.org | 52 33 1008 7801 |
| Mexico (Northern) | | |
| | monterrey@vgroffice.org | 52 (81) 4444 1968 |
| Namibia | namibia@vgroffice.org | 9264-61-229852 |

| Netherlands | europe@vgroffice.org | 31-599-651570 |
| Nigeria | nigeria@vgroffice.org | 234 1 790 3139 |
| Panama | panama@vgroffice.org | (507) 640-9412 |
| Paraguay | paraguay@vgroffice.org | (595) 21 752-787 |
| Peru | peru@vgroffice.org | 51 (1) 534-0031 |
| Philippines | philippines@vgroffice.org | 632-3763253 |

Republic of South Africa                27-11-492-3135
           johannesburg@vgroffice.org

Republic of South Africa
           southafrica@vgroffice.org   27 218 563 110

Republic of South Africa (Durban)
           durban@vgroffice.org       27-31-301-1717

Rep of South Africa (Kimberley)
           kimberley@vgroffice.org   27 (53) 832-0896

Rep of South Africa (Mozambique)
           mozambique@vgroffice.org  27-13-74-57287

Republic of Congo
           brazzaville@vgroffice.org   242-05-55-84-036

| Romania | romania@vgroffice.org | 40-256-411-473 |
| Russia | russia@vgroffice.org | 78124761 786 |
| Togo | togo@vgroffice.org | 228-905-60-26 |
| Uganda | uganda@vgroffice.org | 256-414-577454 |
| Ukraine | ukraine@vgroffice.org | 011 380 5632 60787 |

USA (North West Mexico)
           j.amalong@vgroffice.org   520-743-8211

| Venezuela | venezuela@vgroffice.org | 0251 4471738 |

VGR [ALL OTHER COUNTRIES]
           vogr@branham.org         (812) 256-1177

| Zambia | zambia@vgroffice.org | 260-211-220627 |
| Zimbabwe | zimbabwe@vgroffice.org | 263-4-303-847 |

*Please contact VGR headquarters: web: http://branham.org/ email: vogr@branham.org Tel: (812) 256-1177 if you need to know more about ordering books & tapes, or countries not listed above.

# APPENDIX E

**THE UNIVERSAL DECLARATION OF HUMAN RIGHTS**
Whereas recognition of the inherent dignity and of the equal and inalienable rights of all members of the human family is the foundation of freedom, justice and peace in the world,

Whereas disregard and contempt for human rights have resulted in barbarous acts which have outraged the conscience of mankind, and the advent of a world in which human beings shall enjoy freedom of speech and belief and freedom from fear and want has been proclaimed as the highest aspiration of the common people

Whereas it is essential, if man is not to be compelled to have recourse, as a last resort, to rebellion against tyranny and oppression, that human rights should be protected by the rule of law,

Whereas it is essential to promote the development of friendly relations between nations,

Whereas the peoples of the United Nations have in the Charter reaffirmed their faith in fundamental human rights, in the dignity and worth of the human person and in the equal rights of men and women and have determined to promote social progress and better standards of life in larger freedom,

Whereas Member States have pledged themselves to achieve, in co-operation with the United Nations, the promotion of universal respect for and observance of human rights and fundamental freedoms,

Whereas a common understanding of these rights and freedoms is of the greatest importance for the full realization of this pledge,

Now, Therefore THE GENERAL ASSEMBLY proclaims THIS UNIVERSAL DECLARATION OF HUMAN RIGHTS as a common standard of achievement for all peoples and all nations, to the end that every individual and every organ of society, keeping this Declaration constantly in mind, shall strive by teaching and education to promote respect for these rights and freedoms and by progressive measures, national and international, to secure their universal and effective recognition and observance, both among the peoples of Member States themselves and among the peoples of territories under their jurisdiction.

**Article 1.**

All human beings are born free and equal in dignity and rights. They are endowed with reason and conscience and should act towards one another in a spirit of brotherhood.

**Article 2.**

Everyone is entitled to all the rights and freedoms set forth in this Declaration, without distinction of any kind, such as race, colour, sex, language, religion, political or other opinion, national or social origin, property, birth or other status. Furthermore, no distinction shall be made on the basis of the political, jurisdictional or international status of the country or territory to which a person belongs, whether it be independent, trust, non-self-governing or under any other limitation of sovereignty.

**Article 3.**

Everyone has the right to life, liberty and security of person.

**Article 4.**

No one shall be held in slavery or servitude; slavery and the slave trade shall be prohibited in all their forms.

**Article 5.**

No one shall be subjected to torture or to cruel, inhuman or degrading treatment or punishment.

**Article 6.**

Everyone has the right to recognition everywhere as a person before the law.

**Article 7.**

All are equal before the law and are entitled without any discrimination to equal protection of the law. All are entitled to equal protection against any discrimination in violation of this Declaration and against any incitement to such discrimination.

**Article 8.**
Everyone has the right to an effective remedy by the competent national tribunals for acts violating the fundamental rights granted him by the constitution or by law.

**Article 9.**
No one shall be subjected to arbitrary arrest, detention or exile.

**Article 10.**
Everyone is entitled in full equality to a fair and public hearing by an independent and impartial tribunal, in the determination of his rights and obligations and of any criminal charge against him.

**Article 11.**
(1) Everyone charged with a penal offence has the right to be presumed innocent until proved guilty according to law in a public trial at which he has had all the guarantees necessary for his defence.
(2) No one shall be held guilty of any penal offence on account of any act or omission which did not constitute a penal offence, under national or international law, at the time when it was committed. Nor shall a heavier penalty be imposed than the one that was applicable at the time the penal offence was committed.

**Article 12.**
No one shall be subjected to arbitrary interference with his privacy, family, home or correspondence, nor to attacks upon his honour and reputation. Everyone has the right to the protection of the law against such interference or attacks.

**Article 13.**
(1) Everyone has the right to freedom of movement and residence within the borders of each state.
(2) Everyone has the right to leave any country, including his own, and to return to his country.

**Article 14.**
(1) Everyone has the right to seek and to enjoy in other countries asylum from persecution.
(2) This right may not be invoked in the case of prosecutions genuinely arising from non-political crimes or from acts contrary to the purposes and principles of the United Nations.

**Article 15.**
(1) Everyone has the right to a nationality.
(2) No one shall be arbitrarily deprived of his nationality nor denied the right to change his nationality.

**Article 16.**
(1) Men and women of full age, without any limitation due to race, nationality or religion, have the right to marry and to found a family. They are entitled to equal rights as to marriage, during marriage and at its dissolution.
(2) Marriage shall be entered into only with the free and full consent of the intending spouses.
(3) The family is the natural and fundamental group unit of society and is entitled to protection by society and the State.
**Article 17.**
(1) Everyone has the right to own property alone as well as in association with others.
(2) No one shall be arbitrarily deprived of his property.
**Article 18.**
Everyone has the right to freedom of thought, conscience and religion; this right includes freedom to change his religion or belief, and freedom, either alone or in community with others and in public or private, to manifest his religion or belief in teaching, practice, worship and observance.
**Article 19.**
Everyone has the right to freedom of opinion and expression; this right includes freedom to hold opinions without interference and to seek, receive and impart information and ideas through any media and regardless of frontiers.
**Article 20.**
(1) Everyone has the right to freedom of peaceful assembly and association.
(2) No one may be compelled to belong to an association.
**Article 21.**
(1) Everyone has the right to take part in the government of his country, directly or through freely chosen representatives.
(2) Everyone has the right of equal access to public service in his country.
(3) The will of the people shall be the basis of the authority of government; this will shall be expressed in periodic and genuine elections which shall be by universal and equal suffrage and shall be held by secret vote or by equivalent free voting procedures.
**Article 22.**
Everyone, as a member of society, has the right to social security and is entitled to realization, through national effort and

international co-operation and in accordance with the organization and resources of each State, of the economic, social and cultural rights indispensable for his dignity and the free development of his personality.

**Article 23.**

(1) Everyone has the right to work, to free choice of employment, to just and favourable conditions of work and to protection against unemployment.

(2) Everyone, without any discrimination, has the right to equal pay for equal work.

(3) Everyone who works has the right to just and favourable remuneration ensuring for himself and his family an existence worthy of human dignity, and supplemented, if necessary, by other means of social protection.

(4) Everyone has the right to form and to join trade unions for the protection of his interests.

**Article 24.**

Everyone has the right to rest and leisure, including reasonable limitation of working hours and periodic holidays with pay.

**Article 25.**

(1) Everyone has the right to a standard of living adequate for the health and well-being of himself and of his family, including food, clothing, housing and medical care and necessary social services, and the right to security in the event of unemployment, sickness, disability, widowhood, old age or other lack of livelihood in circumstances beyond his control.

(2) Motherhood and childhood are entitled to special care and assistance. All children, whether born in or out of wedlock, shall enjoy the same social protection.

**Article 26.**

(1) Everyone has the right to education. Education shall be free, at least in the elementary and fundamental stages. Elementary education shall be compulsory. Technical and professional education shall be made generally available and higher education shall be equally accessible to all on the basis of merit.

(2) Education shall be directed to the full development of the human personality and to the strengthening of respect for human rights and fundamental freedoms. It shall promote understanding, tolerance and friendship among all nations, racial or religious groups, and shall further the activities of the United Nations for the

maintenance of peace.

(3) Parents have a prior right to choose the kind of education that shall be given to their children.

**Article 27.**

(1) Everyone has the right freely to participate in the cultural life of the community, to enjoy the arts and to share in scientific advancement and its benefits.

(2) Everyone has the right to the protection of the moral and material interests resulting from any scientific, literary or artistic production of which he is the author.

**Article 28.**

Everyone is entitled to a social and international order in which the rights and freedoms set forth in this Declaration can be fully realized.

**Article 29.**

(1) Everyone has duties to the community in which alone the free and full development of his personality is possible.

(2) In the exercise of his rights and freedoms, everyone shall be subject only to such limitations as are determined by law solely for the purpose of securing due recognition and respect for the rights and freedoms of others and of meeting the just requirements of morality, public order and the general welfare in a democratic society.

(3) These rights and freedoms may in no case be exercised contrary to the purposes and principles of the United Nations.

**Article 30.**

Nothing in this Declaration may be interpreted as implying for any State, group or person any right to engage in any activity or to perform any act aimed at the destruction of any of the rights and freedoms set forth herein.

# NOTES

## Preface and Acknowledgements [Pages ix–xvi]

1   Jorgensen, Owen. *Supernatural: The Life of William Branham,* Vol. I (Tuscan: Tucson Tabernacle, 1994), Back Cover.

2   Allan Anderson, *An Introduction to Pentecostalism* (Cambridge: Cambridge University Press, 2004), p. 58. Daniel G Reid, Bruce L Shelley (Editor), Robert D Linder (Editor), Stanley M Burgess (Editor), Eduard M Van Der Maas (Editor), *Dictionary of Pentecostal and Charismatic Movements* (Grand Rapids, Michigan: Zondervan, 1988), p372; Owen Jorgensen, *Supernatural: The Life of William Branham* (Tucson, Arizona: Tucson Tabernacle (book 2, 1994). *Ephemera of William Marrion Branham: Biography Billy Graham Center, Wheaton College, Illinois, USA (see http://www2.wheaton.edu/bgc/ archives/GUIDES/123.htm); David Edwin Harrell, *All Things Are Possible: The Healing and Charismatic Revivals in Modern America* (Bloomington, Indiana: Indiana University Press, 1978), p25; Walter J Hollenweger, *Pentecostalism: Origins and Developments Worldwide* (Peabody, Massachusetts: Hendrickson Publications, 1997), p229; Eddie L Hyatt, *2000 Years of Charismatic Christianity* (Lake Mary, Florida: Charisma House formerly Strang Communications, 2002), Chapter 25, "The Healing Revival". Robert H Krapohl, & Charles Lippy, *The Evangelicals: A Historical, Thematic, and Biographical Guide* (Westport Connecticut & London: Greenwood Press, 1999), p69; Gordon G Lindsay, *Branham: A Man Sent From God* (Jeffersonville, Indiana: William Branham Evangelical Association, 1950), chapter 14; Angela Smith, *Generation: Remembering the Life of a Prophet* (Elizabethton, Indiana: Believers International, 2006); Julius Stadsklev, *William Branham: A Prophet Visits South Africa* (Minneapolis: Julius Stadskley,1952), http://bcfresourcecenter.com/mm5/ merchant.mvc?Store_Code=BRC&Screen=PROD&Category_C ode=B&Product_Code=APVSA), p131; Don Stewart, *Only Believe: An Eyewitness Account of the Great Healing Revival of the*

*20th Century* (Shippensburg, Pennsylvania: Destiny Image
Publishers Inc., 1999), p48; C. Douglas Weaver, *The Healer-
Prophet: William Marrion Branham (A study of the Prophetic in
American Pentecostalism)* (Macon, Georgia: Mercer University
Press, 2000), 139.

3   http://branham.org/content/AboutUs/williambranham_pg3
    .aspx

4   htp://www.wmb1.com/de/~diego/ChurchSitesA.shtml;
    http://www. williambranham.com/;
    http://branham.org/williambranham;
    http://www.livingwordbroadcast.org/;
    http://www.bibleway.org/home.do;
    http://www.spokenwordchurch.com/swc/;
    http://www.eastleatabernacle.org/;
    http://www.laparoleparlee.com/message_pour_l_epouse_c.
    ws;
    http://branham.org/MessageSearch.htm;
    http://www.bcfellowship.org/; http://www.hbbf.org.uk/

5   Dan. R. McConnell, *A Different Gospel* (Peabody, Massachusetts:
    Hendrickson Publishers Inc., 1988), p166.

6   C Douglas Weaver, *Healer-Prophet: William Marrion Branham
    (A study of the Prophetic in American Pentecostalism)* (Macon,
    Georgia: Mercer University Press, 2000), p111.

7   (http://branham.org/aboutus)

8   2 Timothy, 3:16, KJV.

9   D.A Carson, *The Gagging of God: Christianity Confronts Pluralism*
    (Leicester: Apollo (an imprint of Intervarsity Press, 1996),
    151-152.

10  'Surely the Lord GOD will do nothing, but he revealeth his
    secret unto his servants the prophet' (Amos 3:7, KJV).

11  William Marrion Branham, *An Exposition of the Seven Church
    Ages,* (Jeffersonville, Indiana: Voice Of God Recordings, 1965),
    p13. The prophet consulted the following two of the many
    major reference books thus drawing substantially from
    inspired sections of these and other works when writing the
    *Seven Church Ages.* These works included Clarence Larkin, "The
    Seven Churches", Chapter XXII & other chapters in
    *Dispensational Truth of God's Plan and Purpose in the Ages,*
    Philadelphia/London, 1920; & Rachel C. Hazeltine, *How did it
    happen! A History of the early Christian Churches written by*

*deduction; deduction means just a remaking of events from all of the data collected* (Santa Cruz, California: Voice in the Wilderness, 1958); see also Library of Congress link: http://lccn.loc.gov/58049286 which lists Hazeltine's book in its catalogue. Branham, The Table, 2005, *The Smyrnaean Church Age*, Jeffersonville IN, 1960, para 11 provides evidence to show that the prophet used Hazeltine as a source of reference when in his own words he "read" to his listeners an extract "found in the book ... 'How Did It Happen?' ... by the historian R. C. Hazeltine, the history of the early churches." Other places in his work he acknowledges the substantial contributions scholars of great learning and repute has made to his work.

12  I John 4:1, KJV.

13  http://wmbranham.net/;
    http://wmbranham.net/files/X07ChapterSeven.html#sdendnote67sym

14  Branham, The Table, 2005, *Here Ye Him* Spokane WA, 1962, para F-48.

15  Martin Jacques, *When China Rules The World: The End of the Western World and the Birth of a New Global Order* (London: Allen Lane, 2012).

16  Branham, The Table, *The Time Is At Hand*, Chicago IL, 1956, para E-26

17  Branham, The Table, *The Time Is At Hand*, Chicago IL 1956, para E-26

18  Branham, The Table, *The Handwriting On The Wall*, Jeffersonville, Indiana: Voice Of God Recordings, 1956, paras E14-E15.

# Chapter One [Pages 1–6]

1  Georg Wilhelm Friedrich Hegel, *Philosophy of Right*, trans. Thomas Malcolm Knox (Oxford: Clarendon Press, 1942), 295.

2  Branham, The Table, *A Greater Than Solomon Is Here*, Bloomington Il, 1961, para E-50

3  William Marrion Branham, *An Exposition of the Seven Church Ages*, (Jeffersonville, Indiana:1965), p.348)

4  Branham, The Table, *Expectations*, New York NY, 1950, para E-68.

5  Branham, The Table, *The Anointed Ones At The End Time*,

Jeffersonville IN, 1965, para 100.

6    Branham, Table, *Our Hope Is In God*, New York, 1951, paras E-9-E-10.

7    Hebrews. 8:1, KJV.

## Chapter Two [Pages 7–18]

1    Branham, The Table, *Who Is God?* Cleveland OH,1950, paras E13-E21

2    Branham, Table, *Christ Is Identified The Same In All Generations*, Tampa FL, 1964, paras 69/70.

3    Branham, The Table, *Only Believe*, Tallahassee FL, 1953, para E-6.

4    Branham, The Table, *Prayer Line*, 1953, para E-17.

5    Lerone Bennett, *The Challenge of Blackness*, (Chicago: Johnson Publishing, 1972), 193.

6    William Marrion Branham, *Christ Is The Mystery Of God Revealed* (1963), (Jeffersonville, Indiana: Voice Of God Recordings, published in 1968. Reprinted in 2002), 19.

7    Branham, The Table, *Lifting Him Up Out Of History*, Jeffersonville IN,1958, para E-13.

8    Branham, The Table, *The Revelation of Jesus Christ*, Jeffersonville, IN, 1960, para 255.

9    Branham, The Table 2005, *Seven Church Ages*, Chapters 5, 9 and 10.

10   Luke 24:13-27, KJV.

11   Branham, The Table 2005, *Modern Events Are Made Clear By Prophecy*, San Bernardino CA, 1965, para 18

12   Department of Education & Science, *History from 5 to 16: Curriculum Matters* (London: HMSO, 1988), P.1.

13   Branham, *Seven Church Ages*, 143.

14   http://www.biblicalstudies.org.uk/pdf/eq/gospels_merkley.pdf

15   Branham, The Table 2005, *The Unwelcomed Christ*, Jeffersonville IN, 1955, para105

16   Branham, The Table 2005, *Christ Is Revealed In His Own Word*, Jeffersonville IN, 1965.para 152.

17   Branham, *Seven Church Ages*, page 66.

18   Michel Foucault, *Power & Knowledge: Selected Interviews and Other Writings, 1972-1977* (New York: Pantheon, 1977), 82. Quoted in V.Y. Mudimbe, *The Invention of Africa: Gnosis, Philosophy, and the Order of Knowledge* (Bloomington and

Indianapolis: Indiana University Press; London: James Currey, 1988), 41

19 Mudimbe, *The Invention of Africa*, 41.
20 John 14:16, KJV.
21 Ecclesiastes, 3.1, KJV.
22 Branham, The Table 2005, *Diseases And Afflictions*, Louisville KY, 1950, para 33.
23 Branham, *Seven Church Ages*, 320
24 Branham, *Seven Church Ages*, 320.
25 Branham, The Table 2005, *The Sudden, Secret Going Away Of The Church*, 1958, para E-19.
26 Branham, The Table 2005, *The Greatest Battle Ever Fought*, Jeffersonville, IN, 1962, paras 56-6.
27 Branham, The Table 2005, *The Greatest Battle*, paras 55-3
28 Branham, The Table 2005, Adoption# 1, 1960, Jeffersonville, IN, para106.
29 Frantz Fanon, *Black Skin, White Masks* (New York: Grove Press, 1967), 135.
30 Frantz Fanon, *Black Skin, White Masks*, 135.
31 Karl Marx, *The Eighteenth Brumaire of Louis Bonaparte*, trans. Daniel De Leon (New York: International Publishing, 1898), quoted in Tony Martin, *The Pan-African Connection: From Slavery to Garvey* (Dover, Massachusetts: Majority Press, 1983), 183; See also Karl Marx, *The Eighteenth Brumaire of Louis Bonaparte* trans. Eden & Cedar Paul (Unwin Brothers Limited, London, 1926) , 23.
32 Frantz Fanon, *The Wretched of the Earth* (Middlesex: Penguin, 1967), 166.
33 Karl Marx and Friedrich Engles *Gesamtausgabe* (Berlin: Dietz, 1972), I, iii, 625, quoted in E.H., Carr, *What Is History?* , ed. R.W. Davies, 2nd ed (London: Penguin, 1987),49.
34 Karl Marx, *Capital: A Critique of Political Economy*, vol 1 trans. Ben Fowkes (Harmondsworth: Penguin, 1976), Preface.
35 Branham, The Table 2005, *Hebrews, Chapter Seven* #1, Jeffersonville, IN, 1957, para 30.

# Chapter Three [Pages 9–30]

1 Branham, The Table 2005, *I Will Restore*, Zurich, Switzerland, 1955, para E-14.
2 Branham, The Table 2005, *The Word Became Flesh*, Jeffersonville

IN, 1955, para 44.

3   Oxford University Press, *Oxford English Dictionary*, 2nd edit
    (Oxford: Oxford University Press, 2005), 1487.

4   Rudolph Otto, *The Idea of the Holy* (New York: Oxford University
    Press, 1961).

5   Branham, The Table 2005, *Sign Of The Time*, Bangor ME, 1958,
    para E-45.

6   Branham, The Table 2005, *Satan's Eden*, Jeffersonville IN,
    1965, para 41. Ancient Greek and other historians agree that
    once Lower or Northern Egypt was sea until it was turned into
    land and Southern or Upper Egypt was always land. See also
    Diodorus Siculus. *Library of History*, Vol.II, Book III, trans. C.H.
    Oldfather (Boston, Massachusetts: Harvard University Press,
    1933-35),Vol.I, p.8 & Vol. III, p.106; Griffiths, G.J., *Plutarch's
    De Iside et Osiride* (Cambridge: Cambridge University Press,
    1970), Vol.II, p.367; Herodotus. *The History of Herodotus*,
    trans. George Rawlinson in *Great Books of The Western World*
    (Chicago: Encyclopaedia Britannica, 1952), lib. Ii. Cap. 4; John
    Gardner Wilkinson, *Manners and Customs of the Ancient
    Egyptians*, Vol.I,1837, p.2, p.89; referred to in Alexander
    Hislop, *The two Babylons*, 2nd ed (Neptune, New Jersey:
    Loizeaux Brothers, Inc 1959), 292-294; Cheikh Anta Diop,
    *Civilization or Barbarism: An Authentic Anthropology*, ed (Harold
    J. Salemson and Marjolijn de Jasper, and trans. Yaa-Lengi
    Meema Ngemi (Brooklyn, New York: Lawrence Hill, 1991);
    Cheikh Anta Diop, *The African Origin of Civilization: Myth or
    Reality*, ed and trans. Mercer Cook (Westport: Lawrence Hill,
    1974);68 Branham, The Table 2005, *Satan's Eden*,
    Jeffersonville IN, 1965, para 41.

7   Branham, The Table 2005, *God Of This Evil Age*, Jeffersonville
    IN, 1965, paras, 78; 86; 126-128.

8   Genesis 3: 1-6, KJV.

9   Genesis 3: 1-6, KJV.

10  Genesis 4:3, KJV.

11  Branham, The Table 2005, *Job*, Phoenix AZ, 1955 para E-12

12  Genesis 6:1-2, KJV.

13  Branham, The Table 2005,*The Conflict Between God And Satan*,
    Clarksville IN , 1962, para E47

14  Branham, Table 2005, *Modern Events Made Clear By Prophesy*,
    Jeffersonville IN, 1962, para 54

15  John G. Jackson, *Introduction to African Civilizations* (New York. Citadel Press/Kensington Publishing Corp. 1994 [1970].

16  Genesis 8-10, KJV.

17  Genesis 10:9-10, KJV.

18  Genesis, 11:4, KJV.

19  Branham, The Table 2005, *The Basis Of Fellowship*, Long Beach CA, 1962 para E-27.

20  Diop, *African Origin*, 102. The name Egypt is a Greek corruption of the Egyptian name of Pepi's 6th dynasty pyramid, Men-Nefer. Manetho the Egyptian historian referred to it as Hi-Ku-P'tah "the temple of the vital force of Ka Ptah, written by the Greeks as Ai-gu-ptos, later Latinised as Aegyptus and eventually Egypt". According to historians Egypt was originally a tiny area surrounding the city of Memphis, but the Greeks used it to describe the whole of Egypt. Egypt for the purpose of this study is used in the Diopian sense as 'Ank Tawy', 'that which binds the Two Lands', or Ta Merry, upper Egypt and Lower Egypt, united under its first dynastic king, Menes, about 3100BC.

21  Alexander Hislop, *The Two Babylons Or Papal Worship*, 2nd ed (New Jersey: (Loizeaux Brothers, INC), 1959), 26.

22  Branham, The Table 2005, *The Communion* , Jeffersonville IN, 1957, para 62.

23  Charles Pelham Groves, *The Planting of Christianity in Africa* (London: Lutterworth Press,1948-54),59, quoted in Ben-Jochannan, Yosef, *African Origins of The Major "Western Religions* (New York: Alkebu-Lan Books Associates, 1970),74.

24  Branham, The Table 2005, *Sirs, We Would See Jesus*, Dawson Creek BC, 1961, para E-12.

25  Branham, The Table 2005, *The Mark Of The Beast*, Jeffersonville IN, 1964, para 89.

26  Branham, The Table 2005, *The Mighty Conqueror*, Edmonton AB, 1957, para E-20.

27  Branham, The Table 2005, *The Sardisean Church Age*, Jeffersonville IN,1960, para 47

28  Peter Laslett, *The World We Have Lost*, 2nd ed (London: Metheun Company Limited, 1971), 9.

29  Joe Scott, *The Making of The United Kingdom* (Oxford: Heineman Educational, 1992), p.8.

30  Branham, The Table 2005, *Why Cry? Speak* , Clarkesville IN,

1959, para E-54.

31   Branham, The Table 2005, *The True Easter Seal*, Jeffersonville IN, 1961, para 8.

32   Peter Laslett, *The World We Have Lost* (London: Methuen & Co Ltd, 1965), 74.

33   Branham, *Seven Church Ages*, 290.

34   Branham, The Table 2005, *Jezebel Religion*, Middletown OH, 1961, para 95

35   Branham, *Seven Church Ages*, 340.

36   Branham, The Table 2005, *Who Is Jesus?* Topeka KS, 1954, para 83

37   Branham, The Table 2005, *One In A Million*, Los Angeles CA, 1965.

38   Colossians. 3:6, KJV.

39   II Timothy. 3:1-7, KJV.

40   Department for Children, Schools and Families (DCSF), *Guidance on the place of Creationism and Intelligent Design in Science Lessons*, http:www.teachernet.gov.uk/teaching and learning/subjects/science teaching resources; Francisco J. Ayala, *Darwin and Intelligent Design* (Minneapolis: Fortress Press, 2006); Lesley S. Jones, & Michael J. Reiss, (eds), *Teaching about Scientific Origins: Taking Account of Creationism* (New York: Peter Lang, 2007); Neil A. Manson, (ed), *God and Design: The teleological argument and modern science* (London: Routledge, 2003).

41   Branham, The Table 2005, *Demonology, Physical Realm*, Connersville IN, 1953, para 28.

42   Branham, The Table 2005, *The Seal Of The Antichrist* , Los Angeles CA, 1955, paras E-17-E-18.

43   1 John. 3:12, KJV.

44   Luke 9:33, KJV.

45   Acts 20:27, KJV.

46   Branham, The Table 2005, *Why I'm Against Organized Religion*, Jeffersonville IN, 1962.

## Chapter Four [Pages 31–44]

1    Assemblies of God, General Council. *Minutes of the Annual Meeting of the Assemblies of God in the U.S.A., Canada and Foreign Lands*, Vol.4, 1915, pp. 12f quoted in Robert Mapes Anderson, *Vision of the Disinherited: The Making of American Pentecostalism*

(New York/Oxford: Oxford University Press, 1979), 4.

2   Anderson, *Vision of the Disinherited*, 4.

3   Branham, The Table 2005, *Indictment*, Jeffersonville IN, 1963, para 68.

4   2 Timothy. 3:5, KJV.

5   Branham, The Table 2005, *Why I'm Against Organized Religion*, Jeffersonville IN, 1962, para 32.

6   Branham, The Table 2005, *Why I'm Against Organized Religion*, Jeffersonville, 1962, para, 32.

7   Branham, The Table 2005, *Why I'm Against Organized Religion*, 1962, para 143.

8   Branham, *Seven Church Ages*, 340.

9   Timothy L. Smith, *Revivalism and Social Reform* (New York: Harper & Row, 1965), pp. 45-62; Sidney E. Mead, *The Lively Experiment* (New York: Harper & Row, 1963), pp. 29-35, 55-56, 121-2; Winthrop Hudson, *The Great Tradition of the American Churches* (New York: Harper, 1963), pp. 65-68; quoted in Anderson, *Vision of the Disinherited*, 28.

10  Branham, The Table 2005, *Questions And Answers*, Jeffersonville IN, 1959, para 384-108.

11  Branham, The Table 2005, *Questions and Answers*, Jeffersonville IN, 1959, para 384-108.

12  Branham, The Table 2005, *Make The Valley, Full Of Ditches*, Connersville IN, 1953, para E-30.

13  Branham, The Table 2005, *He Swore By Himself*, Jeffersonville IN, 1954, para 140

14  Exodus 21:1-11, KJV

15  Martin Marty, "Pentecostalism in the Context of American Piety and Practice", in Vinson Synan, ed., *Aspects of Pentecostal-Charismatic Origins* (Plainfield, New Jersey: Lagos International, 1975), 214-15

16  Acts 2:4 (KJV)

17  See Anderson, *Vision of the Disinherited*, 43, 28-46.

18  Mary B.Woodworth.Etter, *Signs and Wonders God Wrought in the Ministry for Forty Years* (Chicago: the author), 1916, 44-45, 48-49, 63-64, 70, 118; quoted in Anderson, *Vision of the Disinherited*, 34-36; see also Mary B.Woodworth.Etter, *Signs and Wonders* (New Kensington, Pennsylvania: Whitaker House, 1997).

19  Branham, The Table 2005, *Is This The Sign Of The End, Sir?*

Jeffersonville IN, 1962, paras 31-32.

20  Branham, The Table 2005, *Debate On Tongues*, Yakima WA, 1960, E-20

21  Branham, The Table 2005, *Debate On Tongues*, para, E-30.

22  Acts 2:38, KJV.

23  Anderson, *Vision of the Disinherited*, 12.

24  Branham, The Table 2005, *Debate On Tongues*, Yakima WA, 1960, para E-2.

25  Branham, The Table 2005, *The Baptism Of The Holy Spirit*, Jeffersonville IN, 1958, para 160

26  Branham, The Table 2005, *Is This The Sign Of The End, Sir?*, Jeffersonville IN, 1962, para 31-2

27  Frank Bartleman, *Azusa Street: Roots of Modern Day Pentecost*, 2nd edit (South Plainfield, New Jersey: Bridge Publishing Inc., 1996) and Frank Bartleman, *The Azusa Street Revival – An Eye Witness Account* (Moreno Valley, California: Revival School, 2008).

28  Kevin Adams, *A Diary of Revival: The Outbreak of the 1904 Welsh Awakening* (Farnham, Surrey: Crusade for World Revival (CRW), 1904).

29  Sarah T. Parham, *The Life of Charles F. Parham: Founder of the Apostolic Movement* (Joplin, Missouri: Tri-State Printing Co., 1930), 276; quoted in Anderson, *Vision of the Disinherited*, 190.

30  Anderson, *Vision of the Disinherited*, 190

31  Nils Bloch-Hoell, *The Pentecostal Movement: Its Origin, Development, and Distinctive Character* (New York: Humanities Press, 1965), 143.

32  Branham, The Table 2005, *This Day This Scripture Is Fulfilled*, Jeffersonville IN, 1965, para 146.

33  II Thessalonians 2:4, KJV.

34  Branham, The Table 2005, *The Unpardonable Sin*, Jeffersonville IN, 1954, para 112

35  Branham, The Table 2005, *Questions And Answers*, Jeffersonville, Indiana, 1954, para 178-181.

36  Branham, The Table 2005, *Questions And Answers*, Jeffersonville, Indiana, 1954, para 178-181.

37  Branham, The Table 2005, *Questions And Answers*, Jeffersonville, Indiana, 1954, para 178-181.

38  Branham, The Table 2005, *Questions And Answers*, Jeffersonville,

Indiana, 1954, para 189-254.

39   Branham, *Seven Church Ages*, Page 185.

40   Branham, The Table 2005, *Question and Answers On Genesis*, Jeffersonville IN, 1953, paras 33-128

41   Branham, The Table 2005, *Proving His Word*, Los Angeles CA, 1965, paras 57, 65.

42   Branham, The Table 2005, *An Ensign*, Connersville IN, 1953, para E-34.

43   Branham, The Table 2005, *The Rejected King*, Jeffersonville IN, 1960, Para 27-2

44   Branham, The Table 2005, *Earnestly Contending For The Faith*, Louisville KY, 1954, para E-26.

45   Branham, The Table 2005, *We Would See Jesus*, New York NY, 1958, para E-8

46   Branham, The Table 2005, *Questions And Answers #1*, Jeffersonville IN, 1964, paras 931-46

47   Branham, The Table 2005, *The Word Became Flesh (India Trip Report)*, Jeffersonville IN, 1954, paras 44, 50.

48   Branham, The Table 2005, *God's Provided Way*, Chicago IL, 1955, para E-6.

49   Branham, The Table 2005, *A Greater Than Solomon Is Here*, Tucson AZ, 1963, para 8.

50   Branham, The Table 2005, *The Great Coming Revival And The Outpouring Of The Holy Spirit*, Chicago IL, 1954, para E-23

51   Branham, The Table 2005, *Law Or Grace*, Jeffersonville IN, 1954, para 161.

52   Branham, The Table 2005, *Law Or Grace*, Jeffersonville IN, 1954, para 161.

53   Branham, The Table 2005, *The Second Coming*, Phoenix AZ, 1955, para E-46

54   Branham, The Table 2005, *Christ Is The Mystery Of God Revealed*, Jeffersonville IN, 1963, para 208.

55   Branham, The Table 2005, *The Resurrection Of Lazarus*, Erie PA, 1951, para E-2.

56   Branham, The Table 2005, *The World Is Again Falling Apart*, Shreveport LA, 1963, para 162

57   Branham, *Seven Church Ages*, page 240.

58   Cheikh Anta Diop, *Civilization or Barbarism: An Authentic Anthropology*, ed. Harold J.Salemson and Marjolijn de Jasper, and trans. Yaa-Lengi Meema Ngemi ( Brooklyn, New York:

Lawrence Hill, 1991).

59   *Civilization or Barbarism*, 19.

## Chapter Five [Pages 45–60]

1    Branham, The Table 2005, *Satan's Eden* , Jeffersonville IN, 1965, para 173.

2    Branham, *The Future Home Of The Heavenly Bridegroom And The Earthly Bride* (Indiana, Jeffersonville, Voice of God Recordings, 1965).

3    Branham, The Table 2005, *God Keeps His Word*, Jeffersonville IN, 1957, para E-4. See Revelation 22:19, KJV.

4    Branham, The Table 2005, *God Of This Evil*, Jeffersonville IN, 1965, para 129.

5    Branham, The Table 2005, *God Of This Evil*, paras 126-131.

6    *Webster's Illustrated Dictionary Encyclopaedia* (New York: Crescent Books, 1984), 75; Noah Webster, *Webster's Concise Dictionary of the English Language* (New York: A.L. Burt & Co., 1919).

7    *Oxford School Dictionary*, 3rd ed (Oxford: Oxford University Press, 2002).

8    II Timothy 3:4, KJV.

9    Anderson, *Vision of the Disinherited*, 29-31.

10   C.I. Scofield, *The Scofield Study Bible, The Holy Bible: Authorised King James Version* (New York: Oxford University Press, 1909); Genesis Chapter 4, Note 2, page 11.

11   Branham, The Table 2005, *God's Power to Transform*, Phoenix AZ, 1965, paras 87-88.

12   Genesis 4:4:16, KJV.

13   See The Reverend Cain Hope Felder, *The Original African Heritage Bible*, King James Version (Nashville: The James C. Winston Publishing Company, 1993), 106; Cheikh Anta Diop, *Civilization or Barbarism: An Authentic Anthropology*, ed. Harold J.Salemson and Marjolijn de Jasper, and trans. Yaa-Lengi Meema Ngemi ( Brooklyn, New York: Lawrence Hill, 1991), xiv, xvi

14   http://epistle.us/inspiration/worldpuzzle.html

15   Hislop's *Two Babylons*, 40-46.

16   Hislop's *Two Babylons*, 21-40

17   Genesis 10:8-11, KJV.

18   C.C.J Bunsen, *Philosophy of Ancient History*, London, 1854,

p.52.

19   Bunsen, *Philosophy of Ancient History*, 52.

20   Branham, The Table 2005, *Adoption*, Jeffersonville IN, 1960, para20.

21   Joseph Augustus Seiss, *A Miracle in Stone or The Great Pyramid of Egypt*, 14th edn (Philadelphia: Porter and Coates, 1880).

22   Acts 7:22, KJV.

23   Hebrews 11:26, KJV.

24   Branham, Table 2005, *I Will Restore Unto You, Saith The Lord*, Los Angeles CA, 1954, para E-13.

25   Martin Bernal, *Black Athena: The Afroasiatic Roots of Classical Civilization, Volume II: The Archaeological and Documentary Evidence* (New Brunswick, New Jersey: Rutgers University Press, 1996), 77, 494, 521

26   George G M. *Stolen Legacy* (San Francisco: Richardson Associates, 1976), 7.

27   James, *Stolen Legacy*, 10-11

28   James, *Stolen Legacy*, 14.

29    Bernal, *Black Athena* vol 1 1, 145.

30   Branham, *Seven Church Ages*, 185-188.

31   Branham, The Table 2005, *Satan's Eden*, Jeffersonville IN, 1965 para 41.

32   Martin Bernal, *Black Athena: The Afroasiatic Roots of Classical Civilization, Volume I: The Fabrication of Ancient Greece 1785-1985*, London: Free Association Books, 1987), 151.

33   Branham, The Table 2005, *God' Power to Transform*, Phoenix AZ, 1965, para 75.

34   Frank Bartleman, *The Azusa Street Revival: Eyewitness Account*, 1925 (Milton Keynes, UK: Revival School), 2008, 70.

35   Branham, The Table 2005, *Adoption #1*, Jeffersonville IN, 1960, para 110

36   Ivan D. Illich, *Deschooling*, (New York: Harper and Row; London: Calder and Boyars, 1971); see also: http://ournature.org/~novembre/illich/1970_deschooling.html.

37   Branham, The Table 2005, *Perseverance*, Phoenix AZ, 1963, para 85.

38   Branham, The Table 2005, *Perseverance*, Phoenix, 1963, para 85.

39   Branham, The Table 2005, *The Voice of the Sign*, Tulare CA, 1964, para 21

40 Hebrews. 11:26, KJV.

41 William Marrion Branham, *The Masterpiece* (Jeffersonville, Indiana: Voice of God Recordings,1964), para 32, p.8

42 Branham, *The Masterpiece*, para 32, p.7

43 C.J. Munford, *Race & Civilization: Rebirth of Black Centrality* (Trenton: Africa World Press, 2001), 19.

44 National Advisory Committee on Creative and Cultural Education (NACCCE), *All Our Futures: Creativity, Culture & Education* (London: DFE and Employment) 1999, 48.

45 Geoffrey Herman Bantock, *Culture, Industrialisation and Education* (London: Routledge & Kegan Paul, New York: Humanities Press, 1968), 2-3.

46 B. Troyna, J. Williams, ed. *Racism, Education and the State* (Kent: Groom Helm, 1986), 15.

47 Peter Laslett, *The World We Have Lost* (London: Methuen & Co Ltd, 1965), 74.

48 Raymond Williams, *Culture and Society 1780-1950*, (Harmondsworth: Penguin,1982); Raymond Williams, *The Sociology of Culture* (New York: Schocken Books, 1982).

49 NACCCE, *All Our Futures*, para. 75, p.47.

50 Laslett, *The World We have Lost*, 75.

51 Branham, The Table 2005, *Identification*, Phoenix AZ, 1963, para 276.

52 Branham, The Table 2005, *The Conflict Between God And Satan*, Clarkesville IN, 1962, para E-39.

53 Blyden, *Christianity, Islam and the Negro Race* (Baltimore: Black Classic, 1994). 115.

54 Branham, The Table 2005, *The End-time Sign Seed*, Tifon GA, 1962, para E-45

55 Branham, The Table 2005, *The God Of This Evil Age*, Jeffersonville IN, 1965, para 129.

56 Marvin Harris, *Cultural Materialism: The Struggle for a Science of Culture* (California: Altamira Press, 2001), 27-28.

57 United Kingdom: *The Guardian*, Thursday 22 March 2011, page 18.

58 Department for Children, Schools and Families *(DCSF Guidance on the place of Creationism and Intelligent Design in Science Lessons, 2008).*

59 Branham, The Table 2005,*The Cruelty Of Sin, And The Penalty That It Costs To Rid Sin From Our Lives*, Jeffersonville IN, 1953,

para 53.

60   Branham, Table 2005, *But It Wasn't So From The Beginning*, Bloomington IL, 1961, para E-30.

61   William Marrion Branham, *An Exposition of the Book Of Hebrews* (Tucson, Arizona: Tuscon Tabernacle Books), n.d), 5.

62   It has been recorded that Charles Darwin, the author of the *Origin of Species* (1859), renounced his theory of evolution and converted to Christianity on his deathbed. This is said to have been reported by Lady Hope who visited Darwin at his home in England before his death. James Richard Moore, *The Darwin Legend* (London: Hodder & Stoughton,1995) attempts to refute this story, while admitting that Hope did exist and visited Darwin. On the other hand, Malcolm Bowen, *True Science Agrees with the Bible* (Bromley: Sovereign, 1998), 259-276 seeks to prove that the story of Darwin's deathbed confession and conversion possesses 'a kernel of truth'.

## Chapter Six [Pages 61–71]

1    Branham, *Seven Church Ages*, 102-103.

2    Larkin, Chapter I, *Dispensational Truth or God's Plan and Purpose in the Ages* suggests that the Bible "is a revelation of God, of the fall of man, the way of salvation, and of God's 'Plan and purpose in the Ages."

3    Kenneth C. Davis, *America's Hidden History: untold tales of the first pilgrims, fallen heroes, and forgotten fighters from Americas hidden history* (New York: HarperCollins, 2008), 8.

4    Kenneth C. Davis, *America's Hidden History*

5    Andrew Clapham, *Human Rights: A Very Short Introduction* (Oxford/New York: Oxford University Press, 2007), 17; quoting Milan Kundera's story 'The gesture of protest against a violation of human rights'; see *Immortality*, (London: Faber and Faber,1991), 150:4.

6    Branham, Table 2005, *The Deity of Jesus Christ* , Jeffersonville, IN, 1949, para 48.

7    2 Corinthians 5:7, KJV.

8    Andrew Clapham, *Human Rights*, 2007), 10

9    Branham, The Table 2005, *As I Was With Moses*, Los Angeles CA, 1951, para E-28; see also Tom Paine, *Rights of Man* (Oxford: Oxford Paperbacks, 2008) and Mary Wollstonecraft, *A Vindication of the Rights of Woman and A Vindication of the*

*Rights of Men* (Oxford: Oxford University Press, 2008).

10   Branham, The Table 2005, *The Angel Of The Lord*, Los Angeles CA, 1951, para E-13

11   Branham, The Table 2005, *Jehovah-Jireh* #3, Grass Valley CA, 1962, para 78.

12   Dominic Raab, *The Assault On Liberty: What Went Wrong With Rights* (London: Fourth Estate, 2009), 3 & 4.

13   Raab, *The Assault On Liberty*, 8.

14   Miles J. Stanford, *Fox's Book of Martyrs*, edit. William Byron Forbush (Grand Rapids, Michigan: Zondervan, 1926).

15   Branham, *Seven Church Ages*, 161.

16   Raab, *The Assault On Liberty*, 9.

17   United Kingdom, Ed Pilkington, New York, 'US legal scholars voice outrage at treatment of Manning', The Guardian, London and Manchester, Monday, 11 July 2011, Front Page.

18   John Locke, *Second Treaties of Government* [1690], ed. Thomas P. Peardon (Indianapolis: Bobbs-Merrill, 2011), 27-31.

19   Branham, The Table 2005, *The Water of Separation*, Chicago Il, 1955, para E-115.

20   I Peter 4:12.

21   Branham, The Table 2005, *A True Sign That's Overlooked*, Jeffersonville IN,1961, para 37

22   Branham, The Table 2005, *The Fourth Seal*, Jeffersonville IN, 1963, paras 282-3 {25}

23   Branham, The Table 2005, *The Breach Between The Seven Church Ages And The Seven Seals*, Jeffersonville IN, 1963, para 103-1 to para 103-6.

24   Branham, The Table 2005, *Adoption* #1, Jeffersonville IN, 1960, para 135

25   Branham, The Table 2005, *The Door Inside The Door*, Klamath Falls, OR, 1960, para E-43

26   Branham, The Table 2005, *Jehovah-Jireh*#3, Grass Valley CA, 1962, para 78

27   Branham, The Table 2005, *Hear Ye Him*, Spokane WA, 1962, para E-2

28   Branham, The Table 2005, *And Thy Seed Shall Possess The Gate Of His Enemy*, Phoexix AZ, 1962, para E-54; see Hebrews 12:5-11, KJV.

29   Branham, The Table 2005, *At Thy Word*, Phoenix AZ, 1948, para E-39; Daniel 3:13-23, KJV.

30  Branham, The Table 2005, *Images of Christ*, Jeffersonville IN, 1959, para, E17

31  Branham, Seven *Church Ages*, 116-117.

32  Branham, The Table 2005, *The Fourth Seal*, Jeffersonville IN, 1963, 282-3 {25}

33  Branham, The Table 2005, *Images of Christ*, Jeffersonville IN, 1959, para, E-17

34  Branham, The Table 2005, *How Can I Overcome?*, Jeffersonville IN, 1963. para, 76

35  Ronald Dworkin, *Taking Rights Seriously* (London: Duckworth, 1977).

## Chapter Seven [Pages 73–88]

1   Branham, The Table 2005, *The Angel of the Lord*, Los Angeles CA, 1951, para, E-13.

2   Robert Bolt (writer), Roland Joffé (director), *The Mission* (1986 film), Kingsmere ProductionsLtd, DVD, distributed by Warner Home Video (UK) Ltd, 2003

3   Adrian Muther, *The Mission Film Reviewer* (see http://www.st-andrews.ac.uk/~histweb/scothist/brown_k/film/closed/revie ws/mission.html)

4   Kenneth C. Davis, *America's Hidden History: Untold Tales of the First Pilgrims, Fighting Women, and Forgotten Founders Who Shaped a Nation* (New York: HarperCollins, 2008), 9; 7-12)

5   http://etc.usf.edu/lit2go/133/historic-american-documents/4956/patrick-henrys-speech-to-the-virginia-hous e-of-burgess-richmond-virginia-march-23-1775/

6   Matthew. 11:12, KJV.

7   Branham, The Table 2005, *Sirs, We Would See Jesus*, Cleveland IN, 1957, para E-32.

8   Branham, The Table 2005, *Questions & Answers*, Jeffersonville, IN 1959, paras 508-176.

9   James Strong, *The Strongest Strong's Exhaustive Concordance of the Bible*, eds John R. Kohlenberger III & James A. Swanson (Michigan: Zondervan, 2005), para 971, p1598).

10  Branham, The Table 2005, *Israel and the Church*, Jeffersonville IN, 1953, para 158

11  Branham, Table 2005, *This Day This Scripture Is Fulfilled*, Jeffersonville IN, 1965, para 133-139

12  Branham, The Table 2005, *The Third Exodus*, Jeffersonville IN,

1963, paras 122-124.

13 Branham, The Table 2005, *O Lord Just Once More*, Hot Springs AR, 1963, para 17.

14 S. Jonathan Bass, *Blessed are the peacemakers: Martin Luther King, Jr.*, eight white religious leaders, and the "Letter from Birmingham Jail" (Baton Rouge, Louisiana: Louisiana State University Press, 2001), 145-147.

15 King, Martin Luther, Jr, *Why We Can't Wait* (New York: New American Library/Harper & Row,1964), 93 (also see pages 76-95); http://www.lokashakti.org/encyclopedia/bios/132-mar tin-luther-king-jr

16 Nelson Rolihlahla Mandela, *Long Walk to Freedom: The Autobiography of Nelson Mandela* (London: Little Brown and Company (UK), 1994, 372-3.

17 Mandela, *Long Walk to Freedom*, 372-3.

18 Branham, The Table 2005, *The Third Seal*, Jeffersonville IN, 1963, para, 266-1 {273}

19 Branham, The Table 2005, *The Third Exodus*, Jeffersonville IN, 1963, para, 148.

20 Branham, The Table 2005, *A Wedding Supper*, Chicago IL, 1956, para E-70,

21 Branham, The Table 2005, *All The Days Of Our Life*, Chicago IL, 1959, para, E-83,

22 John 6:1-45, KJV.

23 Branham, The Table 2005, *All The Days Of Our Life*, Chicago IL, 1959, para, E-83,

24 Branham, The Table 2005, *A Wedding Supper*, Chicago IL, 1956, para E-70,

25 Branham, The Table 2005, Branham, *Seven Church Ages*, 370.

26 Branham, *Seven Church Ages*, 48.

27 Branham, The Table 2005, *Ashamed*, Jeffersonville IN, 1965, para, 223.

28 Branham, The Table 2005, *Does God Ever Change His Mind About His Word*, Jeffersonville IN, 1965, para, 186.

29 Viktor E. Frankl, *Man's Search for Meaning* (London. Sydney. Auckland. Johannesburg: Rider, 2011), 8.

30 Frankl, *Man's Search for Meaning*, xvii; Stephen R. Covey,*The Seven Habits of Highly Effective People* (London. New York: Simon & Schuster, 1992).

31 Viktor E. Frankl, *Man's Search for Meaning*, 32.

32  Covey, *The Seven Habits*, 70.
33  Frankl, *Man's Search for Meaning*, xix
34  Branham, The Table 2005, *Jesus Christ The Same Yesterday, Today, And Forever*, Sanfernando CA, 1955, para, E-68.
35  Branham, The Table 2005, *Jesus Christ The Same, Yesterday, Today, And Forever*, Terre, Haute, IN, 1958, para E-23
36  Branham, The Table 2005, *The Angel Of God*, Phoenix AZ, 1948, para, E-41.
37  Branham, The Table 2005, *The Voice Of God In The Last Days*, Phoenix AZ, para 64.
38  Branham, *Seven Church Ages*, 353.
39  Branham, *Seven Church Ages*, 353; I Corinthians 2: 9- 16
40  Branham, The Table 2005, *Experiences*, Zion IL, 1952, para E-41.
41  A.H. Robertson, *Human Rights in the World: A Introduction to the Study of the International Protection Of Human Rights*, 2nd Ed (Manchester: Manchester University Press, 1982), 24.
42  Clapham, *Human Rights*, 43.
43  Branham, *Seven Church Ages*, 319-320.
44  Branham, The Table 2005, *The Revelation Of Jesus Christ*, Jeffersonville, 1960, para 156.
45  Branham, The Table 2005, *The Supernatural*, Owensboro KY, 1956, para E-37.
46  Branham, The Table 2005, *The Revelation Of Jesus Christ*, Jeffersonville IN, 1960, para 156.
47  Branham, *Seven Church Ages*, 328-329.

## Chapter Eight [Pages 89–100]

1  http://www.vatican.va/holy_father/francesco/speeches/2013/march/documents/papa-francesco_20130322_corpo-diplomatico_en.html ( See Lizzy Davies, "His humility cheers but Vatican reform will test Francis's substance", which states that: "With all this focus on image, it might be tempting to dismiss much of the so called 'Francis effect' as all style and no substance." The Guardian, London and Manchester, United Kingdom, Saturday 20 July 2013, 25).
2  Branham, *Seven Church Ages*, 319-320.
3  The Iron Curtain was the border between Soviet controlled States (Eastern Europe) & the West.
4  Branham, The Table 2005, *The End-Time Sign Seed*, Tifton-GA,

1962, para E-63

5     Walter M. Abbott, *Documents of Vatican II* (Baltimore, Maryland: The American Press, 1966), 295, 296.

6     Branham, *Seven Church Ages*, 192-193.

7     Branham, *Seven Church Ages*, 217.

8     Larkin, *Dispensational Truth*

9     Branham, *Seven Church Ages*, 220.

10    Branham, *Seven Church Ages*, 357.

11    Branham, *Seven Church Ages*, 357.

12    The Catholic University of America, *New Catholic Encyclopaedia*, "Pope Gregory XII", 2nd ed (Michigan: Gale, 2003), 500; http://en.wikipedia.org/wiki/Resignation_of_Pope_Benedict _XVI;    http://en.wikipedia.org/wiki/Pope_Gregory_http:// www.christian-history.org/western-great-schism.html#stha sh.29zBgKVv.dpbsXII: http://en.wikipedia.org/wiki/Western_ Schism

13    http://www.vatican.va/holy_father/francesco/speeches/201 3/march/documents/papa-francesco_20130322_corpo-dipl omatico_en.html

14    http://www.vatican.va/holy_father/francesco/speeches/201 3/march/documents/papa-francesco_20130322_corpo-dipl omatico_en.html

15    http://www.vatican.va/holy_father/francesco/speeches/201 3/march/documents/papa-francesco_20130322_corpo-dipl omatico_en.html

16    Branham, *Seven Church Ages*, 319-320.

17    William Marrion Branham, The Table 2005, Version 2.0, *Why Little Bethlehem*, Phoenix AZ, 1963, para148 (Jeffersonville, Indiana: Voice of God Recordings, 2005)

18    Branham, The Table 2005, *God of This Evil Age*, Jeffersonville IN, 1965, para 124.

19    Alexander Hislop, *The Two Babylons or The Papal Worship proved to be The Worship of Nimrod and His Wife* (New York: Loizeaux Brothers, Inc, 1916), p6.

20    http://www.vatican.va/holy_father/francesco/speeches/201 3/march/documents/papa-francesco_20130322_corpo-dipl omatico_en.html.

21    Branham, Table 2005, *The Angel of The Lord* (1953), Connersville IN, 1953, para E-10.

22    Branham, Table 2005, *What Think Ye of Christ?* Chicago IL,

1954, para E-28; Isaiah 9:6, KJV.

23  Branham, The Table 2005, *Melchisedec. The Great Prince and King*, Jeffersonville IN, 1955, para E-58.

24  http://wahiduddin.net/saint_francis_of_assisi.htm; http://www.franciscan-archive.org/franciscana/peace.html

25  Walter M. Abbott, S. J, *Documents of Vatican II* (Baltimore, Maryland: The America Press, 1966) p. 715. Vatican II did not alter the doctrine of the Catholic Church and did not do away with the decisions of previous Councils.

26  *Secreta Monita Societatis Jesu: The Secret Instructions of The Jesuits*, London, 1723.

27  *The Secret Instructions* (1723), Chap. XVII. Rule VIII.

28  *The Secret Instructions* (1723), Chap. XVII. Rule VII.

29  Pope Francis was named by *Time Magazine* on 11 December 2013 as its "Person of the Year".

30  *The Secret Instructions* (1723), Preface.

31  *The Secret Instructions* (1723), Chap.XVII, Rule 1.

32  *The Secret Instructions* (1723), Chap.II, Rule 11

33  *The Secret Instructions* (1723), Chap I, Rule I.

34  *The Secret Instructions* (1723), Chap II, Rule X

35  *The Secret Instructions* (1723), Chap II, Rule XV

36  *The Secret Instructions* (1723), Chap IV, Rule II

37  *The Secret Instructions* (1723), Chap III, Rule V

38  *The Secret Instructions* (1723), Chap III, Rule V

39  *The Secret Instructions* (1723), Chap XVII, Rule V.

40  *The Secret Instructions* (1723), Chap IV, Rule VI.

41  *The Secret Instructions* (1723), Chap XI, Rule VI.

42  W.C. Brownlee, *Secret Instructions of The Jesuits* (1841), (California: Ulan Press, 2012), 8-29.

43  Jon Phelps, *Vatican Assassins*, 2nd (ed) (Newmanstown, Pennsylvania: Eric Jon Phelps, 2001), 576.

44  Branham, *Seven Church Ages*, 378.

45  Phelps, *Vatican Assassins*, 576.

46  Charles Chiniquy, *Fifty Years In The Church of Rome* (Ontario, California: Chick Publications, 1982).

47  Branham, Table 2005, *The Restoration of the Bride Tree*, 1962, para 50-6

48  Branham, The Table 2005, *A Super Sign*, Grass Valley CA, 1962, para 165

49  Branham, Table 2005, *Letting Off The Pressure*, Green Lake WI,

1962, para E-109.

50   Branham, The Table 2005. *The Laodicean Church Age,* Jeffersonville IN, 1960, para 49

51   Branham, The Table 2005, *The Laodicean Church Age,* Jeffersonville, 1960, IN, para 49

52   https://www.readyforhillary.com;http://articles.washington post.com/2013-09-14/politics/42055556_1_andrews-university-liberty-medal-former-secretary

53   Branham, The Table 2005, *The Mark of the Beast,* Jeffersonville IN, 1954, para 125

54   Branham, The Table 2005, *God's Covenant With Abraham,* Charlotte NC, IN, 1965, para E-44)

55   Branham, The Table 2005, *Why Are We Not A Denomination?* 1958, para 33.

56   Branham, The Table 2005, *But It Was Not So From The Beginning,* Bloomington IL, 1961, para E-47.

57   Branham, The Table 2005, *The Laodicean Church Age,* Jeffersonville IN, 1960, para 49

58   Branham, The Table 2005, *God's Covenant With Abraham,* 1965, para E-44

59   Branham, *Seven Church Ages,* 322.

60   Branham, The Table 2005, The *Greatest Battle Ever Fought,* Jeffersonville IN , 1962, paras 55-3 to 56-6.

61   "U.S Have Unprecedented Voice In Electing New Pope", http://worldnews.nbcnews.com/_news/2013/02/11/.URtTN WbeOok.facebook

62   Branham, Table 2005, *Acts of the Holy Spirit,* Jeffersonville, Indiana, 1954, para 87.

63   Branham, The Table 2005, *The Mark of the Beast,* Jeffersonville, IN, 1954, para 197

64   Branham, The Table 2005, *The First Seal,* Jeffersonville, Indiana, 1963, para 156-1 (266).

## Chapter Nine [Pages 101–109]

1   Frederick Tupper Saussy, *Rulers of Evil: Useful Knowledge About Governing Bodies* (San Francisco, California: Harper Collins, 2001), 296-297, chap. 3, Note 4, p304:

2   Saussy, *Rulers of Evil,* 296-297, chap. 3, Note 4, p304:

3   http://www.vatican.va/holy_father/francesco/speeches/201 3/march/documents/papa-francesco_20130322_corpo-dipl

omatico_en.html
4    http://www.catholicnews.com/data/stories/cns/0801316.h
     tm
5    Brownlee, *The Instructions*, 5-6.
6    Branham, The Table 2005, *Christianity Versus Idolatry*,
     Jeffersonville IN, 1961, para, 176.
7    Brownlee, *The Instructions*, 5.
8    Thomas Edward Watson, *Political and Economic Handbook*
     (Riverside, California: Ulan Press, 2012). 437.
9    Branham, *Revelation of The Seven Seals*, 193, para 289.
10   Ignatius of Loyola, *The constitutions of the Society of Jesus*.
     Translated by George E. Ganss (St. Louis. Institute of Jesuit
     Sources. 1970), p. 249: Franklin Verzelius N. Painter. *A History
     of Education* (New York: D. Appleton and Company, 1903)
     p. 167.
11   Branham, The Table 2005, *The Mark Of The Beast*, Jeffersonville
     IN, 1954, para 108
12   Branham, Table 2005, *Christianity V Idolatry*, Jeffersonville IN,
     1961 para 21
13   Branham, The Table 2005, *Church Ages*, 244-245; *Christianity
     V Idolatry*, Jeffersonville IN, 1961, paras 173-179.
14   Branham, *Church Ages*, 185.
15   Branham, Table 2005, *Wisdom Versus Faith*, Jeffersonville IN,
     1962, paras 28-7.
16   Branham, The Table 2005, *Baptism of The Holy Spirit*,
     Jeffersonville IN, 1958, para 137.
17   Branham, The Table 2005, *Questions and Answers On The Holy
     Ghost*, Jeffersonville IN, 1959, paras 424-71.
18   Branham, The Table 2005, *The Mark of The Beast*, Jeffersonville
     IN. 1954, para 108.
19   Branham, The Table 2005, *Christianity V Idolatry*, Jeffersonville
     IN, 1961, para 179.
20   Martin Luther, *Babylonian Captivity of the Church* [Kindle
     Edition], Amazon, 2012.
21   Ignatius Loyola, *The Spiritual Exercise*, trans. Anthony Mottola
     (Garden City, New York: Doubleday, 1964), pp. 140-141. See
     William B. Ashworth, Jr, "Catholicism and Early Modern
     Science" in David C. Lindberg and Ronald L. Numbers, *God and
     Nature: historical essays on the encounter between Christianity and
     science* (Berkeley; London: University of California Press,

1986), p. 158, n.9. p.l66.

22 Edward Hendrie, *Solving the Mystery of Babylon the Great* (Virginia: Great Mountain Publishing, (2012), 173; *Catechism of the Catholic Church*, § 85 1994 & 2nd ed. 1997, pt. 1, sect. 1, ch. 2, art. 2, III [#100.]

23 Dom. Cuthbert Butler, *The Vatican Council, 1869-1870*, California: Fontana Library, 1962

24 Branham, The Table 2005, *God Is His own Interpreter*, Bakersfield CA, 1964.

25 Saint Ignatius of Loyola, *The Constitutions of the Society of Jesus*. Trans. With an introduction and commentary by George E. Ganss (St. Louis: Institute of Jesuits Sources, 1970), 66-68 & http://www.bibliotecapleyades.net/vatican/esp_vatican13.htm;

26 Mary Francis Cusack, *The Black Pope: A History of the Jesuits* (London: Marshall, Russell & Co; Brighton: D.B. Friend & Co, 1896), 120.

27 Branham, *Seven Church Ages*, 224-225; James M. Powell, *Innocent III: Vicar of Christ or Lord of the World?* (Washington D. C: Catholic University of American Press, 2nd ed., 1994 [1963]).

28 Branham, *Seven Church Ages*, 224.

29 Hislop, *Two Babylons*, 206.

30 John Julius Norwich, *The Popes: A History* (London: Vintage Books, 2011), 1-8.

31 Matthew 8:14-18; Mark 1:29-34; Luke 4:38-41; I Corinthians 9:5; I Peter 3:1-2.

32 Branham, The Table 2005, *The Mark Of The Beast*, Jeffersonville, Indiana, 1954, para 85.

33 Branham, The Table 2005, *Why Are We Not A Denomination?* Jeffersonville IN, 1958, para 69

34 Branham, *Seven Church Ages*, 378-379; Hazeltine, *How did it happen?*, 64-66.

35 Branham, The Table 2005, *I Will Restore*, Phoenix AZ, 1957, para E-29.

36 I Timothy. 2:5, KJV.

37 *The Secret Instructions* (1723), Chap. XVII, Rule VIII.

38 *The Secret Instructions* (1723), Chap. XVII, Rule VII.

39 Edwards, *Spiritual Friend*, p18.

40 Anthony Campolo, *Letters to a Young Evangelical* (New York:

Basic Books, 2006), 149-150.

41   Anthony De Mello, *Sadhana: A Way to God – Christian Exercises in Eastern Form* (St. Louis [Missouri]: Institute of Jesuit Sources in cooperation with Gujarat Sahitya Prakash, Anand Press, 1980; Ray Yungen, *A Time of Departing; How Ancient Mystical Practices are Uniting Christians with the World's Religions* (Eureka, Montana: Lighthouse Trails Publishing, 2006); Brennan Manning, *A Glimpse of Jesus* (London: HarpeCollins, reprint edition, 2004); Leonard Sweet, *Quantum Spirituality: A Postmodern Apologetic* (Dayton, Ohio: United Theological Seminary, 1991); James L. Wakefield, *Sacred Listening: Discovering the Spiritual Exercises of Ignatius Loyola* (Ada, Michigan: Baker Books, 2006); Tilden Edwards, *Spiritual Friend: Reclaiming the Gift of Spiritual Direction* (New York: Paulist Press, 1980); Rob Baker and Henry Gray (eds), *Merton and Sufism: The Untold Story* (Louisville, Kentucky: Fons Vitae, first edition, 2000); Ken Carey, *The Starseed Trans-missions* (San Francisco, California: HarperOne,1992)

42   Branham, The Table 2005, *Jesus Christ the Same Yesterday, Today, and, Forever*, Middletown OH, 1958, para E-5

43   Branham, The Table 2005, *Abraham*, Long Beach CA, 1961, para, E-50.

44   W.C. Brownlee, *The Instructions*, p.18.

45   http://www.sjweb.info/ss/

## Chapter Ten [Pages 111–117]

1   William Marrion Branham, *The Revelation of the Seven Seals* (Jeffersonville, Indiana: Voice of God Recordings, 1963), 105-157.

2   Branham, *The Revelation of the Seven Seals*, 159-203.

3   Branham, *The Revelation of the Seven Seals*, 205-248.

4   Branham, *The Revelation of the Seven Seals*, 205-248.

5   Branham, *The Revelation of the Seven Seals*, 205-248.

6   Branham, *Seven Church Ages*, 189-190; Hazeltine, *How did it happen?*, 53-63.

7   Branham, *Seven Church Ages*, 189.

8   Branham, *The Revelation of the Seven Seals*, 249-295.

9   The Anglican-Roman Catholic International Commission, *Mary: Grace and Hope in Christ* (Harrisburg Pennsylvania /London: Morehouse, 2005), ix. Preface; http://www.vatican.

va/roman_curia/pontifical_councils/chrstuni/angl-comm-docs/rc_pc_chrstuni_doc_20050516_mary-grace-hope-chris t_en.htm

10 http://www.dailymail.co.uk/news/article-2533874/Welby-casts-sin-christenings-Centuries-old-rite-rewritten-language-E astEnders-modern-congregation.html (see Revelation 22:19, KJV; Acts.2:38, KJV: Matthew.28: 19).

11 Branham, *Seven Church Ages*, 192.

12 Branham, The Table (2005), *Countdown*, Jeffersonville, IN, 1962, para 107.

# Chapter Eleven [Pages 119–130]

1 Larkin, Chapter "XXII The Seven Churches", *Dispensational Truth*

2 Branham,The Table 2005, *The First Seal*, Jeffersonville IN, 1963, para 168; Branham, The Table 2005,*The Mark of The Beast*, Jeffersonville IN, 1956, para E-17; Branham,The Table 2005, *The Seed of Discrepancy*,1965, para 76; Branham,The Table 2005, *The Stature of A Perfect Man*, Jeffersonville IN, 1962, paras 56-3.

3 Elizabeth Povoledo, Vatican City, 'Vatican is Urging Overhall of Global Financial Systems', International Tribune, Tuesday October 25, 2011, p. 3; and http://www.catholicity.com /commentary/zmirak/06407.html
William Marrion Branham, *The Revelation Of The Seven Seals*, 1963 (Jeffersonville, Indiana: Voice of God Recordings, 1967. Reprinted 2001), Para 349-350, pp 150-157.

4 http://www.vatican.va/holy_father/benedict_xvi/encyclicals/ documents/hf_ben-xvi_enc_20090629_caritas-in-veritate_en.html, Section 67.

5 http://www.weforum.org/

6 Elizabeth Povoledo, Vatican City, 'Vatican is Urging Overhall of Global Financial Systems', International Tribune, Tuesday October 25, 2011, p. 3; and http://www.catholicity.com/ commentary/zmirak/06407.html
Branham, *Revelation Of The Seven Seals*, para 349-350, pp 150-157.

7 Branham, Table 2005, *First Seal*, Jeffersonville IN, 1963 paras 168-2 (346.

8 Branham, *Seven Church Ages*, 314.

9    Branham, The Table 2005, *The Stature of A Perfect Man*, Jeffersonville IN, 1962-1014M 165, para 58-2; https://open tabernacle.wordpress.com/2010/12/12/the-vatican-and-the-gold-standard/

10   Branham, *Seven Church Ages*, 379.

11   Branham, The Table 2005, *The Handwriting On The Wall*, 1956, paras E14-E15.

12   Martin Jacques, *When China Rules The World: The End of the Western World and the Birth of a New Global Order* (London: Allen Lane, 2012)

13   Branham, Table 2005, *The Time Is At Hand*, Chicago IL, 1956, para E-26.

14   Branham, Table 2005, *The Time Is At Hand*, Chicago IL, 1956, para E-26.

15   Branham, The Table 2005, *The Handwriting On The Wall*, 1956, paras E14-E15.

16   Branham, *Seven Church Ages*, p265; 195.

17   International Tribune, Tuesday October 25, 2011, p. 3.

18   International Tribune, Tuesday October 25, 2011, p. 3.

19   Branham, The Table 2005, *Israel And the Church #2*, Jeffersonville INC, 1953, para 116.

20   Jamie Doward, News, The Observer (Guardian and Observer International: London), Sunday 7 July, 2013, 12.

21   Branham, The Table 2005, *The Feast of the Trumpets*, Jeffersonville IN, 1964, para 150; Branham, The Table 2005, *Israel And the Church #2*, Jeffersonville INC, 1953, para 116.

22   Burke McCarthy, *The Suppressed Truth About the Assassination of Abraham Lincoln*, 1922 (Hong Kong: Forgotten Books, 2012, 32-33.).

23   http://www.people-press.org/2013/06/10/majority-views-nsa-phone-tracking-as-acceptable-anti-terror-tactic/

24   Branham, The Table 2005, *Questions And Answers On Genesis*, Jeffersonville IN, 116, 1953, para 47-Q-6

25   Branham, Table 2005, *The Mark of The Beast & The Seal of God*, Long Beach CA, 1961 para E-48.

26   Branham, The Table 2005, *The Feast of The Trumpets*, Jeffersonville, 1964, para, 48.

27   http://www.timesofisrael.com/pope-francis-accepts-invitation-to-visit-israel/

28   http://www.timesofisrael.com/pope-francis-accepts-

invitation-to-visit-israel/

29  http://jewishisrael.ning.com/profiles/blogs/pope-to-get-seat-
over-the-tomb-of-king-david;
http://www.israelnationalnews.com/Articles/Article.aspx/12
814#.Uc1SYjuThyI

30  http://jewishisrael.ning.com/profiles/blogs/pope-to-get-seat-
over-the-tomb-of-king-david; http://www.israelnationalnews.
com/Articles/Article.aspx/12814#.Uc1SYjuThyI

31  Branham, Table 2005, *God Keeps His Word*, 1957, Sturgis MI,
1957, para E-85.

32  Tom Horn and Chris Putnam, *Exo-Vaticana: Petrus Romanus,
Project LUCIFER* (Crane, Missouri: Defender Publishing Group,
2013), Front and Back Covers, 521-557.

33  Horn and Putnam, *Exo-Vaticana*, 14.

34  Horn and Putnam, *Exo-Vaticana*, 545.

35  Branham, The Table 2005, *Standing In The Gap*, Jeffersonville,
Indiana, 1963, para, 82; Branham, The Table 2005, *Third
Exodus*, Jeffersonville, Indiana, 1963, para 267.

36  see https://www.facebook.com/SeekYeTheTruth;
www.believethesign.com; & http://www.deceptioninthechur
ch.com/williambranham1.html

37  Branham, The Table 2005, *At Thy Word*, Minneapolis MN,
1950, E-32.

38  Branham, Table 2005, *At Thy Word*, Minneapolis, MN, 1950,
para E22; Exodus 13: 21-22, KJV. In an email dated Tuesday
26 November 2013 to the author, Dr. Paul C Boyd, the Library
of Congress Prints and Photographs Division, confirmed that
the image with the "mysterious light" over the head of the
prophet 'is available for viewing in the Prints & Photographs
Reading Room' of the Library of Congress, and 'is readily
accessible in our Biographical File of original prints and photographs from all time periods'. (see also: http://www.loc.gov
/pictures/item/95512174/).

39  Branham, Table 2005, *One In A Million* (1965), Los Angeles,
CA, para 30 http://www.letusreason .org/Latrain4.htmgeles.

40  Branham, Table 2005, *Events Made Clear By Prophecy*,
Jeffersonville IN, 1965, para 129.

41  Branham, Table 2005, *Watchman, What of the Night?*,
Jeffersonville IN, 1958, para E-24).

42  Branham, *Seven Church Ages*, 193-194. The Prophet said:

"Daniel saw the end when the stone was cut out of the mountain without hands, and it rolled into the kingdoms of the world and crushed them. And they became like the trash on the floor, the husk that the winds blew away; but the Stone covered all the earth. That Stone is Christ" (Branham, Table 2005, *The Oneness of the Unity*, Waterloo, IA, 1958, paras 5-9).

43  Horn and Putnam. *Exo-Vaticana*, IX-XXV.

44  Branham, *Seven Church Ages*, 321.

45  Branham, The Table 2005, *God's Wrapped Gift*, Jeffersonville IN, 1960, para 94.

46  Horn and Putnam, *Exo-Vaticana*, 225.

47  Branham, The Table 2005, *The Reproach for The Cause of the Word*, Jeffersonville IN, 1962, para, 14-3.

48  Branham, The Table 2005, *The Uncertain Sound*, 1962), para E-79

49  Branham, The Table 2005, *Perseverance*, Jeffersonville IN, 1962, para 64.

50  William Marrion Branham, *The Rapture*, 1965 (Jeffersonville, Indiana: Voice Of God Recordings published 1970, Reprinted 2001).

51  http://shop.cloudtenpictures.com/dvd/left-behind.html

52  I Thessalonians 4: 14-17; Branham, *The Rapture*, 25, para 128.

53  Branham, The Table 2005, *The Feast of The Trumpets*, Jeffersonville IN, 1964, para 48.

## Chapter Twelve [Pages 131–138]

1   Branham, *Seven Church Ages*, 376-377

2   Branham, *Seven Seals*, para 79, p115.

3   Branham, *Seven Seals*, para 227, p501.

4   Branham, *Seven Church Ages*, 40-41

5   Branham, *Seven Seals*, para 349, p150.

6   Branham, *Seven Seals*, "Questions and Answers on the Seals", para 369, p463.

7   Branham, The Table 2005, *Power of Transformation*, Prescott AZ, 1965, para 213.

8   Branham, *Seven Seals*, 'The Sixth Seal', pp351-407; Branham, The Table 2005, *Questions & Answers #1*, Jeffersonville IN, 1954, paras 70-70 &71-73.

9   Branham, *Seven Seals*, paras 359, p151.

10  Branham, The Table 2005, *The Seventieth Week of Daniel*,

Jeffersonville IN, 1961, para 171

11   Branham, The Table 2005, *Questions and Answers #3*, 1957, Jeffersonville IN, 1957, paras 325-726 and 328-749.

12   Matthew 13:42, 50, KJV.

13   Branham, The Table 2005, *The Ten Virgins, and the Hundred and Forty Four Thousand Jews*, Jeffersonville IN, 1960, para 137.

14   Revelation, Chapter 11, KJV; see also William Marrion Branham, *The Seventy Weeks of Daniel* ((Jeffersonville, Indiana: Voice Of God Recordings 1961. Reprinted in 2006), pp 108-112.

15   Branham, *Future Home*, pages 22-25

16   Branham, *Future Home*, Para 166, p23.

17   Revelation. 5:11, KJV

18   Branham, *Future Home*, para 495, p61.

19   By Eternal City I mean the Holy City, the New Jerusalem in Revelation. The prophet observes that: "papal false Christian Rome (she is even called the eternal city--how blasphemous) now controls by religion even more ably than when pagan imperial Rome controlled by the pure iron of force"(Branham, *Seven Church Ages*, 195).

20   Branham, The Table, *Shalom*, Sierra Vista AZ, 1964, para 162.

21   Branham, *Seven Church Ages*, 102-104; Ephesians 1:4-11, KJV.

22   John 1 3:2, KJV.

23   Branham, The Table 2005, *Questions & Answers 2*, Jeffersonville, Indiana, 1964, paras, 1045-235

24   Branham, The Table 2005, *Questions and Answers 2*, 1964, paras 1045-233.

25   Revelation Chapter 20:13-15, KJV/ Branham, The Table 2005, *Questions & Answers 2*, 1964, para1045-235).

26   Branham, *The Future Home of The Heavenly Bridegroom and The Earthly Bride* (1964), *The Spoken Word* 3, No. 5R, (1968; 2001 reprint): 5-6; see Chapter XXXII "Dispensational Teaching of the Great Pyramid" & Chapter & XXV "Renovation of the Earth" with sub-sections on "the millennium and the New Earth" and a sketch "The Holy City" drawn in the form of a Pyramid-like City" in Clarence Larkin's book, *Dispensational Truth of God's Plan and Purpose in the Ages*, Philadelphia, London, 1920. The prophet has from time to time consulted Larkin's works and has in the past expressed his gratitude for the inspirational aspects of Larkin's and others "views".

http://www.biblebelievers.org.au/great.htm; & Ken Klein, [DVD] *The Great Pyramid: Lost Legend of Enoch.* Ken Klein Productions, 2006; http://www.biblebelievers.org.au/great .htm.

27  Branham, *The Future Home*, 6.

28  Branham , *The Future Home*, 50; see also Revelation Chapter 21, KJV.

29  Branham , The *Future Home*, 45.

30  See:    http://www.biblebelievers.org.au/pyramid.htm#The Great Pyramid – Reflections in Time

31  Branham , The *Future Home*, 45.

32  Branham, *Future Home*, 51. The prominence given to the prophet Enoch, who is recorded in the Bible to have lived before the Flood, and was the Seventh Seed of Adam (Gen. 5:18), walked with God, and was not (Gen. 5:22,24), is shared by other authorities. See Margaret Barker, *The Book of Enoch and its Influence On Christianity* (London: SPCK, 1988) 16; Hugh Nibley, *Enoch the prophet*, (Utah: Deseret Book, 1986) 276. Bruce Metzger and Michael Coogan, ed., *The Oxford Companion to the Bible* (Oxford: Oxford University Press, 1993), 185; J.T. Milik, ed., *The Books of Enoch, Aramaic Fragments of Qumran Cave 4* (Oxford: Oxford University Press, 1976); Hugo Odeberg, ed, *Enoch or the Hebrew Book of Enoch* (New York: KTAV Publishing House, 1973); 139; Geoffrey Bromiley, ed. *The International Standard Bible Encyclopaedia*, Vol .2 (Grand Rapids, Michigan: Eerdsmans, 1982): 103.

33  E.F.C. Rosenmueller, *The Biblical Geography of Central Asia*, Vol.1, trans. N. Morren, London: 1832, SECT. V., page 15.

34  Branham , *Future Home*, 50-51.

35  Branham, *The Future Home*, 51

36  William Marrion Branham, *Who Is This Melchisedec?* (Jeffersonville, Indiana: Voice Of God Recordings, 1965), para 43, p9.

# Summary and Conclusions [Pages 139–151]

1    Edward Fitzgerald, *Rubáiyát of Omar Khayyám: a Critical Edition*, ed. Christopher Decker (Charlottesville: London: University Press of Virginia, 1977). Edward Fitzgerald was born in 1809 and died 1883. Omar Khayyám was born on the 18th May 1048 in Nishapur, Persia (now Iran). He was an astrologer,

mathematician and poet. He died on the 4th December 1131 in the place of his birth. Rubáiyát or 'quatrains' is a poem, unit or stanza of four lines of verse, usually with a rhyme scheme.

2    Exodus 31:8, KJV.

3    Hebrews 9:16-17, KJV.

4    William Marrion Branham, *An Exposition of the Seven Church Ages*, Jeffersonville, Indiana: Voice of God Recordings, 1960), p13.

5    T.S. Eliot, 'The Love Song of T. Alfred Prufrock'.

6    Revelation. 10:6, KJV.

7    Branham, The Table 2005, *Why Little Bethlehem*, Phoenix AZ, 1963, para 4.

8    Branham, The Table 2005, *Why Little Bethlehem*, para 4.

9    Branham, The Table 2005, *Christ Is The Mystery Of God Revealed*, Jeffersonville IN 1963, para 156.

10   Branham, The Table 2005, *I Will Restore Unto You Saith the Lord*, Los Angeles, CA, 1954, para E-12.

11   Branham, The Table 2005, *The Resurrection Of Lazarus*, Erie PA, 1951, paras E-34.

12   Branham, *Seven Church Ages*, p29.

13   Branham, The Table 2005, *The Resurrection Of Lazarus*, Erie PA, 1951, paras E-34.

14   Branham, *Future Home*, para 412, p51.

15   Branham, The Table 2005, *The Resurrection Of Lazarus*, Erie PA, 1951, paras E-33-E-35

16   Branham, The Table 2005, *The Resurrection Of Lazarus*, 1951, para E-35.

17   Branham, Table 2005, *Who Is This Melchisedec*, Jeffersonville IN, 1965, para 43.

18   Branham, The Table 2005, *Who Is This Melchisedec*, 43.

19   Branham, The Table 2005, *Things That Are To be*, RIALTO CA, 1965, para 101.

20   *The LaFontaine Family Live*, 'I Feel the Pull", Track11, DVD (Fountain Records, Toledo, Ohio, 1997).

21   Molefi Kete Asante, *The Afrocentric Idea*. Philadelphia: Temple University Press, 1987), 188.

22   Acts 2:38, KJV

23   Branham, The Table 2005, *Fellowship*, Chicago IL, 1955, para E-52.

24   Luke, 24:27, KJV.

25  Esther Addley, "No rest for the wicked: atheist churches go
    forth and multiply", The Guardian, London/Manchester,
    Saturday 14 September 2013, 13.

26  Branham, *Seven Church Ages*, 328-329.

27  Branham, *Seven Church Ages*, page 65.

# BIBLIOGRAPHY

## PRIMARY SOURCES

## ANCIENT SOURCES

**British Library, London**

Bohen, Peter von. *Introduction to the Book of Genesis*, trans. and ed. James Heywood. London: John Chapman, 1855.

Bunsen, C.C.J. *Philosophy of Ancient History*, London, 1854.

Bower, Archibald. *History of The Popes*, 7 Vols, 1748-66, London, 1807.

Graves, Kersey. *The World's Sixteen Crucified Saviours or Christianity Before Christ*. Boston, Mass: 1875.

Cusack, Mary Francis. *The Black Pope: A History of the Jesuits*, London: Marshall, Russell & Co; Brighton: D.B. Friend & Co, 1896.

Easton, M. G. *Illustrated Bible Dictionary and Treasury of Biblical history, biography, geography, doctrine and literature*. London : T. Nelson & Sons, 1893.

Herodotus. *The History of Herodotus*, trans. George Rawlinson. In *Great Books of The Western World*. Chicago: Encyclopaedia Britannica, 1952.

Iambibichus, of Chalcis. *Iamiblichus on the Mysteries of the Egyptians, Chaldeans, and Assyrians*. trans. Thomas Taylor, Chiswick, 1821.

Josephus, Flavius. The *Complete Works of Flavius Josephus*, trans. William Whinston. London and Edinburgh: Thomas Nelson, 1848.

Knox, John. *History of Reformation of the Church of Scotland*. Edinburgh, 1846-1848.

Landseer, Edwin, *Sabean Researches*, London, 1823.

Larkin, Clarence, *Dispensational Truth of God's Plan and Purpose in the Ages*, Philadelphia, London, 1920.

Laylard, Austin Henry, *Nineveh and Its Remains*, London, 1849.

__*Discoveries in the Ruins of Babylon and Nineveh*. London, 1853.

Petrie,William Matthew Flinders, *The Pyramids and The temples of Gezeh.* London: Field and Tuer, 1883.

Rosenmueller, Ernst Friedrich Carl. *The Biblical Geography of Central Asia, trans.* N. Morren, 17 vols, Edinburgh, 1832.

Seiss, Joseph Augustus, *A Miracle in Stone or The Great Pyramid of Egypt,* 14th edn Philadelphia: Porter and Coates, 1880.

Seiss, Joseph Augustus, *The Gospel in The Stars,* Philadelphia: J.B. Lippincott & Co, 1885.

Siculus, Diodorus. *Historical Library* ... in Fifteen Books to which are added *The Fragments of Diodorus.* Trans. G. Booth, 1814.

Smith, Uriah, *Daniel and the Revelation. The response of history to the voice of prophecy; a verse by verse study of the Book of Revelation,* London: International Tract Society, printed in U.S.A.. 1897

Smyth, Charles Piazzi, *Our Inheritance in The Great Pyramid,* W. Isbister: London: 1864.

Strong, James, *The Exhaustive Concordance of the Bible* ... together with a comparative concordance of the Authorised and Revised Versions. Also brief dictionaries of the Hebrew and Greek words of the original ,,, London: Hodder & Stoughton, 1894.

Taylor, John, *The Great Pyramid: Why Was It Built? And Who Built It.* London: [s.n.], 1859.

Tomkins, Peter, *Secrets of The Great Pyramid.* S.I. Harper and Row, 1971

Wilkinson, John Gardner. *Manners and Customs of the Ancient Egyptians,* 6 vol. London, 1837-41.


### Periodicals

Atallah, Ramez. "The Objective Witness to Conscience: An Egyptian Parallel to Romans 2:15." *Evangelical Review of Theology* 18 (1994): 204-13.

Bernal, Martin, "Black Athena and the APA." In Levine and Peradotto 1989, *Arethusa* 22, No. 17 (1989): 31.

__"Responses to Critical Reviews of *Black Athena,* Volume 1", *Journal of Mediterranean Archaeology* 3, No. 1 (1990): 133.

Blocher, Henri. "The Scope of Redemption and Modern Theology." *Scottish Bulletin of Evangelical Theology* 9 (1991): 80-103.

Boring, E. Eugene. "The Language of Universal Salvation in Paul." *Journal of Biblical Literature* 105 (1986): 269-92.

Bray, Gerald L. " Hell Eternal Punishment or Total Annihilation?" *Evangel* 10 (1992) 19-24.

Carson, D.A. "Current issues in Biblical Research: A New Testament Perspective." *Bulletin for Biblical Research* 5 (1995).

__"When Is Spirituality Spiritual?" *Journal of the Evangelical Theological Society* 37 (1994): 381-94.

Clemens, David M. "The Law of Sin and Death: Ecclesiastes and Genesis 1-3." *Themelios* 19, no. 3 (1994): 5-8.

Colson, Chuck. "Making the World Safe for Religion." *Christianity Today* 37 (November 8, (1993): 31-33.

Fackre, Gabriel. "I Believe in the Resurrection of the Body." *Interpretation* 46 (1992): 42-52.

Grothe, Jonathan F. "Confessing Christ in a Pluralistic Age." *Concordia Journal* 16 (1990): 217-30.

Grounds, Vernon C. "The Final State of the Wicked." *Journal of the Evangelical Theological Society* 24 (1981): 211-20.

Harris, Murray J. "The Translation of *Elohim* in Psalm 45:7-8." *Tyndale Bulletin* 35 (1984): 65-89

Heimerdinger, Jean-Marc. "The God of Abraham." *Vox Evangelica* 22 (1992): 41-55.

Keen, Ralph. "The Limits of Power and Obedience in the Later Calvin." *Calvin Theological Journal* 27 (1992): 252-76.

Moltmann, Jurgen. "Christianity in the Third Millennium." *Theology Today* 51(1994): 75-89.

Moore, Ernest. "'Outside' and 'Inside': Paul and Mark." *The Expository Times* 103

Newbigin, Lesslie. "Certain Faith: What Kind of Certainty?" *Tyndale Bulletin* 44(1993): 339-50.

__"Confessing Christ in a Multi-Religion Society." *Scottish Bulletin of Evangelical Theology* 12 (1994): 125-36.

__"Can the West Be Converted?" *International Bulletin of Missionary Research* 11(1987): 2-7.

Peters, Ted. "The Lutheran Distinctiveness in Mission to a Pluralistic World." *Dialog* (1983): 18-29.

Pinnock, Clark. "The Role of the Spirit in Interpretation. *Journal of the Evangelical Society* 36 (1993): 491-97.

Piryns, Ernest D. "Current Roman Catholic Views of Other Religions." *Missionalia* 13 (1985): 55-62.

Placher, William C. "Revealed to Reason: Theology as 'Normal Science." *Christian Century* (February 1, 1992): 192-95.

Proctor, John. "The Gospel from Athens: Paul's Speech Before the Areopagus and the Evangel for Today." *Evangel* 10 (1992): 69-

72.

Tinker, Melvin. "Battle for the Mind." *Churchman* 106 (1992): 34-44.

Weathers, Robert A. "Leland Ryken's Literary Approach to Biblical Interpretation:

Williams, Stephen. "Revelation and Reconciliation: A Tale of Two Concepts." *European Journal of Theology* 3, no. 1 (1994): 35-42.


**The Spoken Word**

Branham, William Marrion, The Cruelty of Sin, And The Penalty That It Cost To Rid Sin From Our Lives (1953), *The Spoken Word* 25, No. 4 (1990): 7.

__Revelation, Book of Symbols (1956) *The Spoken Word*, 13, No. 6R (1957; 1992 reprint): 5.

__Oneness, *The Spoken Word*, 10, No.2 (1962): 19.

__The Third Exodus 1963), *The Spoken Word* 2, 21R (1967; 2002 reprint): 19-22.

__Christ is the Mystery of God Revealed, *Edmonton Bible Way House* 3, No.7 (1963); 17-20

__How Can I Overcome (1963), *The Spoken Word* 4, No.12 (1969; 2002 reprint):12.

__The Super Sign (1963), *The Spoken Word* 17, No.7 (1982; 1985 reprint): 7.

__Why Little Bethlehem (1963), *The Spoken Word* 19, No. 13R (1984; 1998 reprint): 4-20

__Why? (1963), *The Spoken Word* 20, No. 8 (1985): 14.

__The Future Home Of The Heavenly Bridegroom and The Earthly Bride (1964) *The Spoken Word* 3, No. 5R, (1968; 2001 reprint): 5-6.

__God Is His Own Interpreter (1964), *The Spoken Word* 8, No.6 (1973; 2001 reprint) 14

__The Unveiling of God (1964), *The Spoken Word* 9, No.1R (1974; 2001 reprint): 10.

__Proving His Word (1964) *The Spoken Word* 9, No.6 (1974; 2001 reprint): 30.

__His Unfailing Word Of Promise (1964), *The Spoken Word* 15, No.3 (1980; 2001 reprint): 6.

__Sirs, We Would See Jesus (1964), *The Spoken Word* 19, No. 8 (1984; 2001 reprint): 4.

__A Greater Than Solomon Is Here Now (1964), *The Spoken Word*

19, No. 10 (1984; 2001 reprint): 7.

__The Token (1964), *The Spoken Word* 19, No. 12 (1984; 2001 reprint): 64): 6.

__Shalom (1964), *The Spoken Word* 22, No.1 (1987; 2001 reprint): 6.

__God has Provided Way For This Day (1964), *The Spoken Word* 22, No. 6 (1988; 2001 reprint): 11.

__The Patriarch Abraham (1964), *The Spoken Word* 22, No. 7 (1987; 2001 reprint): 3.

__Countdown (1964), *The Spoken Word* 22, No.9 (1987; 2001 reprint): 5-6.

__When Their Eyes Were Opened They Knew Him (1964), *The Spoken Word* 22, No.15 (1987; 2001 reprint): 13.

__The Investments (1964), *The Spoken Word* 22, No. 17 (1987; 2001 reprint): 10.

__Possessing The Gate Of The Enemy After Trial (1964), *The Spoken Word* 23, No. 6 (1988; 2001 reprint): 3.

__Jehovah-Jireh II (1964), *The Spoken Word* 23, No. 9 (1988; 2001 reprint): 2-3.

__Spiritual Amnesia (1964), *The Spoken Word* 23, No.14 (1988; 2001 reprint): 1-30.

__Then Jesus Came and Called (1964), *The Spoken Word* 36, No.3 (2001): 14.

__Satan's Eden (1965), *The Spoken Word* 2, No.20R (1967; 1990 reprint): 7.

__Events Made Clear By Prophecy (1965), *The Spoken Word* 3, 12R (1977; 2001 reprint):1

__It Is The Rising Of The Sun (1965), *The Spoken Word* 3, 12R (1968; 2001 reprint): 12-14.

__Things That Are To Be (1965), *The Spoken Word* 4, 6R (1969; 2001 reprint): 29-31.

__Christ Is Revealed in His Own Word (1965), *The Spoken Word* 4, No.10R (1969; 1990 reprint): 23-24

__The Anointed Ones at the End Time (1965), *The Spoken Word* 5, No. 3R (1970; 2000 reprint): 28.

__Who Is This Melchisedec? *The Spoken Word* 5, No.10R, (1965).

__The Rapture (1965), *The Spoken Word* 5, 14R (1970; 2001 reprint)

__The Seed Is Not Heir With The Shuck (1965), *The Spoken Word* 6, No. 4R (1971; 2001 reprint): p, 13, 14, 18, 28

__Leadership (1965), *The Spoken Word* 7, No. 7 (1972; 2001

reprint): 31

__Seed of Discrepancy (1965), *The Spoken Word*, 12, No.5 (1977; 2001 reprint).

__Power of Transformation, *The Spoken Word* 17, No.1, (1965).

__God's Power to Transform (1965), *The Spoken Word*, 16, No.5 (1981; 2001 reprint): 13

__Doors In Doors (1965), *The Spoken Word* 17, No. 3 (1982, 2001 reprint): 12.

__The Seed Shall Not Be Heir With The Shuck 1965), *The Spoken Word* 18, No. 5 (1983.; reprint 2001): 12-13

## II. SECONDARY SOURCES

### A. BOOKS

Abbott, Walter M. *Documents of Vatican II* (Baltimore, Maryland: The American Press, 1966),

Achtemeier, Paul J. *The Inspiration of Scripture: Problems and Proposals*. Philadelphia: Westminster Press, 1980.

Adams, Kevin. *A Diary of Revival. The Outbreak of the 1904 Welsh Awakening*, Farnham, Surrey: Crusade for World Revival (CRW), 1904).

Aldwinckle, Russell F. *Jesus-A Savior or the Savior? Religious Pluralism in Christian Perspective*. Macon: Mercer University Press, 1982.

__ *More Than a Man: A Study in Christology*. Grand Rapids: Eerdmans, 1976.

Anderson, Allan, *An Introduction to Pentecostalism* (Cambridge: Cambridge University Press, 2004.

Anderson, Robert Mapes , *Vision of the Disinherited: The Making of American Pentecostalism*, New York/Oxford: Oxford University Press, 1979.

Anglican-Roman Catholic International Commission, *Mary: Grace and Hope in Christ* Harrisburg PA; London: Morehouse, 2005.

Ayala, Fransisco J, *Darwin and Intelligent Design*. Minneapolis: Fortress Press, 2006

Baeta, Christian Gonclaves. *Christianity in tropical Africa. Studies presented at VII International African Seminar Ghana University April 1965*. Oxford: Oxford University Press, 1968.1977.

Baker, Rob and Gray, Henry (eds), *Merton and Sufism: The Untold Story*, Louisville. Kentucky: Fons Vitae, first edition, 2000.

Bantock, Geoffrey Herman, Culture, *Industrialisation and Education*,

London: Routledge & Kegan Paul, New York: Humanities Press, 1968.

Barraclough, Geoffrey, *History in a Changing World*, Oxford: Basil Blackwell, 1955.

Barker, Margaret. *The Book of Enoch and its Influence On Christianity*, London: SPCK, 1988.

Barrett, C.K. *New Testament Christianity for Africa and the World*, ed. M.E. Glasswell and E.W. Fasholé-Luke, London: SPCK, 1974.

Bartleman, Frank. *Azusa Street: Roots of Modern Day Pentecost*, 2nd edit, South Plainfield, New Jersey: Bridge Publishing Inc., 1996.

Bartleman, Frank. *The Azusa Street Revival: An Eye Witness Account*, Moreno Valley, California: Revival School, 2008.

Barton, John. *What Is the Bible?* London: SPCK, 1991.

Bass, S. Jonathan, *Blessed are the peacemakers: Martin Luther King, Jr.*, eight white religious leaders, and the "Letter from Birmingham Jail" (Baton Rouge, Louisiana: Louisiana State University Press, 2001.

Bauval, Robert, and Adrian Gilbert. *The Orion Mystery: Unlocking the Secrets of the Pyramids.* London: Heinemann, 1994.

Bebbington, David. *Patterns in History: A Christian Perspective on Historical Thought.* 2d ed. Grand Rapids: Baker, [1990].

Becker, Markus. *Message Companion: The Changing of the Ministry of William Branham from 1959-1965*, Bieselsberg, Germany: Versammlung bibelgl ubiger Christen, 2013.

Ben-Jochannan, Yosef, *African Origins of The Major "Western Religions.* New York: Alkebu-Lan Books Associates, 1970.

Bennett, Lerone, *The Challenge of Blackness*, Chicago: Johnson Publishing, 1972.

Berkouwer, C.C. *General Revelation*. Grand Rapids: Wn. B. Erdmans, 1953.

Berlin, Isaiah, *Historical Inevitability*, London: Oxford University Press, 1954.

Bernal, Martin. *Black Athena: The Afroasiatic Roots of Classical Civilization*, vol .1 London: Free Association Books, 1987.

___ *Black Athena Writes Back: Martin Bernal Responds to His Critics*, ed. David Chioni Moore. Durham and London: Duke University Press, 2001.

Best, Ernest. *Interpreting Christ*. Edinburgh: T & T Clark, 1993.

Blanchard, John. *Whatever Happened to Hell?* Durham: Evangelical Press, 1993.

Bloch-Hoell,Nils, *The Pentecostal Movement: Its Origin, Development, and Distinctive Character,* New York: Humanities Press, 1965.

Blyden, Edward. *African Life and Customs.* London: C.M. Philips, 1908.

__ *Christianity, Islam and the Negro Race.* Baltimore: Black Classic, 1994.

Bonner, Gerald. *St Augustine of Hippo: Life and Controversies,* rev.ed. Norwich: Canterbury Press, 1986.

Boulaga, F. Eboussi. *Christianity Without Fetishes: An African Critique and Recapture of Christianity.* trans. Robert Barr. New York: Orbis Books, 1984.

Boule, Marcellos and Henri Vallois. *Les Homes Fossile (Fossil Men, 1952).* trans. Michael Bullock, 4th ed. New York: Dryden Press, 1957.

Bowen, Malcolm. *True Science Agrees With The Bible* (Bromley: Sovereign, 1998.

Boyd, Paul C. *The African Origin of Christianity: A Biblical and Historical Account.* London: Karia Press, 1991.

__ *The African Origin of Christianity: Its Place in Modern R.E.* London: Karia Press, 1991.

__ *The Pupil Exclusion Maze: More Answers Than Questions.* London: QEC Publications, 1999.

Branham, William Marrion. *An Exposition of the Seven Church Ages.* Jeffersonville: Voice of God Recordings, privately printed, 1965.

__ *The Revelation of the Seven Seals.* Jeffersonville: Voice of God Recordings, privately printed, 1963.

__ *My Redeemer Liveth (1955),* [DVD-ROM], Jeffersonville: Voice of God Recordings, 2003.

__ *Hebrews.* Jeffersonville: Voice of God Recordings, 1957.

__ *Thy Seed Shall Possess The Gate of The Enemy* (1962), [DVD-ROM], Jeffersonville: Voice of God Recordings, 2003.

__ *At Thy Word (1953),* [DVD-ROM], Jeffersonville: Voice of God Recordings, 2003.

__ *The Revelation Of The Seven Seals* (1963), Jeffersonville: Voice of God Recordings, 1967; 2001 reprint.

__ *Interveil (1956)* [DVD-ROM], Jeffersonville: Voice of God Recordings, 2003.

__ *Conduct Order Doctrine.* Jeffersonville: Voice of God Recordings, 1974; 1991 reprint

__ *The Masterpiece.* Jeffersonville, Indiana: Voice of God Recordings,

1964.

Bromiley, Geoffrey. ed. *The International Standard Bible Encyclopaedia*, Vol .2, Grand Rapids, Michigan: Eerdsmans, 1982.

Brownlee, W. C., *Secret Instructions of The Jesuits* (1841), California: Ulan Press, 2012.

Burgess, Stanley M.; McGee, Gary B.; Alexander, Patrick H. *Dictionary of Pentecostal and Charismatic Movements* (Grand Rapids, MI: Zondervan, 1988)

Burry, John Bagnall. *Edward Gibbon, The History of the Decline and Fall of the Roman Empire*. Lee (Sidney): Methuen Standard Library, 1905.

Butterfield, H. *The Origins of Modern Science 1300-1800*. New York: Macmillan, 1960.

Campbell, William S. *Paul's Gospel in an Intercultural Context*. Frankfurt-am-Main: Peter Lang, 1991.

Campolo, Anthony, *Letters to a Young Evangelica,*New York: Basic Books, 2006.

Capt, E. Raymond, *The Great Pyramid Decoded*, Thousand Oaks, California: Artisan Sales, 1978.

Carey, Ken. *The Starseed Transmissions,* San Francisco, California: HarperOne,1992.

Carr, E.H, *What Is History?,* ed. R.W. Davies, 2nd ed, London: Penguin, 1987.

Carson, D. A, ed. *Biblical Interpretation and the Church*. Exeter: Paternoster, 1984.

Carson, D.A., Douglas J. Moo, and Leon Morris. *An Introduction to the New Testament*. Grand Rapids: Zondervan, 1992.

Carson, D.A, *The Gagging of God: Christianity Confronts Pluralism*. Leicester: Apollo (an imprint of Intervarsity Press), 1996.

Catholic University of America, *New Catholic Encyclopedia*, 2nd, Michigan: Gale Group, 2003.

Cesaire, Aime. *Notebook of A Return to My Native Land*, trans. Mireille Rosello, and Annie Pritchard, Newcastle-upon-Tyne: Bloodaxe, 1995.

Chapman, Colin. *The Christian Message in a Multi-Faith Society*. Oxford: Latimer House, 1992.

Chawner, Charles Austin. *The Life Story and Ministry of Rev. William Branham*. Nelspruit: Emmanuel Press, 1952?

Chiniquy, Charles. *Fifty Years In The Church of Rome* (Ontario, California: Chick Publications, 1982).

Chinweizu. *Decolonising the African Mind*. Lagos, Nigeria: Pero Press, 1987.

Clapham, Andrew, *Human Rights: A Very Short Introduction*, Oxford /New York: Oxford University Press, 2007.

Covey, Stephen R., *The Seven Habits of Highly Effective People*, London. New York: Simon & Schuster, 1992.

Cruden, Alexander. *Complete Concordance to The Old & New Testaments*. Guildford. Lutterworth *Press*. London: Bagster, 1977.

Davidson, David, *The Great Pyramid: Its Divine Message*. London: Williams and Norgate, 1924.

Davis, Kenneth C, *America's Hidden History: untold tales of the first pilgrims, fallen heroes, and forgotten fighters from Americas hidden history*, New York: Smithsonian Books/Collins, 2008.

De Mello, Anthony. *Sadhana : A Way to God – Christian Exercises in Eastern Form* (St. Louis [Mo.]: Institute of Jesuit Sources in cooperation with Gujarat Sahitya Prakash, Anand Press, 1980;

Department of Education and Science, *History from 5 to 16: Curriculum Matters*, London: HMSO, 1988.

Diodorus Siculus, *Library of History*, Vol.II, Book III, trans. C.H. Old father, Boston, Mass: Harvard University Press, 1933-35.

Diop, Cheikh Anta, *The African Origin of Civilization : Myth or Reality*, ed and trans. Mercer Cook (Westport: Lawrence Hill, 1974

Diop, Cheik Anta.*Civilization or Barbarism: An Authentic Anthropology*, ed. Harold J. Salemson and Marjolijn de Jasper, and trans.Yaa-Lengi Meema Ngemi ( Brooklyn, New York: Lawrence Hill, 1991

Dworkin, Ronald, *Taking Rights Seriously*, London: Duckworth, 1977.

Edwards, Jonathan. *Sinners in the Hands of an Angry God*. Phillipsburg: Presbyterian and Reformed, 1992 [1741].

Edwards, Tilden. *Spiritual Friend: Reclaiming the Gift of Spiritual Direction*, New York: Paulist Press, 1980.

Fanon, Frantz, *Black Skin, White Masks* (New York : Grove Press, 1967.

Fanon, Frantz, *The Wretched of the Earth*, Middlesex: Penguin, 1967.

Felder, Reverend Cain Hope, *The Original African Heritage Bible*, King James Version Nashville: The James C. Winston Publishing Company, 1993.

Fitzgerald, Edward. *Rubáiyát of Omar Khayyám: a Critical Edition*, ed. Christopher Decker. Charlottesville: London: University Press of Virginia, 1977.

Foucault, Michel, *Power & Knowledge: Selected Interviews and Other*

*Writings, 1972-1977*, New York: Pantheon, 1977.

Frankl, Viktor E. *Man's Search for Meaning*, London. Sydney. Auckland. Johannesburg: Rider, 2011.

Gartner, Bertil. *The Areopagus Speech and Natural Revelation*. Uppsala: C. W. K. Gleerup, 1955.

Graves, Robert, and Omar Ali-Shah. *Rubáiyát of Omar Khayyám*, Harmondsworth: Penguin, 1972.

Green, Joel B., and Max Turner, ed. *Jesus of Nazareth: Lord and Christ. Essays on the Historical Jesus and New Testament Christology.* Grand Rapids, Eerdmans, 1994.

Groves, Charles Pelham, *The Planting of Christianity in Africa*, London: Lutterworth Press, 1958.

Harrell, David Edwin, *All Things Are Possible: The Healing and Charismatic Revivals in Modern America*, Bloomington, Indiana: Indiana University Press, 1978.

Harris, Marvin, *Cultural Materialism: The Struggle for a Science of Culture*, California: Altamira Press, 2001.

Hazeltine, Rachel C., *How did it happen! A History of the early Christian Churches written by deduction; deduction means just a remaking of events from all of the data collected*, Santa Cruz, California: Voice in the Wilderness, 1958.

Hegel, Georg Wilhelm Friedrich, *Philosophy of Right*, trans. Thomas Malcolm Knox, Oxford: Clarendon Press, 1942.

Hendrie, Edward. *Solving the Mystery of Babylon the Great*, Virginia: Great Mountain Publishing, 2012.

Herbermann, Charles, (ed), *The Catholic Encyclopaedia* New York: The Encyclopaedia Press 1913.

Hislop, Rev Alexander. *The Two Babylons or The Papal Worship*. London: A & C Black, 1926.

Hollenweger, Walter J, *Pentecostalism: Origins and Developments Worldwide*, Peabody, MA: Hendrickson Publications, 1997.

Horn, Tom and Putnam, Chris. *Exo-Vaticana: Petrus Romanus, Project LUCIFER (2013)*, Crane, Missouri: Defender Publishing Group, 2013.

Hudson, Winthrop, *The Great Tradition of the American Churches*, New York: Harper, 1963

Hyatt, Eddie L, *2000 Years of Charismatic Christianity*, Lake Mary, Florida: Charisma House, formerly Strang Communications, 2002.

Ignatius of Loyola, *The constitutions of the Society of Jesus*. Translated by George E. Ganss, St. Louis. Institute of Jesuit Sources. 1970.

Illich, Ivan D, *Deschooling*, New York: Harper and Row; London: Calder and Boyars, 1971.

Jackson, John, *Introduction to African Civilizations*. New York: Citadel Press/Kensington Publishing Corp., 1994 [1970].

Jacques, Martin, *When China Rules The World: The End of the Western World and the Birth of a New Global Order*, London: Allen Lane. 2012.

James, George G.M. *Stolen Legacy*. San Francisco: Richardson Associates, 1976.

Jewett, Paul K. *God, Creation, and Revelation: A Neo-Evangelical Theology*. Grand Rapids; Eerdmans, 1991.

Jones, Lesley S, & Michael J. Reiss, (eds), *Teaching about Scientific Origins: Taking Account of Creationism*, New York: Peter Lang, 2007

Jorgensen, Owen. *Supernatural: The Life of William Branham*, Vol. I., Tuscan: Tucson Tabernacle, 1994.

Josephus, Flavius, *The Antiquities of the Jews*, Vol. 1 trans. William Whiston, Charleston, South Carolina: Bibliobazaar, 2007.

Kaiser, Christopher. *Creation and the History of Science*. Grand Rapids: Eerdmans, 1991.

King, Martin Luther Jr, *Letter from Birmingham Jail*, Stamford, Conn.: Overbrook Press, 1968.

Klein, Ken, [DVD] *The Great Pyramid: Lost Legend of Enoch*. Ken Klein Productions, 2006.

Martin Luther, Jr, *Why We Can't Wait*, New York: New American Library Harper & Row, 1964.

Knox, John. *The History of the Reformation of the Religion within the Realm of Scotland*. ed. Charles John Gutherie. Edinburgh: Banner of Truth Trust, 1982.

Krapohl. Robert H & Charles Lippy, *The Evangelicals: A Historical, Thematic, and Biographical Guide*, Westport Conn. London: Greenwood Press, 1999,

Kush, Indus Khamit, *Enoch The Ethiopian: The Lost Prophet of The Bible*. Brooklyn, New York: A & B Publishers Group, 2000.

Laslett, Peter, *The World We Have Lost*. London: Methuen & Co Ltd, 1965

Leade, Jane. *The Revelation of Revelations*. Edinburgh: Magnum Opus Hermetic, 1981, [1683].

Lemon, Michael C, *The Discipline of History and the History of*

*Thought*, London: Routledge, 1995.

Lindberg, David C. and Numbers, *God and Nature: historical essays on the encounter between Christianity and science.* Berkeley; London: University of California Press, 1986.

Lindsay, Gordon G, *Branham: A Man Sent From God*, Jeffersonville, Indiana: WBEA, 1950.

Locke, John *Second Treaties of Government* [1690], ed. Thomas P. Peardon, Indianapolis: Bobbs-Merrill, 2011.

Loyola, Ignatius, *The Spiritual Exercise*, trans. Anthony Mottola, Garden City, New York: Doubleday, 1964.

Mandela, Nelson Rolihlahla, *Long Walk to Freedom: The Autobiography of Nelson Mandela* London: Little Brown and Company (UK) 1994.

Manning, Brennan, *A Glimpse of Jesus*, London: HarpeCollins, reprint edition, 2004.

Manson, Neil A. (ed), *God and Design: The teleological argument and modern science*, London: Routledge, 2003.

Marshall, I. Howard. *The Origins of New Testament Christology.* Downers Grove: Intervarsity Press, 1976.

___ *I Believe in the Historical Jesus.* Grand Rapids: Eerdmans 1979.

Marx, Karl, *The Eighteenth Brumaire of Louis Bonaparte*, trans. Daniel De Leon, New York: International Publishing, 1898.

Marx, *The Eighteenth Brumaire of Louis Bonaparte*, trans. Eden & Cedar Paul, London, G. Allen & Unwin, 1926.

Marx, Karl, *Capital: A Critique of Political Economy*, vol. 1, trans. Ben Fowkes, Harmondsworth: Penguin, 1976.

Marx, Karl and Friedrich Engles *Gesamtausgabe*, Berlin: Dietz, 1972.

McCarthy, Burke. *The Suppressed Truth About the Assassination of Abraham Lincoln* (1922), Hong Kong: Forgotten Books, 2012

McConnell, Dan. R, *A Different Gospel*, Peabody, MA: Hendrickson Publishers Inc., 1988.

McGrath, Alister. *In the Beginning: The Story of the King James Bible.* London: Hodder and Stoughton, 2001.

Mead, Sidney E. *The Lively Experiment*, New York: Harper & Row, 1963.

Metzger, Bruce and Coogan, Michael, ed., *The Oxford Companion to the Bible*, Oxford: Oxford University Press, 1993.

Milik, J.T. ed., *The Books of Enoch, Aramaic Fragments of Qumram Cave 4*, Oxford: Oxford University Press, 1976.

Moore, Richard. *The Darwin Legend*, London: Hodder & Stoughton,

1995.

Morgan, Robert, and John Barton. *Biblical Interpretation*. Oxford: Oxford University Press, 1988.

Mudimbe, V.Y, *The Invention of Africa: Gnosis, Philosophy, and the Order of Knowledge*, Bloomington and Indianapolis: Indiana University Press: London: James Currey. 1988.

Munford, C. J, *Race & Civilization: Rebirth of Black Centrality*, Trenton: Africa World Press, 2001.

Nibley, Hugh. *Enoch the prophet*, Utah: Deseret Book, 1986.

National Advisory Committee on Creative and Cultural Education, *All Our Futures: Creativity, Culture & Education*, London: DFE and Employment, 1999.

Norwich, John Julius, *The Popes: A History*, London: Vintage Books, 2011.

Odeberg, Hugo, ed. *Enoch or the Hebrew Book of Enoch*, New York: KTAV Publishing House, 1973.

Otto, Rudolph, *The Idea of the Holy*, New York: Oxford University Press, 1961.

Oxford University Press *Oxford English Dictionary*, 2nd edit, Oxford: Oxford University Press, 2005.

Paine, Tom, *Rights of Man*, Oxford: Oxford Paperbacks, 2008.

Painter, Franklin, Verzelius, Newton. *A History of Education*, New York: D. Appleton and Company, 1903.

Parham, Sarah T, *The Life of Charles F. Parham: Founder of the Apostolic Movement*, Joplin, Mo.: Tri-State Printing Co., 1930.

Phelps, Jon. *Vatican Assassins*, 2nd (ed), Newmanstown, Pennsylvania: Eric Jon Phelps, 2001.

Powell, James M. *Innocent III: Vicar of Christ or Lord of the World?* Washington D. C: Catholic University of American Press, 1994 [1963].

Questar, Inc [DVD] *The Exodus Revealed, Search For The Red Sea Crossing*, Chicago: Discovery Media Productions, MMII.

Raab, Dominic, *The Assault On Liberty: What Went Wrong With Rights*, London: Fourth Estate, 2009, 3.4.

Reid, Daniel G, Bruce L Shelley (Editor), Robert D Linder (Editor) *Dictionary of Christianity In America*, Downers Grove, IL: InterVarsity Press, 1990.

Roberts, Alexander and James Donaldson. trans. and ed. *The Ante-Nicene Father: Translations of the Writings of the Fathers Down to A.D. 325*. New York: Grand Rapids. Eerdmans. 1979-1986.

Robertson, A.H., *Human Rights in the World: An Introduction to the Study of the International Protection of Human Rights*, second edition, Manchester: Manchester University Press, 1977.

Rogers, Jack B., and Donald K. McKim. *The Authority and Interpretation of the Bible: An Historical Approach*. San Francisco: Harper & Row, 1979.

Saussy, Frederick Tupper. *Rulers of Evil: Useful Knowledge About Governing Bodies*, San Francisco, California: Harper Collins, 2001.

Schaff, P. (ed), *A Select Library of the Nicene and Post-Nicene Fathers of the Christian Church*, 14 vol, New York: Christian Literature Co., 1892.

Schick. Eduard. *The Revelation of St John*. London. Sheed and Ward. 1977.

Schneiders, Sandra M. *The Revelatory Text: Interpreting the New Testament as Sacred Scripture*. San Francisco/London: Harper Collins, 1991.

Scofield, C.I. *The Scofield Study Bible Authorised King James Version: The Original Scofield Bible*. New York: Oxford University Press, 1909.

Scott, Joe & Fiona Reynoldson. *The Making of The United Kingdom*, Oxford: Heineman Educational, 1992),

Smith, Joe, Angela, *Generation: Remembering the Life of a Prophet*, Elizabethton, Indiana, Believers International, 2006.

Smith, Timothy L., *Revivalism and Social Reform*, New York: Harper & Row, 1965.

Stadsklev, Julius, *William Branham: A Prophet Visits South Africa*, Minneapolis: Julius Stadskley, 1952.

Stewart, Don, *Only Believe: An Eyewitness Account of the Great Healing Revival of the 20th Century*, Shippensburg, PA: Destiny Image Publishers Inc., 1999.

Stanford, Miles J, *Fox's Book of Martyrs*, edit. William Byron Forbush, Grand Rapids, Michigan, 1926.

Sweet, Leonard. *Quantum Spirituality: A Postmodern Apologetic* , Dayton, Ohio: United Theological Seminary, 1999.

Synan, Vinson ed., *Aspects of Pentecostal-Charismatic Origins*, Plainfield NJ: Lagos International, 1975.

Troyna, Barry and Jenny Williams, ed. *Racism, Education and the State*. Kent: Groom Helm, 1986.

Yungen, A Ray. *Time of Departing; How Ancient Mystical Practices are*

*Uniting Christians with the World's Religions*, Eureka, Montana: Lighthouse Trails Publishing, 2006.

Wakefield, James L. *Sacred Listening: Discovering the Spiritual Exercises of Ignatius Loyola*, Ada, Michigan: Baker Books, 2006.

Wallace, Howard N. *The Eden Narrative*. Harvard Semitic Monographs, vol. 32. Atlanta: Scholars Press, 1985.

Watson, Thomas Edward. *Political and Economic Handbook*, Riverside, California: Ulan Press, 2012.

Weaver, C. Douglas. *The Healer-Prophet, William Marrion Branham: A study of the Prophetic in American Pentecostalism*. Macon, Ga: Mercer University Press, 2000.

Webster, Noah, *Webster's Concise Dictionary of the English Language*, New York: A.L. Burt & Co., 1919.

Williams, Raymond, *Culture and Society 1780-1950*, Harmondsworth: Penguin, 1982

__ *The Sociology of Culture*. New York: Schocken Books, 1982.

Wollstonecraft, Mary, *A Vindication of the Rights of Woman and A Vindication of the Rights of Men* (Oxford: Oxford University Press, 2008.

# RECOMMENDED READING AND WEBSITES

## Reading

Branham, William Marrion. *An Exposition of the Seven Church Ages*. Jeffersonville, Indiana: Voice of God Recordings, privately printed, 1965[available at http://branham.org/opc/opc.aspx by typing *Seven Church Ages* into the Product Search box to order]

Branham, William Marrion. *The Revelation of The Seven Seals* (1963), Jeffersonville, Indiana: Voice of God Recordings 1967; 2001 reprint [available at http://branham.org/opc/opc.aspx by typing Seven Seals into Product Search box to place order]

Hislop, Rev Alexander. *The Two Babylons or The Papal Worship*. London: A & C Black, 1926 [available at amazon.com & leading booksellers].

C. I. Scofield. *The Holy Bible, Authorised King James Version* (1909), Centennial Edition, Jeffersonville, Indiana: Voice of God Recordings, 2009 [available at http://branham.org/opc.aspx by typing Scofield Bible]

Bible Expo International, Inc./BibleExpo.com, *The Holy Bible: La Sainte Bible* , Authorised King James English Version (1611) & Louis Segond French Version (1910), Jacksonville, Florida: The New International Version Bilingual Bible [available at http://www.mcssl.com/store/bible-expo-international]

## Websites

**French/English Messages.** Messages spoken by William Marrion Branham and translated into French – http://www.laparoleparlee.com/message_pour_l_epouse_c.ws this is an excellent website for those who wish to listen to the Message in French and or in English and French or French and English.

**The Great Pyramid/Bible Believers.** The following link is a must-read for it explores in some detail the prophet's pronouncement that The Great Pyramid was built by Enoch: http://www.biblebelievers.org.au/great.htm

**Dimensions of The Great Pyramid/ Bible Believers.** This link is a brilliant and refreshing discourse on the dimensions of The Great Pyramid in line with the Prophet's Message: http://www.biblebelievers.org.au/pyramid.htm#The Great Pyramid – Reflections in Time

**The Great Pyramid- Lost Legend of Enoch/ Ken Klein Productions.** An impressive link to the DVD which is well researched: http://www.youtube.com/watch?v=V3OxRuIMLKE

# GLOSSARY

## A

AARON , the eldest son of Amram and Jochebed, a daughter of Levi and older brother of Moses (Ex. 6:20).

ABEL, a breath, or vanity, the second son of Adam and Eve. He was put to death by his brother Cain (Gen. 4:1-16).

ABIGAIL, The name of the woman David married after Nabal's death (1 Samuel 25:14-42). The sister of David, and wife of Jether an Ishmaelite was also called Abigail (1 Chr. 2:16, 17). She was the mother of Amasa (2 Sam. 17:25).

ABIMELECH, father of a king, a common name of the Philistine kings (Gen. 20:1-18) as "Pharaoh" was of the Egyptian kings.

ABOMINATION, defile, unclean, e.g. Egyptians thought they were defiled when they ate with strangers (Gen. 43:32). The Jews copied this practice, and believed that it was unlawful to eat or drink with foreigners (John 18:28; Acts 10:28; 11:3).

ABRAHAM, means father of a multitude, ie, father of many nations. He was a son of Terah (Gen. 11:27). God gave Abraham part of His Name, that is, the H-i-m in El: Elo-him. The H-i-m in God's name is the same as the H-a-m at the end of Abraham's name. Thus, Abraham represented a type of the Father, God.

ABRAM, exalted father. (see ABRAHAM.). First called Abram (Gen. 11:26) then God changed his name to Abraham (Gen. 17:5).

ABSALOM, father of peace; i.e., "peaceful" David's son by Maacah (2 Sam. 3:3; 1 Kings 1:6).

ACCAD, fortress, the high land or mountains, a city in the land of Shinar (Judg. 1:3).

ACCUSER, Satan is called the "accuser of the brethren" (Rev.12:10; Job 1:6).

ACHAN, called also Achar, a troubler (1 Chr. 2:7), known for stealing silver, gold and the Babylonian garment which he hid in his tent (Josh. 7:19-26).

ACRE means a yoke, a space of ground which could be ploughed by a yoke of oxen in a day. It is about an acre of our measure (Isa.

5:10; 1 Sam. 14:14).

ACTS OF THE APOSTLES is the Acts of The Holy Spirit in the Apostles. It was the way the Holy Spirit made the apostles act by the working of signs, wonders, and miracles through them. In (Luke 24:49), Jesus told his disciples, "tarry ye in the city of Jerusalem until you're endued with power from on high" and in (Acts 1:8), He said, "You shall receive power after that the Holy Spirit is come upon you. You'll be witnesses of Me in Jerusalem, Judaea, Samaria, and the uttermost parts of the earth."

ADAM, the generic name for man or humankind. Another form of Adam is Adamah, meaning "earth" or "ground." Sometimes it is used to denote "red" or "handsome". The first Adam lost (Gen. chaps 1-3), (I. Cor.1.45; I Tim. 2.13) the second Adam, Christ, restored again to the human race (I Cor. 15.45).

ADOPTION, placing a son (Eph 1:5-9); (Rom. 8: 15-23). A Christian is predestinated unto the adoption of sons and has to be child trained and tutored by the Holy Spirit before they are adopted (Gal. 5: 17-25).

ADULTERY, a married woman who is unfaithful to her husband or a married man who is unfaithful to his wife. An adulterer was a man who had unlawful intercourse with a married woman.

ADVERSARY, Satan, the devil (1 Pet. 5:8), the enemy, an opponent (Luke.13:17; 1 Kings 5:4).

AGABUS, a vindicated prophet. He prophesied at Antioch of an approaching famine (Acts. 11:27, 28).

AGE, man's allotted time on the earth (Gen. 47:28); continuous period (Eph. 2:7; Col. 1:26) such as the Millennium, that Grand Age, namely, Eternity identified by evidence of the eternal life of the redeemed in their glorified bodies inhabiting the New Jerusalem on earth.

AHAB, uncle, son of Omri, King of Israel (1 Kings 16:29), and a false prophet (Jer. 29:21). Married Jezebel an idolater (I. Kings 16:31).

ALPHA, the first letter of the Greek alphabet, as Omega is the last.

AMALEK, dweller in a valley, Esau's grandson (Gen. 36:12; 1 Chr. 1:36); leader of the Idumean tribe (Gen. 36:16).

AMASA, burden. He was the son of Abigail (2 Sam 17:25), who was sister to King David (1 Chr 2:16, 17).

AMBASSADOR, one who goes on a mission, (Josh. 9:4; Jer. 49:14); a "messenger",(Isa. 30:4; Ezek. 17:15) or a sent one, missionary, representative chosen by God to do His will (2 Cor. 5:20; Eph. 6:20).

AMEN, so be it. It is a Hebrew word meaning firm, and faithful (Rev. 3:14).

AMISH, part of the Mennonite churches and life; an old fashioned way of life following the fundamental teachings of the Bible. They came about as a result of a split with the Anabaptists in Switzerland led by their founder Jakob Ammann in 1693.

ANABAPTIST comes from the Greek word *anabaptista*, meaning "one who baptises over again". Anabaptists were said to be Christians of the Radical Reformation in the nineteenth century who forced their converts to be rebaptised if they were not baptised correctly in the first place; for example, those who were sprinkled when they were infants.

ANGEL, a "messenger". Any vessel God uses to declare his Word, eg, messengers (Job 1:14; 1 Sam. 11:3); prophets (Isa. 42:19; Hag. 1:13) or priests (Mal. 2:7).

ANNA, grace. A prophetess, like Miriam, Deborah, and Huldah (2 Chr. 34:22).

ANOINT, means "to pour on, smear all over or rub into", with olive oil. It was a common sacred practice in the Old and New Testament; e.g., anointing of the high priest (Ex. 29:29; Lev. 4:3) and of the sacred vessels (Ex. 30:26). In modern times Christian ministers talk of the anointing of Holy Spirit.

ANTICHRIST, against Christ, in opposition to Christ, adversary (1 John. 2:18).

ANTIOCH, named as a tribute to Antiochus (Acts. 6:5). Antioch was the metropolis of Syria on the river Orontes, approximately 300 miles north of Jerusalem. It later became the capital of the Roman province in Asia. The disciples were first called Christians in Antioch (Acts 11:26).

ANTITYPE, means original. The antitype is a person or thing symbolised or foreshadowed in the Old Testament to come into existence in the New Testament. For example, the killing of the lamb as a sacrifice in the Old Testament was a symbol of Christ who was going to come to the earth to be sacrificed.

ANUBIS, Greek name for Egyptian Jakal-headed god.

APOSTASY, to give up one's Christian beliefs.

APOSTLE'S CREED, is a symbol or statement of belief used first by the Roman Catholic Church. It begins with the words, "I believe in God the Father Almighty ..". It is traditionally linked to the apostles of Christ, but was never used by them. And it is not in the Bible.

ARABIA, uncultivable land. It is a large piece of land in the southwest of Asia and extends far into the north in the barren deserts of Syria.

ARIA, region in ancient India and ancient Iran.

ARISTOTLE (384 BC-322 BC), Greek philosopher, taught Alexander the Great, educated in Egypt, and was said to have borrowed his ideas and writings from the Egyptians.

ARMINIUS, Jacob (1560 –1609), as a Dutch theologian and leader of the Protestant Reformation focused more on law than grace in his teachings.

ASHER, fortune, happy, Jacob's eighth son; his mother was Zilpah, Leah's handmaid (Gen. 30:13).

ASTARTE, Moon goddess or queen of heaven, mother of the gods, Ashtoreth, I-s-h-t-r. Ashtoreth (Deut. 1:4), pronounced, A-s-t-a-r-t-e, "Astarte." She was called the moon goddess, or "queen of heaven, mother of gods,"

ATHENA, Greek goddess of wisdom, and warfare.

ATONEMENT, means at-one-ment, i.e., to bring at one with Christ or being reconciled to Him 2 Cor. 5:19). Atonement is reconciliation.

AUGUSTINE (A.D.354-430) from Numidia in North Africa. Augustine of Hippo known also as St Augustine was considered a very powerful Church Father in the development and establishment of Western Christianity.

AUL, or awl is a small sharp and pointed tool for boring holes

AZUSA STREET REVIVAL, occurred durtimg the Pentecostal Revival when the Pentecostal Movement spearheaded by Seymour the African American preacher witnessed the outpouring of the Holy Spirit in a big way at Los Angeles, California in 1906.

# B

BAAL, lord, master. He was a sun god. Baal is found in several places in the plural BAALIM (Judg. 2:11; 1 Kings 18:18; Jer. 2:23; Hos. 2:17). Baal is identified with Molech (Jer. 19:5), and known to the Israelites as Baal-peor (Num. 25:3; Deut. 4:3).

BABEL, confusion. The Tower of Babel was built by Nimrod (Gen. 10.10) in the land of Shinar (Gen. 11:1-9).

BABYLON, BABEL in Greek; Babilu in Semitic, meaning, "The Gate of God" or "the city of the dispersion of the tribes" in Assyrian. Babylon was a city in ancient Mesopotamia [now modern day Iraq] built upon the River Euphrates.

BALAAM, destruction (Num. 22:5) or lord of the people (Num. 31:8). Requested by Balak to curse Israel; is forbidden by God to do so (Num. 22:13). Blesses Israel (Num. 23.19; 24).

BALAK, to make empty; spoiler. King of the Moabites (Num. 22:2, 4).

BALANCE, "a reed", "cane", rod or "measuring reed" ( Ezek. 40:3,5; 42:16-18).

BAMBOO CURTAIN is the barrier in politics and ideas which separated the nations in the West from the Communist countries of Asia after the 1919 Chinese Revolution.

BAPTISM, immersion (Acts. 2:38-41; 8:26-39; 19:16). Total immersion in water in the name of the Lord Jesus Christ is the correct form of Christian baptism.

BAPTISM WITH THE HOLY GHOST, It is the Spirit baptising you into the body of Christ. It is the Spirit of God coming in and filling you after you have repented, (having heard His Word) and been baptised in water as an answer of a good conscience toward God (John. 14: 16-23; Acts. 2:38-4).

BAPTISTS, are Christians who believe in the scriptural meaning of baptism by immersion of believing adults as opposed to pouring water over the head of the person being baptised. They also reject the doctrine of sprinkling as a form of baptism, a method of baptism commonly used by some churches when baptising infants.

BARTLEMAN, Frank (1871-1936). American Pentecostal preacher and writer of the book titled *Azusa Street.*

BATH-SHEBA, daughter of the oath (1 Chr. 3:5), daughter of Eliam (2 Sam. 11:3) or Ammiel (1 Chr. 3:5), and wife of Uriah the Hittite. David committed adultery with her (2 Sam. 11:4).

BEL, another form of Baal, the national god of the Babylonians (Isa. 46:1; Jer. 50:2 ;).

BELSHAZZAR, protect the king; the last of the kings of Babylon (Dan. 5:1). Made a great feast and a handwriting appeared on the wall as a warning from God that his kingdom would come to an end, and he was slain (Dan. 5:30).

BELTESHAZZAR, preserve his life. The Chaldee name given to

Daniel by Nebuchadnezzar (Dan. 1.7; 4.8)

BENJAMIN, son of my right hand, fortune. The younger son of Jacob by Rachel (Gen. 35:18).

BERLIN WALL, was built as a barrier by East Germany's Democratic Republic on 15 August 1961. It separated East Berlin from the West. Dotted along the large concrete wall were guarded towers. In practice the walls were used to stop large numbers of its citizens leaving East Germany for the West.

BETHEL, house of God. It was a place in Central Palestine, about 10 miles north of Jerusalem and originally the royal Canaanite city of Luz (Gen. 28:19).

BETHLEHEM, house of bread. It was a city in the "hill country" of Judah, originally called Ephrath (Gen. 35:16, 19; Ruth. 4:11), Beth-lehem Ephrata (Micah. 5:2), Beth-lehem-judah (1 Sam. 17:12), and "the city of David" (Luke. 2:4).

BIBLE, Biblos, ie, Book in Greek or Biblia in Latin meaning "books", or the "Library of Divine Revelation" which is the series of books we have in our Bible today.

BIRTHRIGHT, special privileges conferred on the first born son. In the Jewish tradition the first-born son became the priest of the patriarchal family as in the case of Reuben. That honour was, however, transferred by God from Reuben to Levi (Num. 3:12, 13; 8:18).

BISHOP OF ROME, is referred to as the pope and Sovereign or Supreme Pontiff and leader of the Roman Catholic Church.

BOND, A bond is an I.O.U where the debtor writes on the piece of paper or bond the amount of money they owe. This "government bank" coupon or bond is given to the party to whom the money is owed (creditor) with a promise to repay the debt with interest at a later date or on demand.

BONDAGE, slavery such as the bondage of Israel in Egypt (Ex. 2:23, 25; 5). The word also refers to the Jewish captivity in Babylon (Isa. 14:3).

BOOK, a "writing", a "volume" (Ex. 17:14; Deut. 28:58;) or "roll of a book" (Jer. 36:2, 4).

BOOTH, William (1829-1912). Methodist minister founder and First General of the Salvation Army.

BRANHAM, William Marrion (1909-1965). He was born in the United States of America. He had a healing and prophetic ministry. He is credited by his followers as the end-Time Prophet

Messenger of Malachi 4 and Messenger to the Laodicean Church Age.

BREACH, an opening in a wall (1 Kings 11:27). It is also referred to by the prophet as the period of time between the Church ages and the opening of the seven seals – '*The Breach between the Church Ages and the Seven Seals*', to use the words of the prophet.

BUNSEN, Charles (1791-1860), was a German diplomat and writer of ancient history.

# C

CAESAR, the title of Roman emperors after Julius Caesar including those who ruled Judaea (John. 19:15; Acts 17:7).

CAIAPHAS, a Sadducee (Acts .5:17), and Jewish high priest (A.D. 27-36). He was appointed by the Romans, prophesied concerning Jesus' death (John. 11:50), and is said to have organised Christ's crucifixion (Matt. 26:3,57;).

CAIN, a possession; a spear. He was the first-born son of Eve (Gen. 4.1-16).

CALEB, the son of Jephunneh (Num. 13:6) was one of those whom Moses sent to search the land of Canaan (13:1).

CALVARY (Luke. 23:33). The word Calvary has been interpreted as "the place of the skull" and has the same meaning as Golgotha. Some suggest that it was a hill in the shape of a skull and that is how it came to be called by that name; others argue that calvary was called by that name because it is the place where the skull of Goliath the philistine was buried after David had removed his head (1Sam. Chap.17).

CALVIN, John or *Jean Cauvin* (1509 – 1564). French theologian and pastor who propounded the doctrines of predestination and grace.

CANAAN, The fourth son of Ham (Gen. 10:6). low region (Gen 9:18). The Land of Canaan was named after Ham's fourth son. Canaan is modern day Gaza-strip, Israel, West Bank and the Lebanon.

CANAANITES, inhabitants of Canaan (Judg 1.1); and the descendants of Canaan, the son of Ham.

CANDACE, queen of the Ethiopians (Acts 8:27). The Greeks called the country she ruled Meroe, in Upper Nubia.

CAPTIVE, a prisoner of war. Captives were sometimes carried away into foreign countries, as was the case with the Jews (Jer. 20:5).

CAPTIVITY, imprisonment or confinement. In 606 B.C., Nebuchadnezzar, King of Babylon invaded Jerusalem and captured the city, the treasures of the King of Jerusalem, the vessels of the sanctuary, and Daniel and his companions and took them to Babylon. This began the "seventy years" of Jewish captivity (2 Kings. 24:1; 2 Chr. 36:6, 7; Dan. 1:1, 2; Jer. 25; Dan. 9:1, 2).

CATECHISM, Instructions of the doctrine of Roman Catholicism.

CATHOLIC, means universal. The real Catholic Church is the universal Holy Ghost Church of the world. It is the original Catholic Church, the Bible believing Catholic Church. Thus the true Catholic Church is the continuation of the doctrine of the apostles, the baptism of the Holy Ghost and all the things that the early church stood for. The Roman Catholic Church came later and was the first Catholic Church to form an organisation

CHALDEA or Chaldees, the whole of Mesopotamia (Jer. 50:10; 51:24, 35).

CHALDEANS, were the people who resided in south-eastern Mesopotamia of which Babylon was its capital (2 Kings. 23, Isa. 13:19).

CHILD, covers a variety of ages and stages of ones development. For example, Joseph is called a child when he was approximately sixteen years of age (Gen. 37:3, Benjamin above thirty years (Gen. 44:20) and Solomon referred to himself as a little child when he came to the kingdom (1 Kings. 3:7).

CHRIST, means anointed, the Anointed One or Messiah in Hebrew.

CHRISTIAN, The term was first used at Antioch. This name occurs but three times in the New Testament to mean a follower of Christ or the Christian faith (Acts. 11:26; 1 Pet. 4:16).

CHURCH, means "the called out, the separated."

CHURCH FATHERS, were writers including Christian theologians, teachers or bishops who had a high place of standing in the Church.

CIVILISATION, a people organised, developed, advanced and living in a high cultured society.

CLAY, The expression literally rendered is, "in the thickness of the ground", meaning, "in stiff ground" as in the potter's clay (Isa. 41:25; Rom. 9:21) or as mortar (Gen. 11:3).

CLEOPHAS, Latin, Clopas, Greek, and Cleopas, Aramaic form (Luke 24:18; John 19; Matt. 10:3; 27:56). One of the two men who met Jesus on their way to Emmaus after the resurrection (Luke. 24:13-18).

CLOUD, a covering, symbolising the omnipresence of God, for example, the Shechinah glory of Jehovah on Mount Sinai in a cloud (Ex. 19:9 or the Pillar of Cloud which led the Children of Israel in the wilderness (Ex. 13:22; 33:9,10) by night (Num. 9:17-23).

COLD WAR, was a state of affairs which developed between the two superpowers, the USA and the USSR after World War Two. It lasted from 1947-1991. During these years there was tension between both countries. They carried out a vicious war of words against each other which sometimes led to some fighting. Both sides started to make huge piles of weapons. Sometimes it was thought that there would be a Third World War because of the fighting words they used. The USA was afraid that the USSR would make the whole world communist. And the USSR was afraid that western powers would bring an end to communism.

COLUMBA (A.D.521-597). Saint Columba was born in county Donegal, Northern Ireland to the royal family of Fergus. He was one of Ireland's most prominent religious leaders and messenger to the Thyatirean Church Age (A.D.606-1520).

CONCLAVE, a meeting called by the College of Cardinals to elect a new Pope.

CONSTANTINE, "the great" (A.D.306-337), notorious as the first Roman Emperor to convert to Christianity.

CONSTELLATION, cluster of stars, or stars which appear to be near each other in the heavens, for example, the constellation Orion (Job. 9:9; 38:31). The term was used by the prophet to describe a vision he saw of "a constellation of seven angels in the form of a pyramid."

CONVOCATION, is a Latin term meaning "calling together". It is a group of people formally coming together for a particular purpose. A "holy convocation" is a religious meeting such as the Sabbath (Lev. 23:2, 3), the Passover (Ex. 12:16; Num. 28:25) or feast of Tabernacles (Lev. 23:35, 36).

COSMOS, means the world order.

COVENANT, a binding agreement between two parties, for example, man and man (Gen. 21:32), nations and nations (1 Sam. 11:1), or God and man such as His covenant with Abraham (Gen. 17; Lev. 26:42).

CREATIONISM, is the belief that the universe was created by God, that is, a Supernatural Being.

CRUMPLER, Abner Blackmon, was a Methodist Holiness preacher from North Carolina who founded the Pentecostal Holiness in 1897 which was the first to use the word Pentecostal as a precursor to the Pentecostal Movement.

CUBIT, the lower arm. It is a measurement of the forearm from the elbow to the tip of the middle fingers, approximately 18 inches.

CULTURE, is a national way of life.

CUSH, black. Ham's Eldest son and father of Nimrod (Gen. 10:8; 1 Chr. 1:10). The Land of Cush which the Greeks called Ethiopia (Isa. 18:1; Jer.) derived its name from this son of Ham.

CYPRIAN (A.D.200-258), was one of the early Christian Church Fathers who was Bishop of Carthage in North Africa.

# D

DAEMON, devil. Daemons are evil spirits and enemies of God (Matt. 8:16).

DAEMONIAC, one "possessed with a devil," Such as dumbness (Matt. 9:32), blindness (Matt. 12:22).

DAN, a judge. He was the fifth son of Jacob. His mother was Bilhah, Rachel's maid (Gen. 30:6)

DANIEL, God is my judge or judge of God. Daniel, David's second son of Abigail (1 Chr. 3:1); and Daniel a prophet from the tribe of Judah (Dan. 1:3) carried away into Babylon by King Nebuchadnezzar 606B.C..

DARIUS, governor, holder. Persian kings. Darius the Mede (Dan. 11:1) came to the Babylonian throne on the death of Belshazzar the Chaldean (Dan. 5:31).

DARKNESS, absence of light eg; judgment (Isa. 13:9, 10; Matt. 24:29); a symbol of ignorance (Isa. 9:2; 60:2; Matt. 6:23) and of death (Job. 10:21).

DARWIN, Charles (1809-1882). He is one of the English naturalists responsible for the theory of Evolution. He suggested that all species came from common ancestors which over time changed through a process of what he called natural selection.

DATHAN, a fountain, a Reubenite, who with Korah and their co-conspirators in the wilderness were taken into the bowels of the earth when it opened up and consumed them (Num. 16:1; 26:9).

DAVID, beloved. King, the eighth and youngest son of Jesse, a citizen of Bethlehem (Ruth. 4:22;1 Chr:2). Anointed by Samuel (1 Sam. 16:8). Kills Goliath of Gath (1 Sam. 17:49).

DA VINCI, Leonardo (1452-1519). Italian Renaissance painter.

DAY, The Jews reckoned the day from sunset to sunset (Lev. 23:32). It was originally divided into three parts, evening, morning and noon (Ps. 55:17).

DEATH, means in the natural the termination of life, but a person can be spiritually dead, which is eternal separation from God (Gen. 2:17)

DEMON, See DAEMON. Devil.

DETERMINISM, is the idea that everything happens as a result of natural laws.

DIOCLETIAN (244-311). Roman Emperor from A.D.284-305.

DIOP, CHEIKH ANTA (1923-1986). He was a historian , politician, physicist, and anthropologist, born in Senegal who specialised in the origins of civilisation.

DISPENSATION, is a given period of time in biblical history highlighting the way in which God carries out his purpose in the lives of men.

# E

EAGLE, is a heavenly bird of prey with powerful wings that can go higher than any other bird, 'cause he can see afar off, and see things that's coming ( (Deut. 28:49; 2 Sam. 1:23), (Job 39:27-30). A prophet is sometimes referred to in the Bible as an eagle.

EAR, is used many times in the Bible as a figure of speech to mean that the individual should give their undivided attention to what has been said (Ps. 34:15, Rev. 2:7)). Using the word "ear(s)" figuratively the Bible refers to they that have "ears to hear but can't hear" because they have rejected the Word of God. And their spiritual hearing, their spiritual ears have been sealed even though they can hear perfectly well with their physical hearing; their physical ears remain intact.

EARNEST, pledge (2 Cor. 1:22). The earnest is the down payment on anything that holds it, a surety, secures it.

EARTH, soil or ground, adamah. Husbandman in (Gen. 9:20) is literally "man of the ground or earth".

EASTER, The name "Easter" is the English name of the ancient Assyrian goddess Ishtar, pronounced by the Assyrians exactly as we pronounce "Easter." The Babylonian name of this goddess was Astarte, consort of Baal, the Sun-god. The word Easter is also said to come from the Saxon word (Eostre), a goddess of the Saxons. It was originally a pagan festival celebrated in the springtime (see Acts. 12:4)

EDEN, delight. Eden is Egypt. Our first ancestors dwelt in the Garden of Eden (Gen. 2:8-17).

EDOM, The name of Esau (Gen. 25:30).

EGYPT, Mizraim is the Hebrew name for Egypt.

EGYPTIANS, Citizens of Egypt.

ELAM, highland, the son of Shem (Gen. 10:22), and the name of the country inhabited by his descendants (Isa. 11:11; 21:2).

ELECTION, grace. It is God's foreknowledge, predestination, fore-ordination where we were chosen in Him before the foundation of the world (Eph. 1: 1-12).

ELIAS, the Greek form for Elijah (Matt. 11:14; 16:14).

ELIEZER, God his help. Aliezer was Abraham's servant whom he sent (Gen. 15:2, 3) to select a Bride for Isaac his son. Eliezer represented a messenger or servant of God

ELIJAH, my God is Jehovah. Elijah the Tishbite, a prophet, predicts great drought (1 Kin 17.1; Luke 4.25). Elijah is "the "Elias" of the New Testament.

ELISHA, to whom God is salvation. Elisha became the attendant and disciple of Elijah (1 Kings 19:16-19). He succeeds Elijah, receives his mantle, and divides Jordan (1 King 19:16; 2 Kings 2:13).

EMMANUEL, God with us, (Matt. 1:23).

EMMAUS, hot springs (Luke 24:13); a village "three-score furlongs" from Jerusalem. It is the place to which Cleopas and another of Christ's disciples was going when they met Him on the day of His resurrection (Luke 24:15).

EN MORPHE, from the Greek word *morph* meaning form or shape; an example of to morph, is a caterpillar becoming a butterfly. The prophet said that God *En morphe* means that He changed His mask. The same God in the form of the Pillar of Fire was made flesh and dwelt among us (the Lord Jesus Christ).

ENOCH, initiated. Cain's eldest son, the third from Adam (Gen. 4:17). There was also Enoch, the seventh from Adam (Jude 1:14), the son of Jared, and father of Methuselah (Gen. 5:21; Luke 3:37) who was translated after three hundred and sixty five years on earth (Gen. 5:22-24).

ENSIGN, sign. It is a tall symbol such as a column or high pole (Num. 21:8, 9); a standard or signal or flag placed on high mountains to point out to the people a meeting place when the enemy is advancing (Isa. 5:26). The brazen serpent was the ensign in Moses' day just as Christ is our ensign today.

EPHESIAN CHURCH AGE, The first church age started about A.D. 53, when Paul established the church at Ephesus. He was pastor of the Ephesian church for twenty two years until he was beheaded in A.D.66. After his death Saint John the Divine became the pastor of the Ephesian Church. The Ephesian Church lasted from A.D.53-170 AD. Paul was undoubtedly the messenger to the Ephesian Church Age, for the messenger to every age, regardless of when he appears or goes, is the one who influences that age for God by means of a Word-manifested ministry.

EPHESIANS, inhabitants of Ephesus (Acts. 19.28). Paul's Epistle (Eph. 1).

EPHESUS, was in the western part of Asia Minor, a city of great commerce and trade under Roman government, the language was Greek. Ephesus means aimed high then relaxed. The Church first aimed at high standards then backslid.

EPHPHATHA, is an Aramaic word for "Be opened". For example, the words Christ used when he healed the deaf and dumb (Mark. 7:34, 3:17).

EPHRAIM, fruitful. The second son of Joseph, born in Egypt (Gen. 41:52; 46:20).

EPISTLES, apostolic letters.

ESAIAS, the Greek form for Isaiah (Matt. 3:3; 4:14).

ESAU, hairy. Rebekah's first-born twin son (Gen. 25:25). The name of Edom, "red", was also given to him from his conduct in connection with the red lentil "pottage" for which he sold his birthright (Gen. 25: 30, 31).

ESPOUSE, to betroth. A contract to marry made before the formal ceremony of marriage or it may be used figuratively to illustrate the relationship between Christ and His Bride (Jer. 2:2; 2 Cor. 11:2).

ESTHER, born Hadassah. She was the Jewish queen of the Persian King Ahasuerus. She was also heroine of the biblical Book of Esther (Esther. 2:7).

ETHIOPIA, named "*Aithiops*" or "Ethiopia" by the Greeks, meaning literally "burnt face people". It is the land the Hebrews called Cush connected to the first two rivers in Eden, namely, the Pishon and Gihon.

EVOLUTION, the notion that something, for example, a species, changes gradually over a period of time from one form to another. Darwin uses the term natural selection to explain the extent to which genetic variation of individuals result in the development of new species. But, the prophet is categorical that evolution has a biblical meaning in that : "man evolutes [evolves] from himself"; "every seed"; "living creature"; "bring[s] forth after its kind"; "a bird has been a bird ever since God made him a bird, and a monkey's been a monkey; a man's been a man." "We therefore do not all come from 'one cell'", he proclaims.

# F

FAITH, is "the substance of things hoped for, the evidence of things not Seen" (Heb. 11:1).

FATHER, applies to an ancestor (Deut. 1:11); a title: God is sometimes referred to as Father (Rom. 1:7; 1 Cor. 1:3); the author or beginner of anything (Gen. 4:20, 21).

FIRE, a symbol of God's presence or a sacred purpose (Ex. 14:19; Num. 11:1, 3). Sacrifices were consumed by fire (Gen. 8:20).

FOREKNOWLEDGE, to know in advance what was going to take place (Acts 2:23; Rom. 8:29; 11:2). God, being infinite, in the beginning knew the end from the beginning. Therefore He knew what people would do, so He could foretell what would take place.

FORNICATION is premarital consensual sexual intercourse between a man and a woman; for example, intercourse between an unmarried man and an unmarried woman, or intercourse between a man and woman where either party is already married to another person. Spiritual fornication means "idol worship". That is an illegal union.

FRACKING, also called hydraulic fracturing or hydrofracturing is a way of opening up rocks by drilling deep down into the earth and injecting fluid into the cracks to force them apart to release the gas inside.

FRANCIS OF ASSISI (1181-1226). Italian Catholic Friar and

preacher. Founder of the Franciscan Order.

FRANKL, Victor (1905-1997). He was an Austrian neurologist, psychiatrist and Holocaust survivor.

FREUD, Sigmund (1856-1939). He was an Austrian neurologist and founding father of psychoanalysis

# G

GABRIEL, champion of God. He is the Archangel of God who announces the major events that will take place. He was sent to Daniel to announce the prophecy of the seventy weeks (Dan. 9:21-27). He announced the birth of John the Baptist (Luke. 1:11-17), and the birth of Christ (Luke. 1:26-39).

GARFIELD, JAMES (1831-1881). Elected President of the United States in 1881. He was assassinated after 200 days in office. He was shot at point blank range by Charles J. Guiteau. There was speculation at the time that Guiteau was commissioned by the Jesuits to kill the president. Other reports paint him as someone who was not of sound mind (insane).

GENERATION, fifty years is a generation, considered in the Bible. Four hundred years is eight generations.

GENESIS, generation or beginning. The first Book of the Bible.

GHOST, breath, life, spirit (See HOLY GHOST.)

GIFT, gratuity (Prov. 19:6); present (1 Sam. 9:7); a thing given (Matt. 7:1).

GIHON, a stream. One of the four rivers of Eden (Gen. 2:13).

GLORY, praise, honour (Heb. 2:7).

GLOSSOLALIA, from the Greek *glossa*, tongue, and *lalia*, "talking". Glossolalia is therefore speaking in tongues, utterances.

GOG, Russia. Ezekiel. 38 and 39 deals with Gog and Magog, which is Russia, the north country. The reference to Gog and Magog in Revelation (Rev. 20:8) is a vindication of Ezekiel's prophecy.

GOLAN, exile, a city of Bashan (Deut. 4:43) in the land of Israel, one of the three cities of refuge east of Jordan, about 12 miles north-east of the Sea of Galilee (Josh. 20:8).

GOLD, Deity. In the scriptures gold speaks of Deity. In the Old Testament when the beater was beating gold, the way he knew that he had beaten all the dirt out of it is that he saw the reflection of himself in it like one would see oneself in a polished mirror.

GOLDEN CALF. This was an idol or symbol of worship by the

Children of Israel in the Wilderness, shaped and moulded into a a molten image on Mount Sinai after the fashion of the Egyptians (Ex. 32:4, 8; Deut. 9:16).

GOLGOTHA, "the place of a skull" (Matt. 27:33; Mark 15:22; John 19:17).

GOMORRAH, submersion. It was one of the cities consumed by fire (Gen. 10:19; 13:10; 19:24, 28).

GORBACHEV, MIKHAIL, born 1931. He was leader of the Soviet Union from 1985 to 1991. He introduced reforms which limited the powers of the Communist Party of the Soviet Union and brought an end to the Soviet Union. His contribution ended the Cold War and saw the removal of the Berlin Wall. In 1990 he received the Nobel Peace Prize.

GRACE, favour, kindness, friendship (Gen. 6:8; Tim. 1:9). God's forgiveness and mercy (Rom. 11:6; Eph. 2:5).

GREECE, it was first made up of the four provinces of Macedonia, Epirus, Achaia, and Peleponnesus; country of the Greeks (Acts 20:2).

GREEK, country, language, race of Greece (Acts 16:1), or a Gentile, not a Jew (Rom. 2:9, 10).

# H

HABEAS CORPUS means that you have the body and is known as "the great writ of liberty". It is used to command a person who is detaining another person to bring that person before the courts, particularly where the detainee is held without a cause.

HADES, hell. A Greek word meaning the grave.

HAIL, frozen rain-drops; one of the plagues of Egypt (Ex. 9:23).

HALLELUJAH, praise (Psalms. 106).

HAM, hot. Egyptian word for "black". One of Noah's sons (Gen. 5:32). Egypt is called the Land of Ham in the Bible (Psalms. 78.51; 1 Ch. 4:40).

HAMMURABI, Code of, was that of the sixth Babylonian king, Hammurabi, who enacted this Code to regulate the laws of contract, the family, crime, and other legal matters to protect the rights of individuals within ancient Babylonian society.

HANNAH, favour, grace. one of the wives of Elkanah the Levite, and the mother of Samuel (1 Sam. 1; 2).

HARRIS, Marvin (1927-2001), was an American anthropologist who contributed extensively to the development of cultural materialism.

HAVILAH, sand region. Arabia. A land identified in Genesis rich in gold and bdellium and onyx stone (Gen. 2:11

HEART, the home of the soul. The human heart has a small inbuilt compartment which occupies the human soul confirming that in scriptural terms it is the seat of man's thinking faculties (Prov 23:7

HEAVEN, the firmament (Gen. 2:19); starry heavens (Deut. 17:3); heaven of heavens. The *heavens* mean the atmospheres.

HENRY, Patrick (1736-1799), He was an American Founding Father, politician and governor of Virginia who became a staunch supporter of the American War of Independence evidence in his great oratory, "Give Me Liberty, Give Me Death" speech.

HERMES, is the Greek counterpart of the god Thoth in Egypt, who is said to be responsible for the composition of sacred texts which laid the foundation for Hermeticism.

HERODIANS, Jewish political party that supported the Herodian rulers (Mark. 3:6; 12:13; Matt. 22:16).

HERODIAS, (Matt. 14:3-11; Mark 6:17-28), the daughter of Aristobulus and Bernice. Married to Herod Antipas ((Matt. 6:17).

HERODOTUS (484 BC-425 BC). He was a Greek historian; known as "The Father of History".

HETH, dread, a descendant of Canaan, and the ancestor of the Hittites (Gen. 10:18; Deut. 7:1)

HIDDEKEL, the third of the four rivers of Paradise (Gen. 2:14). The River Tigris.

HIGH PRIEST, Aaron was the first to occupy this office (Ex. 29:7; Lev. 8:12). The High Priest wore a special robe, approached the Lord in a certain way with the blood sacrifice of an animal as he entered the Holy of holies. Christ is now our perfect sacrifice, the High Priest of our confession who makes intercession for us and can be touched by the feeling of our infirmities.

HIGHWAY, a raised road for public use. There's a highway and a way, and the way is the road. A highway has a post on either side of the public thorough way, but in the middle of this highway is the road. You can be in a highway and be in a gutter. But there is a way in the middle of the way. According to Isaiah, "there shall be a highway and a way." "And" is a conjunction which brings the highway down to a way. And here's where you travel, is in the way.

HISLOP, Alexander (1807-1865). Minister of the Free Church of Scotland. Ardent critic of the Roman Catholic Church, and author of *The Two Babylons: Papal Worship Proved to be the worship of Nimrod and his wife*

HISTORY, an era, epoch, period of time; or an indefinite, continuous or eternal unfolding of that Grand Age, namely, Eternity. History has been commonly used to mean "everything that has happened"; or "our actual record of what has happened". In Christendom it is the apocalypse, namely, the unveiling or unfolding of God's purpose.

HOLINESS, of God (Isa. 6:3; Rev. 15:4).

HOLINESS MOVEMENT was founded on the principle of Wesleysian "Christian perfection", that is, one could live a completely perfect life without committing sins which could be immediately achieved through a second work of grace.

HOLY GHOST, the Holy Spirit (Acts. 2:38).

HORUS, ancient Egyptian god, born of the goddess Isis and the god Osiris. Sometimes Horus is represented as the child in the arms of the Egyptian Madonna Isis.

# I

IDOL, anything a person puts before God or honours instead of God.

IDOLATRY, to worship an image or thing, eg. any created object, hero, money, popularity, effigy.

ILLICH, IVAN (1926-2002), was an Austrian writer and Roman Catholic priest, who wrote a critical book titled *Deschooling Society* (1971) where he suggests that we should get rid of schools.

IMMANUEL, God with us (Isa. 7:14; and 8:8; Matt. 1:23).

INDUS, is a main river in Asia snaking its way through Pakistan and India.

INQUISITION, was a body within the Roman Catholic Church's judicial system which tried heretics and protestants. It investigated, hunted down, sentenced, and punished heretics which included burning them at the stakes. In 1542 Pope Paul III permanently established the Papal Inquisition called the Congregation of the Holy Office of the Inquisition. In 1908, Pope Pius X renamed it "the Holy Office". In 1965 Pope Paul VI again changed its name to the "Congregation for the Doctrine of the Faith". It has kept this latter name in the twenty first century.

IRENAEUS, Bishop in Gaul during the Roman Empire. One of the early Church Fathers and messenger to the Smyrnaean Church Age (A.D.170-312).

IRON CURTAIN, was up until 1990 the border guarded between the countries of the Soviet Union and the rest of the world. It was Winston Churchill in his March 1946 speech who first used the term "Iron Curtain" falling down across Europe. He thought that Communism was dividing Eastern Europe from the rest of the world.

IRWIN, Benjamin, once a Baptist preacher from Lincoln, Nabraska helped organise the International Pentecostal Church.

ISAAC, laughter (Gen. 17:19). His birth promised to Abraham (Gen. 15:4). Born (Gen. 21:2).

ISHMAEL, whom God hears, son of Abram (Gen. 16:15; 17:20).

ISIS, pronounced like Aset, was the Ancient Egyptian goddess, worshipped as the wife of the god Osiris, and the Mother with the Child in her arms, that is, the Madonna.

# J

JACOB, supplanter, (Gen. 25:26; Hos. 12:2-4), the second born of the twin sons of Isaac by Rebekah.

JEFFERSON, Thomas (1743-1826), was one of the Founding Fathers in the United States, and the third American President (1801-1809) who was the draftsman of the American Declaration of Independence.

JEHOVAH, Elohim, The Eternal One (Ex. 6:2). The meaning of the word appears from (Ex. 3:14) to be "the unchanging, eternal, self-existent God", the "I am that I am", a covenant-keeping God. (Mal. 3:6; Rev. 1:4, 8.).

JEHOVAH-JIREH, the Lord will provide (Gen. 22:13,14).

JEHOVAH-NISSI, the Lord our banner (Ex. 17:8-15).

JEHOVAH-RAPHA, the Lord that healeth (Ex. 15:26).

JEHOVAH-ROHI (RA-AH), the Lord my Shepherd (Ps. 23).

JEHOVAH-SHALOM, the Lord our peace (Judg. 6:24).

JEHOVAH-SHAMMAH, the Lord is present (Ezek. 48:35).

JEHOVAH-TSIDKENU, the Lord our righteousness (Jer. 23:6).

JEHOVAH WITNESS, was founded by Charles Taze Russell(1852-1916) in the latter half of the nineteenth century in Philadelphia. They were variously called first the International Bible Students, and from 1884 the Watch Tower Bible and Tract Society. Although their teachings are based on the Bible, acknowledging that Jesus is Lord and Saviour, they deny that He is (Jehovah) incarnate. They also reject the fact that Christ is a God-man and contend that He is not part of the Godhead, but that He is inferior to God.

JEREMIAH, raised up or appointed by Jehovah. One of the major prophets.

JERICHO, place of fragrance, a fenced city in Jordan (Josh. 3:16).

JESSE, a gift, a son of Obed, the son of Boaz and Ruth (Ruth 4:17, 22; Matt. 1:5). He had eight boys and David was the youngest. (1 Sam. 17:12).

JESUITS, also called The Society of Jesus was founded by Ignatius Loyola in 1534 and approved by Pope Innocent III 1540. They were the Roman Catholic Church's foot soldiers, secret army or military. The Jesuits were also sometimes referred to as the Soldiers of Jesus Christ.

JESUS, Saviour (Matt. 1:21)

JETHRO, his excellence, a prince or priest. Moses' father-in-law (Ex.18.12).

JEW, their name originated from the patriarch Judah. An Israelite (Esth. 2.5).

JEZEBEL, chaste, wife of Ahab, the king of Israel (1 Kings 16:31).

JOB, a desert (Gen. 46.13); one persecuted (see the Book of Job in the Old Testament).

JOEL, Jehovah is his God. Delivers God judgments (Joel 1-3).

JOHN, the English way of spelling Johanan. Many references to the name John in the New Testament.

JONAH, a dove. Prophet (2. Kin. 14:25). Principal character in the Book of Jonah in the old Testament; and missionary to Nineveh, notorious for being swallowed up by a whale for his disobedience to God (Jonah. 1:17-2:10).

JOPPA, beauty. A town in Dan (Josh. 19:46). Peter dwells (Acts 9:36-43).

JORDAN, is an Arabic Kingdom in the Middle East; situated on the East bank of its principal river Jordan.

JOSEPH, he shall add. Son of Jacob and firstborn of Rachel (Gen. 30:23, 24). The husband of Mary and foster-father of Jesus (Matt. 1:16; Luke 3:23).

JOSHUA, Jehovah the Saviour. "Josh-u-a", is the Name of Jesus in

Hebrew. If it's in English, it's "Jesus."

JUBILEE, the "acceptable year" was the year called, in the Old Writings, "the year of jubilee "which took place every fifty years. A trumpet sounded throughout the land at the year of jubilee. During that year all landed property was returned to its original owner (Lev. 25:13-34), and all who were slaves were set free (Lev. 25:39-54).

JUDA, Judah, son of Jacob (Luke. 3:33; Heb. 7:14).

JUDAH, praise. The fourth son of Jacob by Leah (Gen. 29:35).

JUDAS, Greek form of Judah (Matt. 10:4).

JUDAS, ISCARIOT (Matt. 10:4; Mark 3:19). Betrays Jesus (Matt. 26:14, 47).

JUDE , Judas. Two apostles called by this name. Jude also called Lebbaeus or Thaddaeus (Matt. 10:3; Mark 3:18). The second Jude was Judas Iscariot (Matt. 10:4; Mark 3:19).

JUDEA, land of Judah (Ezra. 5:8).

JUDGE, magistrate or ruler, as opposed to a trial judge. Where there was a dispute the matter was ultimately settled by the Urim and Thummim (Num. 27:21).

JUDGMENT, God's will (Ps. 110:5; 36:6); punishment ((Ex. 6:6; Ezek. 25:11).

# K

KADESH, holy, or Kadesh-Barnea, was a place on the south-eastern border of Palestine, about 165 miles from Horeb. It was the judgment seat of the world during the time the Children of Israel was wandering in the wilderness (Gen. 14:7; Num. 13:3).

KENNEDY, JOHN FITZGERALD (1917-1963). Sometimes referred to as "JFK". John Kennedy was elected President of the United States in 1961. He was assassinated in 1963 allegedly by Lee Harvey Oswald. His killing is alleged to have been instigated by the Roman Catholic Church against Kennedy for his failure to obey their orders. But reports by the U.S. administration found Oswald to be the sole killer. Some sources accuse the U.S. government of a cover-up.

KEY, the opener, shutter (Judg. 3:25); (Matt. 16:19; Rev. 1:18). Christ is the key.

KETURAH, incense. Abraham's second wife after the death of his first wife Sarah. (Gen. 25:1).

KING, Martin Luther, Jnr (1929-1968). American Black Civil

Rights Leader of the nonviolent movement.

KINGDOM OF GOD, (Matt. 6:33; Mark 1:14, 15) "kingdom of heaven" (Matt. 3:2; 4:17). Jesus said "My Kingdom is not of this world, but My Kingdom is in heaven." And He said, "The Kingdom of God will be within you."

KINSMAN, redeem. The Kinsman was called the Goel in Hebrew who was the closest male blood relative living whose duty it was to redeem the inheritance of his next of kin where they were unable to do so (Lev. 25:25, 28; Ruth 3:9, 12). He was also required to redeem his relation who sold himself into slavery (Lev. 25:48, 49). Christ is our Goel.

KLU KLUX KLAN, or KKK, is a far-right extreme reactionary and terrorist organisation in the United States of America which advocated White Supremacy, still has a sizeable membership in the United States. Members of the Klan were and still are White Anglo-Saxon Protestants (WASP) who wore white robes, masks, and carried the cross whilst directing their activities of lynching and burning Blacks, particularly in the Southern States of America.

KNOX, John (1510-1572), a clergyman, founder of the Presbyterian Church and leader of the Protestant Reformation in Scotland.

KORAH, hail. He was a Levite, the son of Izhar, the brother of Amram, the father of Moses and Aaron (Ex. 6:21) who with Dathan and others in the wilderness led a rebellion against Moses (Num. 16:1-3; "but immediately the earth opened and swallowed them" (Num. 16:31-33) and "fire from the Lord" consumed the rest of their followers (Num. 16:35).

KOSMOS means the world order.

KUNDERA, Milan, prominent Czech writer, who wrote the best selling book, *The Unbearable Lightness of Being*.

KUSH, was ancient Ethiopia. Cush was the son of Ham and the father of Nimrod (Gen. 10:8; 1 Chr. 1:10).

# L

LABAN, white. Laban lived in Haran, Mesopotamia. He was the son of Bethuel, who was the son of Nahor, Abraham's brother. His sister Rebekah was married to Isaac, Abraham's son. (Gen. 24). Jacob and Esau were a product of this marriage. But Jacob fled to the house of his uncle Laban whose daughters Leah and Rachel (Gen. Chap 29)) he married.

LAODICEA, people's rights. Once known as Diopolis (City of Zeus) in honour of their god, it was situated in the regions Phrygia and Lydia, about 40 miles east of Ephesus (Rev. 3:14), on the banks of the Lycus.

LAODICEAN CHURCH AGE, is the seventh and final church age. It began around the turn of the Twentieth Century. The prophet messenger of that age has been identified as William Marrion Branham by end time message believers.

LASLET, Peter (1915-2001). He was an English historian.

LAZARUS, Greek form of Eleazar, whom God helps. Brother of Mary and Martha raised from the dead (John. 11:1-44).

LEAH, weary. Laban's eldest daughter, sister of Rachel (Gen. 29:16). Married to Jacob (Gen. 29:23).

LEO, the lion in the Zodiac is the symbol of the Second Coming of Christ. It represents judgment. Christ leaves the intercessory throne as a slain Lamb to be a Lion, King, to bring the world to judgment in these last days.

LEONARDO DA VINCI, (1452-1519). Italian Renaissance painter.

LEVI, associate. Jacob's third son by Leah (Gen. 29:34).

LEVITE, descendant of the tribe of Levi (Ex. 6:25; Lev. 25:32); and the Levitical Priesthood (Ex. 32; Num. 4:3).

LIFE, physical life (Gen. 2:7; Luke 16: and spiritual life (John 3:16, 17); but there is only one form of life, namely, eternal life (John 3:15).

LIGHT, the Word of God, Jesus. The Bride today is "the light of the world" (Matt. 5:14).

LINCOLN, ABRAHAM (1809-1865). He was President of the United States from 1861-1865. He helped abolish slavery. He was assassinated in 1865 at point blank range allegedly by a Jesuit motivated killing. Roman Catholicism denies anything to do with Lincoln's killing, thus blaming the allegation on an anti-Catholic conspiracy theory. Lincoln was assassinated by the actor John Wilkes Booth.

LION, the most powerful carnivorous animal. The lion is King of the jungle just as Christ is King of Kings.

LITTLE BOOK, a symbol of the Word of Life, the (Rev.10:8), the Bible, the Word of God from Genesis to Revelation. "Lo, I come (in the volume of the book it is written of me,) to do thy will, O God", saith the Lord. (Heb.10:7; Ps. 40:7). John saw the Book in the right-hand of Him that sat upon the throne, and there was no man in heaven, or in earth, or beneath the earth that was worthy to take the Book to open it, or to loose the seals. And there come a Lamb that had been slain since the foundation of the world. And He was worthy. And He took the Book, and loosed the seals, and opened the Book.

LOCKE, John (1632-1704), was an English philosopher the most prominent leader of the Enlightenment.

LORD'S DAY, The Lord's Day is when the days of man are over. The Lord's Day is neither the Sabbath Day, that is, Saturday nor Sunday, the first day of the week.

LOT, a covering; veil, the son of Haran, and nephew of Abraham (Gen. 11:27). Resided in Sodom (Gen.13:5-13). When the Lord reined judgment on Sodom, Lot escaped (Gen. 19:1-26).

LOVE, *agape, phileo*, (John 21:16, 17). These are the two Greek words for "love." *Phileo* love is natural love and affection, the love for one's wife. *Agape* is the divine love of God. This love would cause a man to pray for his enemy's lost soul instead of wanting to kill him. *Phileo* love would want you to kill your enemy.

LOYOLA, Ignatius (1491-1556). He founded the "Company of Jesus" or Jesuits in 1534. The name the "Company of Jesus" was later changed to the Society of Jesus and was approved by Pope Innocent III in 1540.

LUCIFER, brilliant star, angel of light, light-bearer (Isa. 14:12). In the beginning Lucifer was God's right hand man, archangel, the son of the morning or morning star.

LUCRE, from the Latin *lucrum*, "gain". (1 Tim. 3:3), "not given to filthy lucre", that is, money.

LUTHER, Martin (1483-1546), Roman Catholic priest and monk from Germany, who was the first to openly protest against the Catholic Church. His actions triggered the Protestant Reformation in the sixteenth century as he denounced such practices of church members having to pay their way out of purgatory or to avoid punishment by buying their way out of sin and hell. He was the messenger to the Sardisean Church Age (1520-1750).

LYBANS, inhabitants of Lyba.

# M

MADONNA, comes from the Italian root words "ma" or my, and "donna" or lady. The Madonna is sometimes referred to by

Roman Catholics as Mary with the child Jesus in her arms.

MAGNA CARTA, is a Latin expression for the Great Charter of the Liberties of England, forced on King John of England in 1215 to grant certain liberties to the barons and agreeing not to abuse his power, for example, by acknowledging that no "freeman" would be punished except by the law of the land.

MAGOG, Russia, North Country. He was Japheth's second son (Gen. 10:2; 1 Chr. 1:5). In Ezekiel (Ez. 38:2; 39:6). It is the name of a nation (Russia).

MALACHI, messenger or angel, the last of the minor prophets, and the writer of the last book of the Old Testament (Mal. 4:4, 5, 6). He is the end-time prophet messenger of Malachi 4. Malachi prophesied that in the last days which we are in now, the Lord God will send Elijah the prophet before the great and terrible day of the Lord, and he will restore the faith of the children back to the fathers, just before the world is destroyed.

MAMMON, wealth, riches, god of riches (Luke. 16:9-11). The word "mammon", translated means, "the world." If you love the world, or the things of the world, it's because the real love of the Father is not even in you. You can't love the world and God at the same time.

MAN, natural, spiritual. He made the original man, Adam, from the dust (body); the breath of live was breathed into him and he became a living soul (Gen. 2:7; Eccl. 12:7; 2). "The first man is of the earth, earthy: the second man is the Lord from heaven (I Cor. 15:47).

MANDELA, Nelson (1918-2013), a former anti-apartheid campaigner, and Ex President of the African National Congress and politician who became President of South Africa from 1994-1999 as the first Black African to occupy that position.

MANGER, stable. (Luke. 2:7, 12, 16) where Jesus was born (Luke. 13:15) It was a stall on which the hay or other food of the animals such as cattle was placed.

MANTLE, a large over-garment. This was Elijah's mantle (1 Kings. 19:13, 19; 2 Kings. 2:8, 13). The same Holy Spirit that was upon Christ was His mantle that God gave Him, the anointing of the Holy Spirit. And they went up at Pentecost and waited in the upper room which was the antitype of Elijah, was taken up from death and resurrected; He sent back the mantle to Elisha (the Church, the Bride of Christ). The same Holy Spirit that was upon

Jesus fell on the Church.

MARK OF THE BEAST, the mark of the beast (Rev. 13:11) is the mark of apostasy, that is, to reject the Seal of God through the Baptism of the Holy Spirit. In his exposition of the mark of the beast the prophet says that "the churches are controlling politics and at the opportune time will manifest exactly how great is that control ... *when* [*when* is my word or insertion] all the people have to belong to the world church system or be at the mercy of the elements for they cannot buy or sell without the mark of the beast in the hand or head. This mark in the head means that they will have to take the doctrine of the world church system ... and the mark in the hand which means to do the will of the world church. With this great power the church systems will persecute the true bride. This image will try to keep the bride from preaching and teaching, etc. Her ministers will be forbidden to give comfort and truth to the people who need it. But before the antichrist (in person) takes over this complete world system of churches the true church will be taken away from this world to be with the Lord God will catch away His bride for the great Marriage Supper of the Lamb" (*Church Ages*, pp. 376-377)

MARRIAGE is a voluntary union for life between one man and one woman to the exclusion of all others. First instituted in Paradise (Gen. 2:18-24). This definition applies equally to the invisible union between the Bride and Christ. Thus, the Bride of Christ can no more be married to the world and to Christ at the same time.

MARTIN, Of Tours (315-399). Hungarian and Bishop of Tours. He was the messenger to the Pergamean Church Age (A.D. 312-606).

MARYOLATRY, idolatrous worship of Mary as the Mother of God.

MCKINLEY, WILLIAM (1843-1901), was United States President from 1897 until he was assassinated in 1901. He was shot at point blank range by the Polish, Leon Frank Czolgosz, an anarchist. Other sources claim that Czolgosz was co-opted by the Jesuits to eliminate the President. Roman Catholicism's response to this claim is that this is an anti-Catholic conspiracy spread by Protestants.

MEDIA, situated in northwestern Iran in ancient times, but today is located in the regions of Azerbaijan and Kurdistan.

MEDIATOR, one who intervenes between two parties and tries to reconcile them together to the position they would have been in had the relationship not broken down. The Bible declares, that "God was in Christ, reconciling the world unto Himself"(2 Corin. 5:19). Christ is the only mediator between God and man (1 Tim. 2:5; Heb. 8:6).

MELCHISEDEC, king of righteousness, the king of Salem (Jerusalem) (Gen. 14:18-20). In modern times our Melchesidec is Jesus. And the great Melchisedec of heaven, the King of, not the natural Jerusalem, but the King of the heavenly Jerusalem, the New Jerusalem, will meet the Bride and she will be served again the wine and the bread.

MEMPHIS, capital of Egypt during the Old Kingdom.

MERCY, compassion for the miserable.

MEROË, capital of the Kingdom of Kush (called Ethiopia by classical writers) was situated on the east bank of the Nile.

MESOPOTAMIA, the region between the rivers Euphrates and the Tigris (Gen. 24:10).

MESSENGER, angel ((Job. 1:14; 1 Sam. 11:7; 2 Chr. 36:22). A messenger bears record to some individual, and that individual carries out the word.

MESSIAH, Christos, that is, anointed (John. 1:41 and 4:25). Jesus Christ is the Messiah (Matt. 26:54; John 5:39).

METHODIST, is a follower of the teachings of John Wesley.

MICHAEL, who is like God. One of the Archangels (Dan. 10:13, 21; 12:1).

MICHELANGELO (1475-1564), Italian Renaissance painter, sculptor.

MIDIAN, strife. The fourth son of Abraham from his second wife Keturah, ancestor of the Midianites (Gen. 25:2; 1 Chr. 1:32).

MILLENNIUM, a thousand years (Rev. 20:1-7). Christ will come to the earth to establish His Kingdom at the beginning of the millennium. His saints will rule and reign with Him throughout this period. At the end of the thousand years He and His saints will judge the world.

MINERVA, Roman goddess of wisdom, art, and trade.

MIRACLE, a supernatural occurrence (John 2:18; Matt. 12:38).

MIZRAIM, mound, fortress. One of Ham's sons. Descendants of Mizraim. (Gen. 10:6, 13; 1 Chr. 1:8, 11). The Hebrew name for Egypt.

MOAB, the seed of the father. Lot's firstborn son by his eldest daughter (Gen. 19:37)

MOABITE, the descendants of Moab. (Gen. 19:37)

MOLOCH, king; god of fire (Amos 5:26). In (Lev. 18:21) he is known as Molech.

MOON, with the sun created "for signs, and for seasons, and for days, and years" (Gen. 1:14-16). Figuratively the moon is the wife of the sun. When the sun goes away, the moon reflects the light of the sun. It's just exactly like Christ and the Church. When Christ had gone away from the earth, He shines back His power on the Church which reflects His Light. That's just like the Bride and the Bridegroom.

MORMONS, are members of The Church of Jesus Christ of Latter Day Saints. They date back to the first half of the nineteenth century when they were first established by Joseph Smith. They are a religious and cultural Christian group with their main headquarters at Utah in the United States, though their main membership is drawn from outside the United States. Mormons live a strict life of chastity and follow the principles of their founder, Joseph Smith. He is believed to be the one through whom Christ restored His Church; so they follow the Scriptures and the Book of Mormons.

MOSES, drawn, saved from the water. Prophet. Moses was a shadow of the coming of Christ. He himself said that "the Lord thy God shall send a prophet like unto me, Him ye shall hear" (Deut. 18.15). He was the leader of the Children of Israel who took them out of Egypt and led them into the wilderness.

MYSTERY, a previously hidden truth, now made manifest by the revelation of God.

MYSTICISM, used in relation to far eastern occultism and the mysteries of Chaldea, Babylon and Egypt. It is an idolatrous practice where the individual through contemplation direct their human soul to be one with the divine. It is an out of body [transcendental] religious experience of the ultimate reality of God, achievable through "contemplative prayer and meditation".

# N

NAPHTALI, my wrestling. Son of Jacob (Gen. 30:8).

NAZARETH, branch. City in Palestine where Joseph and Mary lived (Luke. 2:39); Gabriel appeared to Mary (1:26-28) and where Jesus was raised (Luke. 4:16)).

NAZARITE, Israelites who made a vow (Num. 6:2-2), separated themselves from the world of sin and consecrated themselves to the Lord; did not drink alcohol or cut their hair.

NEBUCHADREZZAR or Nebuchadnezzar, a short cut (Jer. 21:2). These names refer to one and the same person and are interchangeable. They mean Nebo, that is, protect the king. Nebuchadnezzar was the most powerful and renowned Babylonian king.

NEIT, also Neith, was an Egyptian goddess of war and hunting.

NICENE COUNCIL. In A.D.325 Constantine called the First Council of bishops at Nicaea (now present day Iznik in Turkey) to set up for the first time the organisation of the great universal Christian church we know today as the Roman Catholic Church. It also introduced the idea of the trinity, namely, three persons in one God, and ratified praying to dead saints.

NIMROD, son of Cush, Ham's grandson and Noah's great grandson (Gen. 10:8-10).

NINEVEH, city in Assyria built by Nimrod (Gen. 10:11). The city where Jonah was commissioned by God to go to preach (Jonah. 3).

NINUS, means son. He was king of Assyria and founder of Nineveh. Married Semiramis who was portrayed at times as the Madonna, the mother with the babe in her arms.

NOAH, rest, wondering. Grandson of Methuselah (Gen. 5:25-29. Constructed the Ark at God's command (Gen. 6:14-16) which took one hundred and twenty years to build before the Great Flood (Gen. 7).

NOD, exile. The place where Cain found refuge after he was thrown out of the Garden of Eden by the Lord (Gen. 4:16).

NUBIA, region embracing Southern Egypt and Northern Sudan, from which emerged the Kingdom of Kush in ancient times.

# O

OATH, solemn promise, pledge. (Deut. 6:13); God made an oath to Himself (Heb. 6:13-18).

OBED, serving; worshipping. Son of Boaz and Ruth (Ruth. 4:21, 22). David's grandfather (Matt 1:5).

OIL. Olive oil was used for a number of purposes e.g. anointing the body ( (Ex. 29:7); lamps (Ex. Matt. 25:3). Oil in scripture is a symbol of the Holy Spirit.

OLIVES, Mount; named after the olive trees growing on this mountain in Jerusalem (1 Kings. 11:7).

OMEGA, last letter of Greek alphabet (Rev. 1:8).

OSARIS, ancient Egyptian sun-god; god of the afterlife and underworld, who was the husband and brother of Isis, and worshipped as Horus reincarnated.

OTTO, RUDOLF (1860-1937), was a renowned German Lutheran theologian.

# P

PALESTINE, the Holy Land. Early history designated this area as the Land of Canaan (Ex. 15); later period "the Land of the Hebrews" (Gen. 40:15) and "Land of Israel" (1 Sam. 13:19).

PAPAL SCHISM, sometimes called the Western Schism, was a period in church history where there was a division in the Roman Catholic Church from 1378 to 1417. During this period two men at the same time claimed to be the legitimate heirs to the papacy – each man said that he was the truly elected pope.

PARABLE, the word come from Greek meaning comparison. It is a short story used to teach one or more principles by comparing natural, that is, "an earthly story with a heavenly meaning".

PARADISE a royal park. A place of rest for the immortal souls (Rev. 2:7).

PARHAM, Charles (1873-1929), was initially a Methodist preacher who later contributed to the advancement of Pentecostalism and the belief that the initial evidence that a person had received the Holy Spirit was speaking in tongues.

PATMOS, a tiny island in the Aegean Sea (Rev. 1:9). It was a penal colony where Saint John the divine was exiled by the Roman emperor Domitian (A.D. 95); and where he was inspired to write the Book of Revelation.

PAUL, Small; little. The apostle Paul was Saul before his conversion. Saint Paul has been identified as the messenger to the first Church Age, namely, the Ephesian Church Age (A.D.53-170).

PENTECOST, fiftieth. Feast of Weeks (Lev. 23.15). Holy Spirit given at (Acts. 2).

PENTECOSTAL, is a Christian who believes that they should have a personal experience with Christ through the baptism of the Holy Ghost which is manifested through the individual by their initial experience of speaking in tongues as evidence of receiving the

Holy Spirit. The true meaning of Pentecostal comes from Pentecost which is a Greek name for the Jewish Feast of Weeks, but for Christian believers the Day of Pentecost was marked by the outpouring of the Holy Spirit in the New Testament. Pentecostals major on the gifts, signs, wonders and miracles and speaking in tongues.

PEREZ, Pharez, breach. Son of Judah (Neh. 11:4).

PERGAMEAN CHURCH AGE, the Pergamean Age lasted about three hundred years, from A.D.312-606. The Messenger to the Pergamean Church was Martin, a Hungarian born in A.D.315.

PERGAMOS, Pergamum (ancient name) was situated in Mysia.

PERSEUS, a Greek demi-god, and in Greek legend founder of Mycenae.

PERSIA, is now present day Iran. In ancient times Persia was a Kingdom within Iran.

PHARAOH, the sun. Title of the Egyptian kings.

PHAREZ, breach. The first twin of Judah (Gen. 38:29) from which came David (Ruth. 4:18-22).

PHARISEES, means: "actors, put on"; "the separated". A Jewish religious sect of which Paul professed he once belonged (Acts. 23:6-8).

PHENICIA, land of palm trees (Acts. 21:2). It is also known as Phoenicia).

PHILADELPHIA, brotherly love, a city in Asia Minor which hosted one of the "seven churches" (Rev. 3:7-12).

PHILADELPHIAN CHURCH AGE, called The Age of Brotherly Love, lasted from 1750 to about 1906. The messenger to this age was John Wesley.

PHOENICIANS, Canaanite inhabitants along the coastline of the Mediterranean, present-day Lebanon.

PILATE, Pontius, armed with a javelin (?), Governor of Judea at the time of the ministry of Christ and his death (Luke. 3.1).

PILGRIM FATHERS, were first the French Pilgrims then the one hundred puritans who travelled to the New World on the ship called the *Mayflower* in search of religious freedom.

PILLAR. Pillar had various meanings: support for a building (Judg. 16:26, 29); and the column of fire in the wilderness which led the Children of Israel (Ex. 13:2).

PILLAR OF FIRE, is the Angel of God which appeared to Moses in a burning bush in a form of a Pillar of Fire (Ex. 13:21) that led the children of Israel. The Pillar of Fire, which was the Angel of the Covenant, was the Logos which was Christ.

PINNACLE , small wing or parapet perched on top of a porch on the roof of a temple court, some 350 feet (Matt. 4:5; Luke. 4:9).

PLATO (428 BC-348 BC), philosopher of classical Greek, mathematician, student of Socrates and educated in Egypt.

POPE CLEMENT XIV (1705-1774). Head of Roman Catholic Church from 1769-1774.

POPE EMERITUS BENEDICT XVI, name at birth Joseph Aloisius Ratzinger 1927, but was made Supreme Pontiff Emeritus of the Catholic Church in 2013. He served as pope from 2005-2013.

POPE FRANCIS, born 1936 to Italian parents. They named him Jorge Mario Bergoglio. Between 1973-1979 he served as Argentina's Provincial Superior of the Jesuits. He is sovereign pontiff of the Vatican state and Bishop of Rome. He was elected on the 13th March 2013 by the conclave after the resignation of Pope Benedict XVI.

POPE GREGORY XII (1326-1417). He was leader of the Catholic Church from 1406-1415. His resignation brought to an end the Western Schism.

POPE INNOCENT III (1160-1216). He was leader of the Roman Catholic Church from 1198-1216. He popularised the idea of the Pope as the Vicar of Christ – Supreme Sovereign of the Church.

POPE JOHN PAUL II (1920-2005), Polish. He was leader of the Roman Catholic Church from 1978 to 2005. John Paul II was the second pope in history to remain in office for such a long time. He was said to be the most charismatic and influential leader of the twentieth century who contributed to ending communism in his homeland Poland, and removing the Iron Curtain.

POPE PAUL III (1468-1549). He was leader of the Roman Catholic Church from 1534-1549. In 1542 he permanently established the Papal Inquisition called the Congregation of the Holy Office of the Inquisition.

POPE PIUS X (1835-1914). He was Head of the Roman Catholic Church from 1903-1914.

POPE PIUS XVII (1876-1958). Leader of Roman Catholic Church from 1939-1958.

PORCH, Solomon's, a colonnade on the eastern side of the temple.

PRESBYTERIAN, is a member of the Presbyterian church who follow the teachings of Calvin which focuses on the Christian doctrine that by grace are we saved through faith.

PRIEST, a person who offers sacrifices.

PRINCE, chief of state.

PRISCILLA, Aquilla's wife (Acts. 18:2).

PROPHECY, foretell. It is a shadow of something that is going to happen.

PROPHET, comes from a Greek word meaning advocate. A prophet is a teller forth or a forth teller. A prophet also means a seer (1 Sam. 9:9) and "a revealer of the Word that's written in his own life." His own work reveals and vindicates the Word of that day. A prophet in short is God's mouthpiece.

PROPITIATION, provision, or perfect sacrifice for our sins (1 John. 2:2).

PROSELYTE, a stranger, "a newcomer to Israel"; (1 Chr. 22:2); "a sojourner in the land"; (Ex. 12:48); a convert to Judaism.

PROVERB, maxim. A simple saying that expresses a truth.

PURITANS, were an identifiable group within the Protestant Movement who were often regarded as "extremists", and were therefore prevented from making changes within the established churches. The laws of the land restricted their religious activities. Therefore, many of them left England for the New World to practice their religion freely in places like the United States of America.

PYTHAGORAS (570 BC-495 BC), born on the island of Samos, was an Ionion Greek Philosopher and mathematician. He visited Egypt where he received his education, and founded the Pythagorean Theorem.

# Q

QUAKERS, as a group are known as the Religious Society of Friends or Friends in short. Their fundamental belief is that of universal priesthood, namely that the ministry or the priesthood is for all believers; so that early on in their ministry from the seventeenth century most of the travelling Quaker preachers were women.

QUEEN, king's wife. Christ came first to redeem His Bride; then He comes to receive His Bride; finally He comes with His Bride, as King and Queen, to reign through the millennium.

# R

RACHEL, daughter. Laban's second daughter and a wife of Jacob (Gen. 29:6).

RAHAB, large. The Harlot who saved spies and her household rescued (Josh. 6 and 7).

RAIN, is *moreh* or former rain (Joel. 2:23); and Melqosh or latter rain (Prov. 16:15). Rain is a symbol of the Holy Spirit. God promised that in these last days He would show the same signs that He did in the beginning; and that the former and latter rain would come together.

RAINBOW is "caused by the reflection and refraction of the rays of the sun shining on falling rain". The rainbow has seven perfect colours which represents the Seven Church Ages, and God's covenant that he will not destroy the world with water again.

RAMA, a city; Greek form of Ramah (Matt. 2:18).

RAMESES, RAAMSES (Gen. 47:11).

REBEKAH, means a noose, captivating, the daughter of Bethuel, and the wife of Isaac (Gen. 22:23; 24:67). Isaac is a symbol of Christ; and Rebekah, a symbol of the Bride.

RECONCILIATION, is a change of heart where two estranged parties are brought back into friendship again. Christ is the propitiation of your sins, to call you to reconciliation, to Him, to love.

REDEEMER, Goel. Heb. a kinsman whose duty it was to restore a person to the position they would have been in had the wrong not taken place (Lev. 25:48, Ruth. 4:1). Christ redeems the sinner to bring them back into fellowship with Him.

REDEMPTION, to buy back something that is lost by the payment of a ransom. Christ paid the full price of the human redemption through His death on the cross.

RELIGION is a covering, that is, a basic set of man-made beliefs or moral principles called, tenets, dogma or doctrines practised by its followers or devotees who are members of its organisation or denomination.

RENAISSANCE means to be reborn in Italian. It was a cultural, artistic, architectural, and intellectual revival which started in Italy from about the 14th century spreading across Europe until the seventeenth century.

RESURRECTION is to rise from the dead. When God revealed to the prophet Job that Christ would come to take away the sin of the

world, and would rise again, he foresaw the resurrection of the
Lord. He immediately proclaimed, "I know my Redeemer liveth,
and at the last days He will stand on the earth. And though the
skin worms destroy this body, yet in my flesh shall I see God"
(Job. 19:25-27). He knew he would see Christ in the last days,
because there would be a resurrection, a general resurrection.
Resurrection is a central theme of the Bible that because Christ
rose from the dead you will also rise from the dead in newness of
life.

REUBEN,behold a son. The eldest son of Jacob and Leah (Gen.
29:32).

REVELATION, unveiling that which had previously been hidden.

ROCK, symbol of Christ, the "rock from which the stone is cut
signifies the divine origin of Christ."

ROSE, various types. Christ is often referred to as the "rose of
Sharon".

RUTH, a friend. Story of (Ruth. 1-4).

# S

SABAOTH, the Lord of hosts (Rom. 9:29; James 5:4).

SABBATH, rest (Gen 10:7). The Sabbath day, means rest day. But, in
the New Testament Paul revealed that Sabbath had a deeper
meaning suggesting that if Jesus had given them rest, namely, a
rest day, then would he not afterwards have spoken of another
day. Paul was clear that under the Mosaic law that the Sabbath
meant rest day. When Christ came under the law of grace the
true meaning of Rest was demonstrated when the Holy Ghost
was first given to the people on the day of Pentecost. That is the
Rest, the Sabbath to the people of God. According to Paul, "there
remains... a Sabbath to the people of God who has entered into
his rest"(Jesus' Rest). "Come unto Me, all ye that labour and are
heavy laden, I'll give you Rest" (Matt.11:28) "for he has ceased
from his own work, as God did from His" (Heb.4.10) at the
beginning. The Holy Spirit, Christ is the true Rest.

SADDUCEES, named after their founder Zadok. The sect was
characterised as priestly and righteous (Matt. 16:1-4; 22:23).

SAINT, believer totally separated from the world to serve the Lord
(Rom. 1:7; 8:27).

SALEM, peace. Name of Jerusalem (Gen. 14:18; Heb. 7:1, 2).

SALMON, shady (Ps. 68:14). Salmon was the son of Nahshon who married Rahab of Jericho. Boaz was the product of this marriage ( 1Chron. 2:10-11; and Matt. 1:4).

SALOME, perfect (Acts. 27:7). Daughter of Herodias (Mark. 6:17-29; Matt. 14: 3-11)

SALVATION, deliverance, especially from sin.

SAMARIA, a watch-tower. Shomeron is its other name, meaning, guard( 1 Kin.16:24). Its name comes from the ancient city of Samaria, capital of the Kingdom of Israel.

SAMSON, like the sun (Judg.13-16). Delivered up to the Philistines (Judg. 16.21). His death Judg(15:32).

SAMUEL, heard of God. He was the son of Hannah, one of the two wives of Elkanah (1. Sam. 1:20). A Nazarite (1 Sam. 1:23-2:11). Leader and prophet of ancient Israel (1 Sam. 7). Anointed the first two kings Saul (1 Sam. 10:1) and David (1 Sam. 16:12-13).

SANCTIFICATION, cleansed and set aside for service. The vessels of the old temple were cleaned and set aside for service.

SANCTUARY, the temple (1 Chr. 22:19); the tabernacle (Ex. 25:8); or the holy place ( Lev. 4:6).

SANHEDRIN, Sanhedrin, the supreme judicial and ecclesiastical council of the ancient Jewish nation, composed of approximately 70 men, begun by Moses (Num. 11:16, 17).

SARAH, princess. Abraham's wife and half-sister (Gen. 11:29; 20:12).

SARDIS, means, the escaped ones. It was the capital of ancient Lydia. Seat of the fifth of the seven churches in Asia minor

SARDISEAN CHURCH AGE, the Sardisean or fifth church age lasted from 1520 to 1750. It is usually called the Age of the Reformation. The messenger to this age is the best known messenger of all the ages. He was Martin Luther. He entered the Augustinian convent at Erfurt, Germany in 1505. During the time of Pope Leo X, John Tetzel sought to sell indulgences for sin which caused Luther to denounce this practice as anti-Scriptural. Luther then wrote his famous 95 theses which on October 31, 1517 he nailed to the door of Castle Church, triggering the reformation.

SATAN, called many names including, the adversary (Job 1:6-12; 2:1-7). the devil or accuser.

SAUSSY, Frederick Tupper (1936-2007). A United States author, composer and singer.

SAVIOUR, is a person who saves or delivers one from evil. In

Christendom, Christ is our only Saviour. The message of the gospel is that Christ has come to save the world from sin and that we should accept Him as our personal saviour.

SCOFIELD, Cyrus Ingerson (1843-1921). He was a popular American best selling Bible writer, minister and theologian.

SCRIBES, belong to the sect of the Pharisees, and were lawyers (Matt. 22:35; Mark. 12:28). They interpreted the letter of the ancient written law in the spirit of their traditions (Matt. 23).

SCRIP, a small bag used by shepherds and travellers (Matt. 10:10).

SEAL, small metal or clay device with imprint of its uses, for example, a ring engraved with an impression of the owner. A Seal signifies (i) a finished work; (ii) ownership, for example, when you are bought by the Blood of Jesus Christ and sealed by the Holy Ghost, you no longer belong to the world or anything pertaining to the world. You are owned by God; (iii) security. A Seal means you are safe and secure until you reach your final destination.

SECT, initially used to refer to a religious party such as the various sects of the Sadducees (Acts. 5:17); Pharisees (Acts. 15:5); and Nazarenes (Acts. 24:5). It later was used to identify groups who held beliefs contrary to the Word of God (2 Pet. 2:1; Gal. 5:20).

SEER, a prophet, that is one who sees things before they come to pass and what's going to be afterwards.

SEISS, Joseph (1823-1904). He was a Lutheran minister, American theologian, and a writer on the Great Pyramid and the cosmos from a Christian perspective.

SERAPHIM, it means burners. The Seraphim is the one who receives the sacrifice, and cleanses the worshipper, and then presents him to God. In Isaiah 6 the Seraphims were angelic beings, and they are the very next ones to God, right at the altar – they receive the sacrifice.

SERPENT, the serpent is mentioned in two senses in Scripture, venomous (Gen. 49:17; Jam. 3:7; Jer. 8:17); and in connection with healing as the brazen serpent in the wilderness. The serpent in this respect wasn't a healer. But God put His gift of healing upon that serpent. Therefore someone who was ill and looked upon the serpent and believed was cured. They knew then that God was testifying through that serpent, that He was Jehovah-rapha, the Healer.

SETH, APPOINTED; a replacement. Seth the third son of Adam and

Eve took the place of Abel (Gen. 4:25).

SEVEN, a number identified with perfection. It is God's perfect number. God rested on the seventh day (Gen. 2:2, 3). There are seven church ages, seven lamps, seven seals, seven thunders, seven stars, seven rainbow colours, and so on; for example, God said, "Six days shall you labour, seven days…" All down through the age including the seventh Church Age, seven is God's number of worship.

SEVEN CHURCH AGES. The seven golden candlesticks in the *Book of Revelation* represents the Seven Church Ages: Ephesian (A.D.53-170), Smyrnaean (A.D.170-312), Pergamean (A.D.312-606), Thyatirean (A.D.606-1520), Sardisean (1520-1570), Philadelphian (1750-1906), and Laodicean (1906-present).

SEVEN REDEMPTIVE NAMES. God has seven redemptive or compound names: "our provider", "our healer", "our banner", "our peace", "our shepherd", "our righteousness", and "our presence".

SEVENTH-DAY ADVENTIST, believes that Saturday, their Sabbath, the once Judeo-Christian Seventh Day of the Week, should be the day set aside for worship. It is a Christian protestant Church founded in 1863 by supporters of its doctrine such as Ellen White.

SEYMOUR, William (1870-1922), was an African American preacher who founded the Pentecostal Movement.

SHADRACH, Chaldean name given to Hananiah, one of the three Hebrew boys (Dan. 1.7)

SHAKERS, also called Believers in Christ's Second Appearing was a protestant group in eighteenth century England which later moved to America led by a prominent figure and charismatic preacher known as Anne Lee. The Shakers came to be known as the "Shaking Quakers" as a means of distinguishing them from other Christian movements and in light of their forms of worship, "singing and dancing, shaking and shouting."

SHEBA, QUEEN OF. Jesus said that "the queen of the south (which was the queen of Sheba, that is, Ethiopia) she'll rise in this generation and condemn it: for she came from the uttermost parts of the earth to hear the Wisdom of Solomon" (Matt. 12:42; Luk. 11:31).

SHEM, Noah's first son (Gen. 5:32; 6:10). Noah had three sons: Shem, Ham, and Japheth. The Semitic languages is said to have derived from the name of Shem. The nation of Israel can be traced to the ancestral lineage of Shem (Gen. 11:10-26; 1 Chr. 1:24-27).

SHEPHERD. The word "pastor" means "shepherd." And the Holy Ghost has made him overseer over a certain flock to feed them. When the pastor ministers the Word of God, he is God's angel or messenger to the church.

SHILOH, Messiah (Gen. 49:10). Shiloh is also a place of rest (Judg. 21:19).

SHINAR, The Land of, Chaldees. Mesopotamia, Babylonia (Gen. 11:1-6).

SIBERIA, covers a wide geographical area embracing most of North Asia, the Ural Mountains, and Arctic Ocean, and the hills of north central Kazakhstan and to the borders of Mongolia and China.

SIMEON, hearing. Jacob's Second son by Leah (Gen. 29:33).

SIN, is unbelief.

SKULL, It means "the place of a skull". Calvary and Golgotha has the same meaning as skull. One source said that this meaning comes from the fact that it was on top of a hill shaped like a human skull.

SLAVE (Jer. 2:14), servant, bondservant. In the year of Jubilee, the fiftieth year in the Old Testament, a man who had been sold into slavery was free to leave his master once the trumpet sounded no matter how long he had been in slavery. But if he wanted to remain with his master he would be taken into the temple and an awl would be used to pierce his ear as a sign that he had sold his birthright and is now his master's property for life.

SMALE, Joseph, pastor of First Baptist Church in Los Angeles who founded the First New Testament Church.

SMYRNA was the seat of the fourth church in Asia. The city of Smyrna was a little north of Ephesus at the mouth of the Smyrna Gulf. The word Smyrna means, "bitter", being derived from the word, myrrh. Myrrh was used in embalming the dead. Thus we have a twofold significance found in the name of this age. It was a bitter age filled with death. The two vines within the framework of the church were drifting further apart with an increased bitterness toward the true vine on the part of the false.

SMYRNAEAN CHURCH AGE, lasted from A.D.170 until A.D.312.

The Messenger for this age was Irenaeus.

SMYTH, John (1570-1612), was an Anglican priest in England and founder of one of the earliest Baptist Churches in Holland (1609) where he fled after breaking away from the Church of England. He later returned to England where he set up a Baptist Church

SOCIAL DARWINISM, is the notion that concepts of biology relating to Darwin's theory of evolution can be applied to sociology and politics.

SOCRATES (469 BC-399 BC), classical Athenian Greek philosopher, educated in Egypt.

SODOM, burning; the city and its inhabitants destroyed by fire from heaven (Gen. 19:1-2).

SODOMA,(Rom. 9:29), the Greek form for Sodom.

SODOMITES, inhabitants of Sodom and persons who were as wicked as the inhabitants of Sodom (1. Kin. 14.24).

SOLOMON, peaceful. Son of David by Bathsheba (2 Sam. 12; 1 Chr. 22:5).

SON OF MAN; is God united in man; the Son of God manifesting Himself through human flesh. God was on earth dwelling with us in a Man who was His Son Jesus Christ. And Christ is now living in His Bride. The Son of Man is therefore Christ in His Bride unveiling Himself and doing the greater works.

SOOTHSAYER, a diviner, one who claims to be able to tell what will happen in the future (Josh. 13:22).

SORCERY, invocation of evil spirits to control others, black magic, spells.

SOUL, is the nature of the spirit. The human soul has two senses: faith and unbelief. One of them governs the individual.

SOVEREIGN PONTIFF, is the pope. "The College of Cardinals, with the Pope at its head, is just the counterpart of the Pagan College of Pontiffs, with its 'Pontifex Maximus', or 'Sovereign Pontiff', which had existed in Rome from the earliest times, and which is known to have been framed on the model of the grand original Council of Pontiffs at Babylon" (Hislop's *Two Babylons*).

SPIRIT, Holy; also referred to as the HOLY GHOST.

STAR, Morning, Jesus has been described as the Bright and Morning Star, the greatest Star of all the stars of heaven.

STRANGER, a foreigner living in Palestine. Such persons enjoyed many privileges in common with the Jews, but still were separate from them (Deut. 24:14-21). Christians professed to be pilgrims and strangers on this earth, affirming that here we have no continuing city but seek one to come (Heb. 13:10-14).

STRIPES, inflicted as a punishment (Deut. 25:1-3). The Scriptures declare that Jesus was offered up as a sacrifice for us at Calvary and that He was wounded for our transgressions, and with His stripes we are healed.

SUN, created in consort with the moon as one of the two great lights of heaven (Gen. 1:14-18). God created the firmament before He made the sun. This suggests that there is light besides sunlight. The apostle said that our whole body is full of light (Luke. 11:36). X-rays prove that there is plenty of light besides the sunlight.

SUPPER, this was served in the evening as the main meal of the day (Mark. 6:21; John 12:2).

SURETY, an undertaking or pledge; a certainty; one who becomes liable for the actions of another. Thus for a surety our "Attorney" is our "Judge". He is both "Attorney" and "Judge. Jesus was made a surety of a better testament (Heb. 7:22)

SUSIANA, with its capital Susa was situated to the east of Mesopotamia (corresponds to modern day Iraq), is sometimes referred to as Elam (located in Iran) in ancient literature, but was a separate state with its own structure and government.

SWORD, pointed or two-edged. Symbolised the Word of God (Heb. 4:12; Eph. 6:17; Rev. 1:16).

SYNAGOGUE, an assembly or place of assembly (Ps. 74:8) where Jews congregate for worship.

SYROPHENICIAN, Greek, a Syrophenician by nation (Mark 7:26). Jesus Himself compared a Gentile woman, to dogs when He said to her "It's not meet to take the children's bread and give it to the dogs" (Mark 7:24-30). He was here referring to Gentiles, non-Jew.

# T

TABERNACLE, a house or dwelling-place (Job. 5:24) which Jehovah commanded Moses in the wilderness to build after the "pattern", (Exodus. 29:42), that is, "the fashion", (Acts. 7:44). The tabernacle in the wilderness was merely a shadow of things to come when it would become flesh, that is, body (2 Cor. 5:1, 4). Jehovah, God, the Father, tabernacled Himself in His Son Jesus

Christ. In these last days Christ is tabernacled in His people, the Bride. Peter talks about being "in this tabernacle" which he "must put off", referring to his own body (2 Peter. 1:13-14).

TABLES, slab, board, leather or wood on which meals were served and people sat round to eat. In the Old Testament Jews kept the commandments which were written on tables of stone. But in theses last days, God promised that He would write these laws upon the fleshly tables of our heart. He said that He will no longer write His laws in "tables of stone, but in the fleshy tables of the heart", demonstrating that the dwelling place of God would be in the human heart, not the human head (2 Corin. 3:3; Heb. 8:10).

TABLET, small flat surface, slab of stone, wood or paper on which was written or engraved.

TALENT, largest unit of weight and circular in appearance made of silver or gold (2 Sam. 12:30); a gift or skill as in the parable of the talents (Matt. 18:24; 25:15).

TARES, weedy plants which look exactly like the wheat until the ear appears. In the *Parable of the Weeds* or the *Parable of the Wheat and the Tares* (Matt. 13:25-30) Jesus tells the story of how in the end time "the children of the evil ones (the tares or weeds) will be separated from the Bride of Christ (the wheat). Just before the second coming of the Lord the church would go back to being a Wheat Seed Bride again while the tares would be harvested and burned in the lake of fire.

TELEOLOGY, comes from the Greek word "telos" meaning "end" or purpose in that God begins with the end in mind and continues until He achieves His purpose.

TEMPLE, the tabernacle, "the temple of the Lord" (1 Sam. 1:9). When Christ said "destroy this temple, and I'll raise it up in three days". He was speaking of His body. Solomon's temple represented the Temple spiritual. We are baptised into the Temple of God, into the Body of God, the Body of Jesus Christ. And we're in Christ by Holy Spirit baptism ( I Corin. 12). The Bride of Christ is the temple of the living God (John. 2:19, 21).

TESTIMONY, witness, evidence (2 Thess. 1:10).

TERTULLIAN (A.D.155-222). He was one of the early Christian Fathers from Carthage. the Roman province in Africa. He is the first Christian writer to introduce Latin into the Church through his literature.

THRONE, chair a sovereign occupies; royal seat ((Deut. 17:18)

THUMMIM, light and perfection, revelation and truth ( Ex. 28:30). The Urim Thummim was a Light that flashed over the breastplate of Aaron hanging in the temple. The Urim Thummim was used to answer questions, for example, whether a person was innocent or guilty, or whether a dream or prophecy was from God. If a prophet prophesied or a dreamer dreamed a dream, and the Lights didn't flash, this was a divine answer that neither the dream nor the prophecy was from God.

THUNDER, a loud cracking sound or rumbling blast from the skies; in Scripture a thunder is the Voice of God (John. 12:29; Rev. 19:6).

THYATIRA, the seat of the fourth of the seven churches in Asia. It is a city situated between the border of Lydia and Mysia and Ionia. Thyatira means, "Dominating Female."

THYATIREAN CHURCH AGE, begins in A.D.606 and lasted throughout the dark ages until 1520. The messenger to the Thyatirean Church Age was Saint Columba.

TIGRIS, is one of the two great rivers used together with the Euphrates to give Mesopotamia its meaning, that is, "land between rivers".

TITLE, is a word or phrase given to a book or subject in order to identify the work, subject matter or person in question, for example, the name of a particular book. Jesus' commission to the disciples to baptise is a good example of the meaning of the term title: "Go ye therefore and teach all nations, baptizing them in the Name (not in names), in the Name of the Father, Son, and Holy Ghost" (Matt. 28:19). Father's not a name; Son's not a name; Holy Ghost is not a name. It's a title to a Name. It's the name of three attributes that belong to one God. And that name is Jesus.

TOMB, excavation of a rock where the dead are buried; grave; cave (Judg. 8:32; 2 Sam. 2:32).

TONGUES, positive use of tongues eg gift of tongues (Acts. 2:4; Mark. 16:17) and; negative use of tongues e.g. confusion, Babel (Gen. 11:1-8).

TOWER, of Babel, men built a tower in Babylon which they hoped would reach up to heaven, and the Lord scattered them into different languages (Gen. 11).

TRADITION, an established practice or belief handed down to the descendants of a given society (Mark. 7:3).

TRANSFIGURATION, a total change in outward form or appearance from a mortal body to a glorified state, as when Jesus was
transformed in the presence of His three disciples on Mount
Transfiguration (Matt. 17:1-8; Mark. 9:2-8; Luke. 9:28-36).
God came out in the old days, and led the Church of God from
bondage out of Egypt into freedom. He has come down again in
the same manner to lead His Church spiritual, the Bride, out of
the bondage of sin first, by the Holy Spirit and then into glory. He
will take this body and change it from mortality to immortality,
that is, the transfiguration or transformation of our human
bodies into the perfect image of the Son of God.

TREE OF LIFE, the Tree of Life is mentioned three times in Genesis
and three times in Revelation. The first time it was mentioned
in Genesis was in Eden (Gen. 2:9; 3:22) and that Tree which is
the source of Eternal Life was Jesus. The Tree of Life was
mentioned three times in Revelation as Christ in paradise (Rev.
2:7; 22:2, 14). Thus the Tree Of Life is the Person of Life, and
that is Jesus.

TREE OF THE KNOWLEDGE OF GOOD AND EVIL (Gen. 2, 3) is also
a person, namely, Satan. Thus the Righteous One and the
Wicked One stood side by side there in the midst of the Garden
of Eden. Ezekiel 28:13 "Thou (Satan) hast been in Eden, the
garden of God."

TRIBULATION, oppression, distress of times, persecution and
sufferings (Deut. 4:30; Matt. 13:21). The Great Tribulation in
the Bible is the period of time where there would be weeping and
wailing and gnashing of teeth. The sleeping virgins who
belonged to a Christian religious organisation and didn't have
enough oil in their lamps will be persecuted. It is during this
period of persecution and martyrdom that Israel will go through
a purging and receive the message of the Kingdom by the two
prophets of Revelation 11.

TRINITY, not mentioned in the Scripture but used by Bible
commentators to explain the Godhead (Mark 12:29, 32; John.
10:30). One God was confirmed in three manifestations. God
manifested Himself as a Father, then He manifested Himself in
the Son, then He manifests Himself in the Holy Spirit, the same
God every time.

TRUMPET, means political disturbance: wars. In Matthew 24, Jesus
spoke of it. He said, "You'll hear of wars and rumours of war..."

which is a trumpet sounding. A trumpet also denotes a feast day. It is a gathering together of the people. Paul said, "For if the trumpet give an uncertain sound, who shall prepare himself for battle?" (1 Corin. 14:8) or peace or other event or happening.

TRUTH, a reality; the Word of God. Jesus said: "I am the way, and the Truth and the Life" (John. 14:6). The Truth is the vindicated Word of God (Gal. 2:5; 2 Tim. 3:7; 4:4).

TYNDALE, WILLIAM (1494-1536), was a scholar, theologian and a leading figure in the English Protestant Reformation. He was credited with the translation of the Bible into English. It was the first English Bible to be translated directly from Hebrew and Greek. He wrote it in "proper English" so that the ordinary man and woman would be able to read and understand it. In 1536 he was put to death by being strangled and burnt at the stake for heresy and treason. But in 1538 Henry VIII authorised The Great Bible for the Church of England. Tyndale's Great Bible formed the basis of the "Authorised King James Version of the Bible".

TYPE, pattern, representation, or symbol in the Old Testament which is a shadow of things to come in the New Testament and beyond. Moses was a type of Christ.

TYPOLOGY, is the study or use of types, for example, in Christianity there is the belief that what is written in the New Testament was prefigured or symbolised in the Old Testament as the shadow of things to come.

# U

UNBELIEF, sin, death. Unbelief is separation from God.

UNCTION, anointing, (1 John. 2:20, 27).

UR, City where Abram dwelt before moving to Canaan (Gen. 11:29, 31).

URIAH, light of the Lord God Jehovah, Hittite. Bathsheba's husband (2 Sam. 11:2-12).

URIM, lights, revelation (Ex.28:30).

USURY, moderate interest (Lev. 25:36, 37).

# V

VEIL, vail, covering (2 Cor. 3:13-15; Ex. 34:33, 35). In the Old Testament, there was a veil that hung between the holy place and the Holy of Holies. Only Aaron or the high priest, alone, was to go in there once a year.

VERSION, a translation of the Bible.

VINE, a stem plant; grape vine; a vital produce of Palestine. Jesus likens His heritage to a vine or tree. In Saint John 15, He said, "I am the Vine, and ye are the branches." The vine can't bear fruit, although the fruit is in the vine. It has to have the branch to bear the fruit. The vine with all of its energy cannot produce anything unless the branch is willing to receive the energy. God is depending on the Bride as a member of His Body to bear fruit of His Spirit. If the branch is getting its life out of the vine, well, it's the same kind of life that's in the vine. Our hands, and our lips, and our eyes, are God's hands, lips, and eyes through which He can operate to perform signs, wonders and miracles and to proclaim the message of the hour.

VIPER is a venomous snake. A snake was little, lowdown, and sneaky; so Jesus used the word figuratively when He said to the Pharisees and Sadducees, "O generation of vipers" (Matt.12:33-35) and John the Baptist rebuking them cried out, "You generation of snakes, who has warned you to flee from the wrath that's to come?" (Matt. 3:7)

VIRGIN means "pure, holy." Isaiah says, "a virgin shall conceive, and bear a son..." Here a virgin is a girl who has not had sexual intercourse.

VISION, a divine gift to see what has or will take place. According to the prophet, a vision is to dream while you are awake; for it materialises before your very eyes, just like a picture flashed across a television screen. Jesus did not do a thing within Himself until God showed Him a vision of what was being done. According to Saint John 5:19 Jesus said: "Verily, verily I say unto you, the Son can do nothing in Himself, but what He sees the Father doing: that doeth the Son likewise."

VOW, is a solemn promise to serve or do something; a marriage vow.

# W

WAGES, rate; payment (Matt. 20:2; Matt. 20:1-14 ). "The wages of sin is death" (Rom. 6:23). Sin is death and death is unbelief.

WATCHES, a span of time from sun up to sun down, from dawn to dusk, sunrise to sunset. The night was not divided in hours, in the Bible time, it was divided in watches. There were three watches. Now, the first watch started from nine until twelve, the second watch started from twelve to three, and the third watch of the night was counted from three to six. In the New Testament there were four watches. This may have been based on the way the Romans divided up time.

WEEK, begun when the universe was first created, and consisted of seven days, six working days and one rest day (Gen. 2:2).

WELL, hole or shaft dug into the earth to get water, for example, Jacob's well (John. 4:6). Jacob's well symbolised Christ, the Word of God. He said to the woman from Samaria who went to Jacob's well to draw water: "...whosoever drinketh of the water that I shall give him shall never thirst; but the water that I shall give him shall be in him a well of water springing up into everlasting life" (John. 4:14).

WESLEY, Charles (1707-1788). Younger brother of John Wesley, the founder of the Methodist Movement. Charles was also a minister and hymn writer within the Methodist Church.

WESLEY, John (1703-1791), founder of the Methodist Church. He became the most forthright proponent of Arminian theology. Arminianism still remains the principal doctrine of Methodism today. He was the messenger to the Philadelphian Church Age (1750-1906).

WHEAT, staple diet cultivated by man from the dawn of civilisation

WHITE represents purity (2 Chr. 5: Rev. 3:18). In the Book of Daniel, the Ancient of Days, whose hair was as white as wool is reminiscent of the ancient judges, like the high priests in Israel who wore white, woolly-like hair and beard to signify the supreme authority of the judges. Today the English judges sitting in judgment must wear a white wig to show that there's no other authority and their word is absolute – it is the law of the land.

WHITFIELD, George (1714-1770). He was an English Anglican minister who helped found and propagate Methodism.

WIFE, a woman who is married to a man; marriage was ordained in Eden (Gen. 2:24; Matt. 19:4-6). God spoke to Abraham and told him that his wife Sarah was going to have a baby. And God speaks to Christ, and we are His Wife, His Bride. Here Christ is in His Church. The Bride and Christ are one, like husband and wife are one. The Church and Christ are moulded together as one Person, the same Holy Spirit.

WILDERNESS, uncultivated and inhospitable region. The area in which the Children of Israel were wandering for forty years before they came into Israel was called the wilderness (Ex. 13:18).

WINE, an alcoholic drink made from fermented grape juice. At Cana Jesus changed water into wine (John 2:1-10). The water would have been wine someday anyhow, but it would have had to go through the regular procedure of growing up into the grape vine, coming out into the grape, and being harvested and changed into wine. Jesus just bypassed the vine and made the water into wine, because He is God and has control of all things.

WISE, wisdom (Job, 28:12-28; Prov). There is a worldly wisdom and a godly wisdom. The Holy Spirit moved men to write the Bible; without the Holy Spirit, no matter how well you're educated, you'll never understand It. Jesus thanked God that He'd hid It from the eyes of the wise and prudent, and revealed It to babes such as would learn. And every one of the disciples was more or less illiterate and unlearned people. Paul who was learned confessed that he had to forget all he ever knew in order to find Christ. He therefore told the Corinthian church, that he didn't come with the wisdom of men and great speech, because then their faith would be in the wisdom of men, but he came to them in the power and demonstration of the Holy Spirit, that their faith would rest upon the works of the Holy Spirit according to the Word of God.

# X

XAVIER, Francis (1506-1552). He was a Spaniard and one of the co-founders of the Society of Jesus, that is, the Jesuits.

# Y

YEAR, means "repetition" or "revolution" (Gen. 1:14; 5:3). The Biblical year has three hundred and sixty days, divided into twelve equal months, thirty days in each month. During the tribulation the two prophets of Revelation 11 come on the scene in Palestine to preach the Gospel to the Jews. They preach a thousand, two hundred and three score days, according to the Biblical calendar. This calendar has exactly thirty days in the month, which is three and one-half years mentioned in Daniel which is allotted to the Jews. That's Daniel's last part of the seventieth week which covers the period from the going up of the Church (the Bride) until the coming back of the Church (the Bride).

YOKE, a crossbar with two U shaped pieces put round the necks of two oxens to enable them to draw the plough (Num. 19:2; Deut. 21:3). In the New Testament, the yoke meant that Christ was not yoked or entangled with anything on this earth. He was not yoked or entangled with any affiliation or organisation. "Be not entangled in the yoke of bondage"(Gal. 5:1); "yoke yourself not amongst unbelievers; be ye separated" (2 Corin. 6:17), declares the Bible. Christ is yoked to one thing, and that's His Church, which is not an earthly organisation, but a heaven-born group of people, namely, the Bride of Christ, that's regenerated by the Blood of His Own sacrifice. For He had no yoke of this earth, neither has His Bride.

# Z

ZION, sunny; height (2 Sam. 5:7; Rev. 14:1). Mount Zion in Jerusalem is that place where the Bible records Abraham was seeking a city whose Builder and Maker is God (Heb. 11:10).

ZWINGLI (1484-1531). He was a champion of the Protestant Reformation in Switzerland.

# INDEX

## A

Abel 48, 235, 272
Abraham xiii, 22, 35, 71, 138,
   205, 208, 219, 221, 229,
   235, 243, 253, 254, 255,
   256, 257, 258, 261, 270,
   281, 283
Adam 31, 58, 63, 64, 68, 70,
   81, 214, 235, 236, 245,
   246, 259, 271
Age of Reason 57
Alien Savoir 126
Alpha 19
American Civil War 34, 47
American Declaration of
   Independence 61, 64, 67
Amish 43, 237
Anabaptists 40, 237
Andronicus 114
Anglican Church 116
Anglo-Saxon 81, 256
Ankerberg Theological
   Research Institute 101
Antediluvian 129, 137
Antichrist 113, 114, 115,
   131, 191, 237, 260
Anubis 52, 237
Apocalypse xii, 140, 252
Apostasy 30, 90, 116, 237,
   260
Aria 51, 238
Arizona 126, 184, 198
Armada 95
Armageddon 114, 116

Arminius, Jacob 24, 238
Asia Minor 52, 86, 247, 265,
   270
Atheist 20
Athena 52, 196, 218, 223,
   238
Atlantic 65, 120
Atomic 129
Augustine, Saint 22, 104,
   112, 224, 238
Authentic xi, xv, 11, 12, 45,
   104, 105, 153, 189, 194,
   195, 226
Avignon 90
Azusa Street 38, 39, 193,
   196, 223, 238, 239

## B

Babylon 21, 22, 42, 50, 53,
   68, 92, 105, 107, 108,
   128, 207, 217, 227, 239,
   240, 242, 244, 262, 274,
   277
Bamboo Curtain 97, 239
Barons 66, 107, 259
Bartleman, Frank 54, 103,
   196, 223, 239
Benedict III 90
Benedict XVI 91, 92, 102,
   120, 266
Biàn li n 109
Biblos 139, 240
Bill of Rights 66, 67, 68
Birmingham, King's Letter 78,
   201, 223, 228
Black horse rider 112, 113
Boleyn, Anne 116
Book of Daniel x
Book of Life 134, 135
Booth, William 32, 240
Brass 48, 128

Bride of Christ 5, 129, 130, 132, 138, 148, 151, 259, 260, 276, 283

Bridegroom 133, 195, 213, 220, 262

British Library xiv, 93, 152, 154, 155, 156, 161, 162, 163, 166, 167, 169, 217

Buddism 43

Buddha 83

Bunsen C. F 50, 195, 196, 217, 241

## C

Cainitic 48

Calendar 7, 8, 282

Calvin, John 24, 74, 219, 241, 267

Calvinists 25, 104

Campolo, Anthony 109, 207, 226

Canaan 50, 75, 76, 241, 251, 264, 279

Caribbean 10, 43, 96, 146

Carpathia, Nicolae 123

Carthage 22, 244, 276

Catesby, Robert 96

Catherine of Aragon 116

Césaire, Aimé 146

Chaldea 52, 108, 244, 262

China xiv 42, 122, 186, 228, 273

Christendom 5, 12, 146, 252, 271

Chronologists 9, 57, 129

Chronology 8

Church of England 24, 25, 26, 115, 116, 279

Civilisation, meaning 45, 47, 242

Clinton, Hilary 98

Columba 27, 243, 277

Comet 127

Communion 24, 41, 104, 105, 164, 190

Communism 15, 16, 17, 18, 99, 243, 253, 266

Congregation of the Holy Office 101, 102, 256, 266

Constantine 22, 23, 116, 263

Cosmos 54, 128, 243, 271

Counter Reformation 102

Covey, Stephen 83

Creation 15, 19, 21, 28, 29, 59, 60, 120, 142, 143, 148, 228

Creationism 59, 191, 192, 193, 104, 195, 196, 197, 228, 244

Cromwell, Thomas 115

Croton 52

Crumpler, Abner Blackmon 35, 244

Culture, meaning 55, 56, 57, 197, 222, 227, 232, 242, 244

Cupid 100

Cush 21, 22, 50, 244, 248, 256, 263

Cybele 42

Cyprian 22, 244

Cyprus Italy 120

## D

Daniel x, 128, 150, 189, 212-213, 218, 240, 242, 244, 249, 281, 283

Dark Ages 27, 90, 102, 112, 277

Darwin, Charles 29, 59, 60, 191, 198, 222, 229, 244, 248, 274

Debate On Tongues 37, 193
Defender of Faiths 57, 150
Deity 133, 144, 198, 249
Delano Kenneth J 127
Deous 42
Determinism 16, 17, 81, 245
Dickens, Charles xi, 7
Diop, Cheik, Anta 22, 44, 86,
    189, 190, 194, 195, 226,
    245
Diopolis 86, 257
Dispensation 119, 149, 245
Dominica 10
Dramatis personae 142

**E**

Ecumenical Council 109, 116
Eden 25, 27, 53, 54, 58, 63,
    206, 229, 246, 263, 278
Egypt 6, 20, 22, 42, 45, 48,
    49, 50, 51, 52, 53 54, 55,
    108, 137, 189, 190, 196,
    218, 238, 240, 246, 247,
    250, 251, 261, 262, 263,
    266, 267, 274, 278
Election 69, 75, 97, 98, 99,
    102, 125, 246
Elijah 2, 88, 132, 151,
    166, 167, 246
Emancipation 34, 35
Emmaus 20, 148, 206
En morphe xii, xiii, 138, 144,
    145, 246
End-time prophet messenger x,
    5, 150, 259
Enlightenment 57, 58, 64, 65,
    85, 258
Enoch 48, 51, 137, 214, 223,
    228, 229, 230, 234, 246
Ephesus 27, 117, 247, 257,
    273

Eternal City 133, 135, 140-
    141, 213
Eternal Life 61, 62, 70, 76,
    134, 142, 236, 257, 278
Ethiopia 51, 228, 241, 244,
    248, 256, 261, 272
Evangelisation 92, 109
Evolution xii, 29, 59, 198,
    244, 248, 274
Exo-Vaticana 126, 128, 211-
    212, 227
Extragalactic 126

**F**

Finney, Charles 36, 160, 161
Fire Baptised 44
Flying saucers 126, 129
Foot soldiers 95, 102, 254
Fort Caroline 73, 74
Fox's Book of Martyrs 66, 73,
    104, 199, 231
France 64, 90, 96
Francis Pope 89, 91, 92, 102,
    115, 125, 202, 294, 248,
    266
Francis of Assisi 92, 103
Frankl, Viktor xiii, 81
French Declaration 64, 66, 85
French Pilgrims 61, 73, 74,
    265

**G**

Gadara 21
Garden of Eden, location 20
Garfield, James 97, 249
Gérard, Balthasar 96
Giza 51
Godhead 5, 254, 278
Gold 69, 70, 71, 120, 121,
    128, 131, 143, 235, 249,
    251, 276

Gorbachev, Mikhail 89, 250
Gossolalia 38, 249
Grand Age 15, 142, 212
Grecian 128
Greece 22, 52, 120, 196, 250
Gregory XII 90, 91, 203, 266
Guaraní 73
Gunpowder Plot 95

# H

Habeas corpus 66, 250
Ham 21, 50, 51, 241, 244,
    250, 256, 261
Hammurabi 68
Harris, Marvin 59, 197, 227,
    250
Hegel, Friedrich xvii, 2, 227
Henry IV King of France 96
Henry VIII 24, 115, 279
Henry, Patrick 74, 200, 251
Heresy 101, 106, 279
Heritage xi, xii, 56, 78, 141,
    148, 195, 226, 280
Herodotus 52, 189, 217, 251
Hieroglyphics 51
Hinduism 43
Hislop, Alexander 13, 22, 50,
    92, 107, 108, 157, 189,
    190, 195, 203, 207, 233,
    252
History, meaning xi, xii, 185,
    186, 187, 226, 252
Holiness 33, 34, 35, 36, 40,
    47, 104, 244, 252
Horn, Tom 126, 127, 129,
    211, 212, 227
Horus 52, 252, 264
Huguenots 104

# I

Illich, Ivan 54, 196, 228, 252

Illuminated 43
India 40, 122, 176, 194, 238,
    252
Industrial Revolution 23, 26,
    57
Indwelling 43
Infallible 11, 116
Innocent III 107, 207, 230,
    254, 258, 266
Inquisition 100, 102, 107,
    252, 266
Inspiration xi, xii, xv, xvi, 2,
    14, 17, 50, 51, 106, 213,
    222
Investigating Angels 128, 129
Iran 67, 122, 214, 238, 260,
    265, 275
Ireland ix, 25, 103, 120, 243
Irenaeus, 27, 253
Iron Curtain 89, 97, 202, 253
Isaiah 12, 133, 204, 247,
    251, 271, 280
Isi 42
Isis 22, 42, 53, 253, 284
Islam 43, 108, 109, 197, 224
Iswara 42
Italy 52, 90, 99, 120, 268
Iznik, Turkey 22, 263

# J

Jacksonville 72, 233
Jacques, Martin xiv, 122, 186,
    210
Jerusalem 35, 71, 125, 130,
    132-133, 135-, 137, 140-
    43, 213, 236-237, 240,
    246, 261, 264, 269, 283
Jesuit Constitution 106
Jesuit Treason Plot 195
Jethro 6, 45, 254
Job 69, 70, 189, 235, 237,

243, 244, 245, 254, 261,
    268, 269, 270, 275, 282
John Paul II 89, 266
John the Baptist 2, 249, 280
Jorgensen, Owen ix, 184, 228
Junius 114
Jura, perjura, veritatem que
    denega 94
Justification 33, 34

# K

Kangaroo Courts 101
Kennedy, John F 80, 97, 98,
    255
Kentucky ix, 98, 208, 222
Khayyam, Omar 139
King John 66, 107, 259
King, Martin Luther 77, 78,
    79, 80, 201, 206, 223,
    228, 255
Klu Klux Klan 39, 256
Knox, John 217, 228, 256
Kosmos 46, 128, 133, 256
Kundera, Milan 62, 198, 256

# L

LaFontaine 146, 147, 174,
    215
Lady Hope 59, 60, 198
Laity 93, 111, 123
Lamb 16, 131, 134, 138, 139,
    140, 141, 237, 257, 258,
    260
Laodicea 86, 87, 88, 257
Larkin, Clarence 90, 119,
    185, 198, 203, 209, 213,
    217
Laslett, Peter 26, 56, 58, 190,
    191, 197, 228
Law and the Prophets 76
Left Behind 123, 129, 130, 132

Leonardo, da Vinci 53
Libyans 51
Lincoln , Abraham 35, 97,
    210, 229, 253, 257
Logos 143, 144, 266
Loyola, Ignatius 103, 207,
    206, 208, 227, 229, 232,
    254, 258
Lucifer 29, 127, 211, 227,
    258
L.U.C.I.F.E.R, Project 126,
    127, 129
Luther, Martin 24, 104, 166,
    206, 270

# M

Madonna 22, 53, 104, 252,
    253, 258, 263
Magisterium 195
Magna Carta 66, 67, 68, 107,
    259
Malachi 12, 28, 88, 151, 241,
    259
Mandela 79, 80, 81, 201,
    229, 259
Mark of the beast 131, 190,
    205, 206, 207, 210, 260
Marley, Bob 76
Marx, Karl 17, 18, 188, 228
Maryolatry 104, 260
Masterpiece 61, 142, 176,
    194
Mather, Andrew 74, 200
Mayflower 61, 265
McCarty, Burke 124
McKinley, William 97, 260
Media 51, 260
Median-Persian 128
Mediation 108
Melchisedec xiii, 204, 214,
    215, 221, 261

Memphis 51, 190, 261
Menéndez 74
Meroe 51, 241
Messiah 4, 68, 132, 158, 242, 261, 273
Methodist 2, 20, 26, 27, 32, 33, 35, 38, 41, 43, 47, 240, 244, 261, 264, 281
Mexico 51, 177
Michelangelo 55
Middle East 49, 91, 121, 122, 125, 254
Midian 6, 45, 261
Millennium 133, 134, 213, 219, 136, 261, 267
Minerva in Rome 52
Mission 17, 54, 73, 74, 94, 103, 115, 121, 200, 210, 236
Mississippi 51
Mizraim 50, 246, 261
Mohammedanism 43
Mormons 40, 43, 156, 262
Moses 2, 6, 12, 29, 51, 55, 132, 139, 149, 198, 235, 241, 241, 254, 256, 262, 265, 270, 275, 279
Mount Graham 126, 129
Mount Transfiguration 29, 278
Mouthpiece xi 11, 28, 267
Mystery Babylon 92
Mysticism 108, 109, 262

**N**
NATO 120
Nazi 20
Nebuchadnezzar 150, 240, 242, 244, 263
Neit 52
New Jerusalem 71, 135, 137, 140, 141, 142,143, 213, 262
Nicaea 22, 29, 114, 116, 263
Nicene Council 22, 23, 263
Nico 111
Nicolaitanes 111
Nile 51, 261
Nimrod 21, 22, 40, 50, 157, 203, 238, 244, 252, 256, 263
Ninus 22, 53, 263
Noah 21, 129, 250, 263, 272
Nod, land of 48, 263
Norwich, Julius 107, 207, 230
Nubia 52, 241, 263
Numidia 22, 238

**O**
Omega 10, 236, 264
One World Government 88, 116, 120, 121, 151
Osiris 22, 42, 50, 53, 252, 253
Otto, Rudolf 18, 189, 264

**P**
Pach n, Adolfo Nicolás 102
Pagan Rome 23, 108
Palestine 52, 125, 137, 240, 255, 262, 264, 274, 280, 282
Papal Rome 23, 108
Parham, Charles 38, 39, 193, 230, 264
Patrick, Saint 103
Pentagon 126
Pentecost 2, 35, 38, 42, 132, 148, 149, 193, 223, 259, 264, 265, 269
Pergamos 27, 117, 265
Perseus 52, 265

Persia 51, 52, 214, 265
Peru 51, 177
PewResearch 124
Pharaoh 55, 234, 265
Philadelphia 27, 117, 265
Phut 50
Pilgrims Holiness 40
Pillar of Fire xiii, 127, 138,
    144, 170, 246, 265, 266
Pius X, Pope 102, 252, 266
Piux XVII, Pope 103
Plato 52, 266
Pontiff 91, 106, 107, 115,
    240, 266, 274
Portuguese 74
Predestination 5, 16, 17, 24,
    241, 248
Prefect of the Congregation
    102
Presbyterian 20, 23, 35, 36,
    226, 256, 267
Profane 12, 13
Protestant Reformation 24,
    26, 104, 115, 238, 256,
    279
Ptolemy I 82
Purgatory 108, 114, 258
Puritans 62, 265, 267
Purple Curtain 97, 99
Pyramid-like Mountain 133,
    135, 137
Pyramid, The Great 51, 136,
    137, 196, 213, 214, 218,
    225, 226, 228, 234, 271
Pythagoras 52, 267

Q
Queen Elizabeth I 95

R
Rapture xiii, 5, 130, 132, 133,
212, 221
Ratzinger, Josef 102, 266
Redeemed 135, 137, 138,
    140, 141, 142, 143, 236
Religion, meaning 19, 20, 268
Renaissance 53, 55, 245, 257,
    261, 268
Repent 42, 147, 239
Resurrection 12, 132, 141,
    142, 149, 194, 215, 219,
    243, 246, 268, 269
Revelation, meaning xii, 269
Robben Island 79
Roman Empire 22, 89, 101,
    123, 225, 253
Roman martyrology 112
Russia 67, 89, 99, 177, 249,
    259

S
Salvation Army 32, 240
Samaritan woman 80
Samos 52, 67
Sanctification 26, 33, 34, 69,
    270
Sardis 27, 117, 270
Saudi Arabia 122
Saussy, Frederick Tupper 102,
    205, 270
Schofield, C. I 48
Seals 5, 110, 114, 199, 206,
    208, 209, 212, 224, 233,
    241, 258, 272
Second World War 11, 125,
    129
Seer 10, 19, 267, 271
Segregation 38, 77, 78, 79, 80
Semiramis 30, 59, 218
Seymour, William 38, 39,
    238, 272
Shakers 40, 272

Shakespeare xiii
Shem 21, 246, 272, 273,
Shinar 50, 51, 235, 238, 273
Silver 128, 235, 276
Smale Joseph 39, 273
Smyrna 27, 117, 273
Smyth, John 25
Socialism 15, 87
Society of Jesus or Jesuits 103,
    206, 207, 227, 254, 258,
    282
Socrates 52, 266, 274
Sodom 128, 129, 258, 274
South Africa 79, 80, 81, 154,
    177, 184, 231, 259
Soviet Union 89, 250, 253
Sparkbrook 56
St Christopher 52
Stokes, Brian 6, 45
Stonehenge 19
Sun worshippers 43
Superior General, Jesuit 102
Superman 112, 114
Supranational 120
Susiania 51
Swiss Alps 121
Syria 52, 125, 237, 238

T
Teleology xii, 15, 276
Tertullian 22, 276
Testator 139, 140
Thyatira 27, 90, 111, 117,
    277
Tomb of David 125
Tower of Babel 21, 22, 27, 92,
    238
Transfiguration 29, 278
Tribulation 69, 70, 130, 131,
    132, 151, 278, 282
Trinity 22, 145, 263, 278

Turkey 22, 263
Type x, 1, 6, 15, 16, 59, 60,
    150, 235, 279

U
UFOs 128, 129
Universal Declaration of
    Human Rights (UN) 85,
    86, 178, 179

V
Vatican II 203, 204, 222

W
Welsh Revival xvi, 38
Wesley, Charles 26
Wesley, John 26, 33, 261,
    265, 281
White horse, rider 100, 111,
    112, 113, 116
White throne judgment, great
    134
Whitfield, George 26, 281
William of Orange 96
William the Conqueror 23
William Tyndale 115
Woodworth-Etter, Mary B 36
World Council of Churches
    43, 116, 131
World Economic Forum 121

X
Xavier, Francis 103, 105, 282

Z
Zechariah 12
Zeus 86, 257
Zodiac 143, 257
Zwingli, Huldrych 24, 283